Orthodox Christianity, New Age Spirituality and Vernacular Religion

Bloomsbury Advances in Religious Studies

Bettina E. Schmidt, Steven J. Sutcliffe and Will Sweetman

Founding Editors: James Cox and Peggy Morgan

Bloomsbury Advances in Religious Studies publishes cutting-edge research in the Study of Religion/s. The series draws on anthropological, ethnographical, historical, sociological and textual methods amongst others. Topics are diverse, but each publication integrates theoretical analysis with empirical data. The series aims to refresh the interdisciplinary agenda in new evidence-based studies of 'religion'.

Appropriation of Native American Spirituality, Suzanne Owen
Becoming Buddhist, Glenys Eddy
Community and Worldview among Paraiyars of South India, Anderson H. M. Jeremiah
Conceptions of the Afterlife in Early Civilizations, Gregory Shushan
Contemporary Western Ethnography and the Definition of Religion, Martin D. Stringer
Cultural Blending in Korean Death Rites, Chang-Won Park
Globalization of Hesychasm and the Jesus Prayer, Christopher D. L. Johnson
Individualized Religion, Claire Wanless
Innateness of Myth, Ritske Rensma
Levinas, Messianism and Parody, Terence Holden
New Paradigm of Spirituality and Religion, Mary Catherine Burgess
Post- Materialist Religion, Mika T. Lassander
Redefining Shamanisms, David Gordon Wilson
Reform, Identity and Narratives of Belonging, Arkotong Longkumer
Religion and the Discourse on Modernity, Paul- François Tremlett
Religion as a Conversation Starter, Ina Merdjanova and Patrice Brodeur
Religion, Material Culture and Archaeology, Julian Droogan
Secular Assemblages, Marek Sullivan
Spirits and Trance in Brazil, Bettina E. Schmidt
Spirit Possession and Trance, edited by Bettina E. Schmidt and Lucy Huskinson
Spiritual Tourism, Alex Norman
Theology and Religious Studies in Higher Education, edited by D. L. Bird and Simon G. Smith
The Critical Study of Non-Religion, Christopher R. Cotter
The Problem with Interreligious Dialogue, Muthuraj Swamy
Religion and the Inculturation of Human Rights in Ghana, Abamfo Ofori Atiemo
UFOs, Conspiracy Theories and the New Age, David G. Robertson

Orthodox Christianity, New Age Spirituality and Vernacular Religion

The Evil Eye in Greece

Eugenia Roussou

BLOOMSBURY ACADEMIC
LONDON · NEW YORK · OXFORD · NEW DELHI · SYDNEY

BLOOMSBURY ACADEMIC
Bloomsbury Publishing Plc
50 Bedford Square, London, WC1B 3DP, UK
1385 Broadway, New York, NY 10018, USA
29 Earlsfort Terrace, Dublin 2, Ireland

BLOOMSBURY, BLOOMSBURY ACADEMIC and the Diana logo are trademarks of
Bloomsbury Publishing Plc

First published in Great Britain 2021
Paperback edition published 2022

Copyright © Eugenia Roussou, 2021

Eugenia Roussou has asserted her right under the Copyright, Designs and
Patents Act, 1988, to be identified as Author of this work.

For legal purposes the Acknowledgements on p. ix constitute an extension
of this copyright page.

All rights reserved. No part of this publication may be reproduced or transmitted
in any form or by any means, electronic or mechanical, including photocopying,
recording, or any information storage or retrieval system, without prior
permission in writing from the publishers.

Bloomsbury Publishing Plc does not have any control over, or responsibility for,
any third-party websites referred to or in this book. All internet addresses given
in this book were correct at the time of going to press. The author and publisher
regret any inconvenience caused if addresses have changed or sites have ceased
to exist, but can accept no responsibility for any such changes.

A catalogue record for this book is available from the British Library.

Library of Congress Cataloging-in-Publication Data
Names: Roussou, Eugenia, author.
Title: Orthodox Christianity, new age spirituality and vernacular religion :
the evil eye in Greece / Eugenia Roussou.
Description: New York : Bloomsbury Academic, 2021. |
Series: Bloomsbury advances in religious studies |
Includes bibliographical references and index.
Identifiers: LCCN 2020052981 (print) | LCCN 2020052982 (ebook) |
ISBN 9781350152793 (hardback) | ISBN 9781350152809 (pdf) |
ISBN 9781350152816 (epub)
Subjects: LCSH: Greece–Religion. | Christianity and other religions–New Age
movement. | Orthodox Eastern Church–Greece. | New Age movement–Greece.
Classification: LCC BL980.G8 R68 2021 (print) |
LCC BL980.G8 (ebook) | DDC 299/.9309495–dc23
LC record available at https://lccn.loc.gov/2020052981
LC ebook record available at https://lccn.loc.gov/2020052982

ISBN:	HB:	978-1-3501-5279-3
	PB:	978-1-3502-2539-8
	ePDF:	978-1-3501-5280-9
	eBook:	978-1-3501-5281-6

Series: Bloomsbury Advances in Religious Studies

Typeset by Integra Software Pvt Ltd

To find out more about our authors and books visit www.bloomsbury.com
and sign up for our newsletters

To I. P.,
For the gift of spiritual protection

Contents

List of figures		viii
Acknowledgements		ix
1	Introduction	1
2	The New Age of Greek religiosity: Orthodox Christianity and beyond	29
3	*Matiasma*: The energetic interplay of senses and emotions	51
4	*Ksematiasma*: Healing, power, performance	83
5	Creative syntheses through material culture: The evil eye in the spiritual marketplace	113
6	The pluralistic landscape of Greek religiosity: Religion and spirituality at a Global Age	141
7	Conclusion	165
Notes		176
References		181
Index		193

Figures

1	*Palo santo* and the evil eye	2
2	A typical Rethymniot alley	16
3	Aristotelous Square	17
4	Feng shui and Orthodox Christianity at home	30
5	Household icon stand	37
6	Church small shrine for lighting a candle	42
7	New Age and Orthodox household items for positive energy	53
8	Social proximity in the Old Town of Rethymno	57
9	The *paralia* of Thessaloniki	58
10	*Ksematiasma* performed alongside Orthodox icons and New Age crystals	84
11	Icon stand and *ksematiasma*	86
12	The most typical ritual of *ksematiasma*	86
13	The Cretan *ksematiasma* with the use of a towel	88
14	Sensory engagement through touch during the ritual healing	89
15	Evil eye objects outside a Rethymniot shop	114
16	Religious icons as *matakia*	117
17	Religious icons in a Thessalonikan household	119
18	A *Panagia* (Virgin Mary) combined with an evil eye	123
19	An evil eye amulet, sold at an ecclesiastic shop	126
20	Material co-inhabitation of religious icons and the evil eye	128
21	A New Age spiritual symbol meets the evil eye at a spiritual healing centre	137
22	'Feng Shui World'	142
23	Eastern spirituality meets the evil eye	143
24	Feng shui protective object against the evil eye	150
25	A conscious spiritual amalgamation of New Age and Orthodoxy	152

Acknowledgements

This book is the outcome of a long journey that began during my undergraduate studies and was consolidated when I chose the 'evil eye' as the main research subject of my doctoral thesis. I am more grateful than I can ever express to all my interlocutors in Crete and northern Greece; without their generous help, this work would never have been accomplished. In Rethymno, special thanks go to: Mrs Anthoula Simantiri and Alexandros Simantiris, whose hospitality and kindness made me warmly comfortable, as if living in a familial environment; Mrs Ntina Lempidaki, who brightened my life from the very first moment I met her at the Painting Workshop; Dr Aris Tsantiropoulos for his advice on Cretan culture; and Dora, Vaggelis and the family, Mary, Despina, Zavi, Evita, Persefoni, Nikos, Marcela and Katerina for the laughs and the evil eye conversations we shared. In Thessaloniki, I wish to thank Katerina and Andreas for making my everyday life throughout fieldwork sparkle with humour and joy; and Tzeni, Dorita, Dora, Mrs Eleni and Mr Lazos, Maria, Anna, Sofia and Kitsa for not hesitating to speak in front of a recorder, and for their friendship and help.

Some of my ethnographic data and their analysis included in this book have already appeared in previous publications, and I am very grateful to the editors and publishers for their permission to reuse the content here. More specifically, Chapter 6 of the book is based primarily on my article entitled 'The New Age of Greek Orthodoxy: Pluralizing Religiosity in Everyday Practice', which was included in the volume *The Best of All Gods: Sites and Politics of Religious Diversity in Southern Europe* (ISSN 978-90-04-25523-4), edited by José Mapril and Ruy Blanes, and published by Brill in 2013. Chapter 3 includes a section that is derived, in part, from my article 'Believing in the Supernatural through the "Evil Eye": Perception and Science in the Modern Greek Cosmos', published in the *Journal of Contemporary Religion* on 9 September 2014, available online: http://wwww.tandfonline.com/10.1080/13537903.2014.945726. Chapters 1–3 include some sections that were previously included in my article 'Orthodoxy at the Crossroads: Popular Religion and Greek Identity in the Evil Eye Practice', published in 2011 by the *Journal of Mediterranean Studies* (ISSN: 1016-3476).

My appreciation goes to the Department of Anthropology at UCL, London, UK, for the financial support of this project through the award of a Postgraduate

Departmental Bursary in 2005–6. Part of the ethnographic data that appear in the book was collected between 2011 and 2017, during my frequent fieldwork visits to Greece in the context of my postdoctoral project (grant reference: SFRH/BPD/72003/2010), funded by the Portuguese Foundation for Science and Technology (FCT), to which I owe all my gratitude. The writing up of the book has been made possible through my position as a senior researcher at the *Centro em Rede de Investigação em Antropologia* (CRIA), ISCTE-IUL, Lisbon, Portugal and under the financial support from FCT in the context of the strategic plan of CRIA (UIDB/04038/2020), to which I am indebted.

I am grateful to Camilla Erskine, Lalle Pursglove and Lily McMahon at Bloomsbury Publishing, who have worked with me in different stages of the publishing process with determination and efficiency, for all their valuable help. I wish to extend my gratefulness to the series editors of Bloomsbury Advances in Religious Studies for agreeing to include this book in their series, and, especially, to Steven J. Sutcliffe for the encouraging comments, inspiration and the influence his work has had on my writings and on my understanding of the always difficult concepts of 'New Age' and 'spirituality'. I would also like to thank immensely the anonymous reviewer for the sharp comments and thoughtful remarks, which were delivered with extraordinary kindness and certainly improved the text of the final manuscript.

I am very thankful to Charles Stewart, who supervised my PhD thesis on the 'evil eye' at the Department of Anthropology, UCL, for generously offering his expertise on Greek culture, through his thoughtfulness, encouragement, intellectual strength, insightful understanding and scrupulous discussions and readings of texts of much of the work presented here. I am more indebted than I can ever express to Brian Morris; without his captivating teachings, inspiring personhood and encouragement during my MA studies at Goldsmiths College, I would not have chosen to turn my anthropological research attention to religion in the first place. The communication we shared in the years that followed always constituted the most reassuring trait that I should hang in there in times of academic disenchantment. I am also grateful to Ritsa Deltsou, Penelope Papailias, Athena Athanasiou, Victoria Goddard, Allen Abramson and Vassiliki Chryssanthopoulou for provoking intellectual stimulants, insights and inspiration, while discussing various ideas on the 'evil eye' during my undergraduate and postgraduate years of studying anthropology. My indebtedness goes to Diana Riboli: her brilliant intellect, inspiring work, constant encouragement, the common vision we share about what anthropology is and/or should be, our discussions on religion and spirituality, together with her very useful suggestions on this work, have made me a better anthropologist.

There are many friends and colleagues in my anthropological path who, during our shared PhD experience at UCL in London, our postdoctoral research phase at the Centre for Research in Anthropology (CRIA) in Lisbon, my current position as a researcher at CRIA, co-attendances at international conferences and elsewhere, have encouraged my efforts, supported me in times of disillusionment and/or provided academic aid and inspiration.

In London, during the years that a large amount of this text was written as part of my doctoral thesis, I could not have asked for better fellow travellers than Gladys San Juan, Koshin Machida, Diana Espírito Santo, Fabio Gygi, Dafne Acorroni, Tomoko Hayakawa, Devorah Romanek, Constantinos Tsikkos, Marjorie Murray, Sergio Gonzalez Varela and Sharon Ferlesch, among many others; my deep gratitude goes to all of them for their precious academic companionship and/or friendship in that challenging yet extremely fruitful period.

In Lisbon, I wish to warmly thank Anastassis Panagiotopoulos, Anna Fedele, Antónia Pedroso de Lima, Paulo Raposo, Clara Saraiva, José Mapril, Ruy Blanes, Valerio Simoni, Pedro Antunes, Inês Lourenço, Giullia Cavallo and Joana Martins, among others, for making my academic home at CRIA feel like such a creative cluster of anthropological inter/action. I am also especially grateful to Cátia Miriam Costa who, through her always positive spirits, great intellect and humour, made the long hours of working within the limitations of an office space far less lonely and much more enjoyable; the lunches and conversations we have shared with Cátia and Ana Margarida Santos at ISCTE, and their encouragement during the final stages of writing this book, have been precious.

My thankfulness goes, furthermore, to valued colleagues around the world: in particular, Denise Lombardi, Katerina Ferkov, Anna Clot-Garrell, Maria Vivod, Athena Peglidou, Efi Mastorodimou, Natasha Chanta-Martin, Kostis Kalantzis, Taj Khan Kalash, Árdis Ingvarsdóttir, Borja Martín-Andino, Evgenia Fotiou, Silvia Rivadossi, Bea Vidacs, István Povedák, Irina Stahl, Clara Lemonnier, Alexandra Antohin, Urmila Morhan, Kim Knibbe, Stefania Palmisano and Victor Roudometof, some of whom have also become dear friends and whose research, anthropological sharing and exchange of ideas have influenced and supported this work, one way or another.

During the phase of amending the manuscript I could not have asked for a better refugee than the *Tasca do Jaime* in Lisbon, which creatively enhanced my inspiration through the melodic influence of *fado*. There, an enormous *obrigada* goes particularly to Laura Nunes for her warmth, affection, strength and for always welcoming me with open arms; and to the grand *fadista* João Soeiro for his sensitivity, kind attitude and profound voice that has accompanied and inspired my writing constantly and consistently. My appreciation also goes to my weekly yoga group in Lisbon, and especially to Carly, Cláudia, Camille and Luisa, who have created for many years a safe and trusting space to share and learn about spiritual healing and mindful embodiment.

My warm thoughts of gratefulness go to those dear friends who, each one separately, and on his/her own unique way, have cared and lifted my spirits intentionally, or without actually realizing it, during various periods of writing up this work: Aristea, Salomé, Kimon, Alexandre, Vassia K., Dora, Debbie, Eleni, Roula, Nia, Despina, Christos, Gogo, Stratis, Dimitris, Ersi, Erida, Grigoris, Anastasia, Nikolas, Stefanos, Eri, Vassia G.-V., Nasos, Vaggelio, Despina: thank you so much for all the love, laughter, hugs, chats, spiritual exchanges and beautiful encounters.

Finally, I am completely indebted to those few special individuals who have displayed persistently their care and, as a result, have helped me keep sane. A deep 'thank you' then needs to be expressed to Mimi, Christina, Eva, Tânia, Elli, Olga and Georgia who, through their loving support, understanding, creativity and by always being nearby somehow, even if far away, never cease to prove that our long-term friendship cannot but be considered priceless, and to João for being present through a special connection of interactive empathy, telepathy, affection and tender vulnerability.

Above all, I owe my innermost thanks to my parents: to my late father, Ioannis N. Roussos, who encouraged me to love learning, reading and researching, and to my mother, Anthoula Tsilfidou-Roussou, whose unconditional love and care, constant support and evil eye 'expertise' have always been invaluable; without them, none of my goals and dreams would ever be achieved.

1

Introduction

Ariadne,[1] a northern Greek woman in her early forties, is making all the necessary preparations to show me how she performs the ritual healing against the evil eye. It is in the summer of 2019, and hers is the last interview I will conduct before closing my almost fifteen years of on-and-off research on the practice of the evil eye. I sit on the sofa, waiting for her to return from the kitchen, where she went to fill a coffee cup with water and get some olive oil, namely the necessary materials to perform the ritual on me – it has become a common ethnographic strategy to sense how the evil eye healing works on my own body. While I wait, I notice the feng shui lucky charms, the New Age crystals and other similar objects in her living room; a rosary, which, as Ariadne has told me, was given to her by a female relative for spiritual protection, after a visit to a Greek Orthodox monastery, also claims its own space in the room. Ariadne comes back but immediately realizes she has forgotten something, so she excuses herself and leaves the room again to go and get it. I wonder what she could have possibly forgotten, as all the necessary things for the healing are already standing here in front of me.

Ariadne comes back with a piece of wood sitting inside a small porcelain saucer; she does not need to explain to me what it is. I had recently discovered *palo santo*,[2] and I had also bought a small saucer depicting an eye from a popular retail chain shop to burn it inside for positive spiritual energy (see Figure 1). I am stunned by the coincidence but I try not to show it to Ariadne, since I do not want to impose my own choices, ideas, beliefs and explanations – at a personal and at an auto-reflexive ethnographic level – on her. So, uninterrupted, she describes what *palo santo* is and mentions the fact that she bought the little saucer from a particularly popular shop from where she had brought lately various objects depicting eyes, because she wanted to be protected from all kinds of negative energies, evil eye and otherwise; she has also bought some napkins with the eye symbol on it; 'perhaps it can protect me from the evil eye and from

Figure 1 *Palo santo* and the evil eye.

the admiration of people when I cook a very tasty dinner for them', she jokes. Ariadne usually keeps the evil eye saucer and the *palo santo* in her bedroom where, almost every night, she lights the little piece of wood before she goes to sleep and she meditates, so as to 'fill my bedroom with its spiritual aroma, to protect me, and bring peaceful energy in my dreams'. Ariadne lights up the piece of wood, passes it around the room and makes a smoky circle with it around my body, before leaving it to slowly burn off on the table in front of us. She then proceeds with the ritual healing against the evil eye, murmuring a religious prayer and using the oil and the water.

The evil eye (*kako mati* or simply *mati*) refers to the phenomenon where certain individuals, possessed by envy, meanness and general bad – but sometimes also good – feelings in their soul, transmit a form of energy to fellow human beings. It is a belief that exists since Greek antiquity, with a terminological and analytical emphasis being placed on the 'eye', since it is through the sense of vision and the exchange of gazes that the evil eye is supposed to primarily occur. Despite the important role of vision and its subsequent influence in defining the practice of the evil eye linguistically, as it will be argued later in the book, the evil eye is a practice that involves all the senses but also goes beyond them. The emotional broadcast in the evil eye occurs during daily sensory communication, when people interact with one another visually, verbally and aurally. Such interactions commonly result in evil eye affliction (*matiasma*). This is followed by a state of bodily distress, where the afflicted person (*matiasmeni*) experiences the evil eye effects, in the form of ill-health symptoms, on his/her body. What follows is a ritual healing known as *ksematiasma*, which is predominantly performed by lay specialists. Finally, in addition to the spiritual beliefs and practices involved, people draw on a panoply of evil eye material objects (*matakia*), which are mainly used as prophylactic amulets against any form of evil.

Placing the belief in the evil eye at the centre of the analysis, this book explores the practice of vernacular religiosity in a southern European country, by examining the dynamic ways in which lay people in Greece, and more specifically in Crete and northern Greece, practise their religion and spirituality during their everyday lives. Stepping away from the theoretical and analytic stereotype of perceiving religion and spirituality as antithetical, the objective of this ethnography is to analyse the complex and creative ways in which religion and spirituality are amalgamated in vernacular performances of religiosity, while approaching contemporary spirituality as 'lived religion' (McGuire 2008). With the popular belief in the evil eye and its various elements as a vehicle, it will be shown how people in Greece redraw the boundaries between religion and spirituality, creating a dynamic field of spiritual freedom through individual action, as 'traditional forms of religion, particularly Christianity, are giving way to holistic spirituality, sometimes still called New Age' (Heelas and Woodhead 2005: x).

The analytical value of choosing the practice of the evil eye as the main theme of study rests on the fact that it stands between Orthodoxy and New Age spirituality, merging both in its everyday performance. It furthermore designates that something has changed in Greece nowadays. Orthodoxy's defences have dropped, and its concrete walls have become porous and do not deny the reception of other spiritual influences. Greeks do not simply 'tolerate' (Hayden 2002) other religions any longer. They are not afraid to be religiously, spiritually and ritually creative. They now produce their own syntheses of believing, and they actively practise their belief. Through the evil eye, it is shown how contemporary Greek religiosity is going through a process of 'individualization' (Pollack 2008), and how New Age spirituality has become an active part of Greek religiosity. Orthodoxy appears to be losing its exclusive authority, as Greeks have the choice to follow other spiritual paths. Cretans and northern Greeks attend church liturgies and do sun salutations at home; they practise reiki and simultaneously perform religious-orientated healing treatments; they place Christian icons next to feng shui objects; they possess religious amulets and healing crystals; they believe in the divine, the supernatural and in flowing energy. Namely, they combine Orthodox religion and New Age spirituality, based on their individual spiritual needs and beliefs.

This spiritual amalgamation between (Orthodox) religion and (New Age) spirituality that is currently experienced and practised in Greece constitutes a fundamental development. It shows that the link between Orthodoxy and Greek identity does not stand by itself uncritically any longer. Namely, Greek religious identity has ceased to be 'assumed' (Stewart 2004: 280), since its Orthodox boundaries have become transcended. Greeks, therefore, have taken a crucial step towards freeing themselves from having Orthodoxy as a given part of their identity. Given the historical bond between Orthodox Christianity and Greek identity and the resulting predominance of Orthodoxy in the country for centuries, people in Greece today are doing more than simply transforming Greek popular religiosity. Instead, they are rebelling against an – up until recently – predetermined religiosity without, however, abandoning doctrinal religion altogether (as have many of their European counterparts). Greeks, then, act creatively while they handle their religiosity in dynamic ways through their pluralistic choices to follow more than one spiritual path along the way. Perhaps it is not so random, therefore, that the evil eye practice has been transformed, keeping its complicated yet everlasting relationship with Orthodoxy, but simultaneously incorporating new forms of spirituality. In the context of the evil eye belief and practice, a crossing of paths between religion and spirituality has occurred: a belief and practice that are considered religious and magical, Orthodox and pagan, natural and supernatural, scientific and mystical. In the words of Bruce (1998: 230):

> As cultures become more diverse and as individuals claim greater authority to decide not only what they want to do but also what they want to believe, the shared ground for communal beliefs is reduced. This in turn reduces the

plausibility to any individual of any religion but it does not prevent people from idiosyncratically entertaining diverse views of the life hereafter. Indeed, because there is no longer a dominant tradition with the power to stigmatise alternatives as deviant, it positively encourages low salience flirtation with an exotic array of alternatives.

As shown in the ethnographic example of Ariadne above, vernacular religiosity and spiritual creativity go hand in hand within the field of religious practice (Primiano 1995, 2012; Bowman and Valk 2012). In this book, emphasis is placed on the transformation of the Greek religious landscape at the level of everyday religious practice, where the so-called New Age spirituality (Heelas 1996; Hanegraaff 1996; Sutcliffe 2003; Heelas and Woodhead 2005; Kemp and Lewis 2007; Sutcliffe and Gilhus 2013) has become a new lived religiosity. Christianity and contemporary spirituality have always co-existed, interacted and continue to intermingle in the religious landscape of southern Europe. At the same time, as recent anthropological works (Rountree 2010; Fedele 2012; Cornejo Valle 2013; Fedele and Knibbe 2013; Roussou 2011, 2013) demonstrate, the presence of alternative spirituality in countries like Italy, Spain and Greece has become apparent, claiming an important role within the religious landscape of European countries that have been directly linked to Christian belief.

Especially during the current socioeconomic crisis in southern Europe, new forms of spirituality have provided an alternative to denominational religion, predominantly Christianity, for the latter has left people feeling largely unsupported and disillusioned in these difficult times. And although most of Christian believers do not let go of the Church completely or at all, the majority of the individuals quoted in this ethnographic work have questioned the position that Orthodox Christianity holds in contemporary Greece and have begun to follow non-Orthodox spiritual itineraries.[3] Their need to pursue other spiritual directions in parallel to practising Orthodoxy is inspired by global trends and their desire to discover new ways of communication with the sacred. The aim of the book is to follow the(ir) diverse spiritual trajectories of vernacular religiosity, as people in Greece are gradually letting go of the churches and 'believe without belonging' (Davie 1994), without, however, abandoning their religious heritage.

Orthodox Christianity and Greek socio-cultural identity share a long-established intimacy. According to statistical surveys, around 97 per cent of the Greek population is – at least nominally – Orthodox (Alivizatos 1999: 25). Nowadays, however, practices of New Age spiritual orientation challenge the almost exclusive role of Orthodox Christianity as the autochthonous religion in contemporary Greece. Orthodox Christianity and New Age spirituality interact and amalgamate, leading contemporary Greek religiosity towards a dynamic path of creative spiritual synthesis. It is true that, up until recently, Orthodox Christianity seems to have dominated the religious field of contemporary Greece. However, the recent popularity of New Age spirituality challenges religion in contemporary Greece and pushes it in novel directions. More particularly, New Age spirituality has entered the evil eye practice as a result of a porous Orthodoxy and of the pursuit of new spiritual and cultural trends. Greeks do not perceive these new paths of spirituality as threatening. The evil eye practice remains socio-culturally Greek, even when accompanied by reiki or yoga, or when the ritual healing is performed to keep the negative energy away and while New Age crystals, feng shui objects and religious icons reside in some other part of people's homes to protect from evil energies. Consequently, from articulating discourses on energy, to practising yoga, and from adopting a feng shui lifestyle to enhancing *ksematiasma* with reiki healing embodiments, the religious landscape in contemporary Greece appears to have escaped Orthodox Christianity. As Stewart (2004: 280) argues: 'Now, with around 96 per cent of the populace at least nominally Orthodox, religious boundaries and identity have become more assumed than defended.'

With only a few exceptions (e.g. Rountree 2010; Palmisano 2010; Fedele 2012; Cornejo Valle 2013; Palmisano and Pannofino 2017; Roussou 2017, 2018; Clot-Garrell and Griera 2019), when it comes to countries of southern Europe such as Greece, Portugal, Spain and Italy, studies have continued to reproduce the traditional stereotype that connects southern Europe to the single-faith, namely Christian, approach. The present work escapes this stereotype and it is one among a very scarce number of studies that present a different image of contemporary Greek religiosity, disconnecting Greece from the stereotypical assumption that follows it, as a southern European country, that (Orthodox) Christianity dominates the religious landscape of the country. The objective is to demonstrate how contemporary Greek religiosity is characterized by open religious horizons, where a creative amalgamation of Christianity and New Age spirituality takes place at the level of vernacular religious practice.

Conceptualizing religion and spirituality

Despite their usefulness as analytical means of negotiating contemporary issues of belief and religiosity, religion and spirituality are two concepts that are complex, vague and can be considered as 'umbrella terms'. For that reason, it is important to clarify their signifieds and, through such a clarification, to contextualize the main focus of the book, namely the practice of the evil eye, within the interactive yet challenging relationship between the two. For the needs of my argument and analysis, then, religion is employed in the book as synonymous to the prevailing organized religious institution in Greece, namely Orthodox Christianity. Spirituality is used in order to signify non-institutional and more subjectivized New Age practices that have recently entered the spiritual field of contemporary Greece. It must be emphasized again, however, that religion and spirituality are not perceived as – necessarily – opposed to one another. Orthodox Christianity consists of and can be regarded as spirituality. New Age practices consist of and can be regarded as religion. Namely, both Orthodox and New Age practices possess elements of both religion and spirituality equivalently.

Using religion as synonymous to Orthodox Christianity does not imply a portrayal of contemporary Greek religiosity as mono-religiously oriented. Furthermore, as mentioned above, it is a fact that New Age practices may well be regarded as religious; yet, when my interlocutors in Crete and northern Greece mentioned religion during our conversations, they referred to Orthodox Christianity, which they thought to be the prevailing institutional, doctrinal, official religion of Greece. During my ethnographic research religion (*thriskeia*) was perceived as synonymous to Orthodoxy. Consequently, for the needs of the analysis, I follow the emic interpretation of *thriskeia* as synonymous to Orthodoxy, while being aware of the possible limitations such an approach can entail.

In addition, 'alternative spirituality', 'new (forms of) spirituality' and – especially – 'New Age spirituality' are all considered to be umbrella terms and have received criticism in recent years (Sutcliffe and Bowman 2000; Sutcliffe 2003; von Stuckrad 2005; Wood 2007). As has been argued, 'the scholarly field of New Age studies is fraught with a tendency to lack theoretical underpinning, empirical evidence and comparative considerations' (Wood 2007: 9). Taking thus into consideration the difficulties and the complications these terms entail, they are used interchangeably in the present text, in order to denote the non-Christian and more individualized paths that my interlocutors follow during their everyday lives. Adopting an emic analytical model and ethnographic perspective, the analysis is based on the fact that Rethymniots and Thessalonikans – the residents of the Cretan town of Rethymno and the northern Greek city of Thessaloniki, equivalently, where I conducted my ethnographic fieldwork – use themselves the terms alternatively in order to describe their practices and utilize the terminology accordingly.

Shimazono (1999) has proposed the term 'New Spirituality Movements and Culture' as an alternative. In his words (Shimazono 1999: 125):

> Using 'movements' in the plural shows that the term embraces various types of 'New Age' groups. The word 'spirituality' is used because many people in these movements consider that they belong to a New Age of 'spirituality' that is to follow the age of 'religion' as it comes to an end. 'Spirituality' in a broad sense implies religiousness, but it does not mean organized religion or doctrine. Rather, it is used to mean the religious nature expressed by an individual's thoughts and actions.

According to Shimazono's approach, spirituality does not belong to any official doctrine. It is not collectively organized but individually driven and practised, while moving culturally forward, gradually leaving religion behind. As happens with 'New Religious Movements', 'New Spiritual Movements' imply an antithesis between religion and spirituality, where religion is understood as the officially organized doctrine and spirituality as the individual experience of the sacred in everyday life.

In my analysis, I follow Shimazono's (1999) approach, without, however, adopting the implied antithesis between religion and spirituality. Knoblauch (2008: 145) asserts that 'spirituality differs from religion by the stress laid on subjective experience of great transcendences by "ordinary" people. Students of Weber may detect the fundamental change with respect to traditional religion: charisma is not restricted to virtuosi or administered by organizations but becomes generalized and subjectivized'. People in my Greek fieldsites have shown that Orthodoxy and New Age spirituality should be considered as complementary – the boundaries between them are blurred. Certainly, there is a long tradition of spirituality within Orthodoxy. Thus, the synthesis of Orthodox and New Age spiritual practices in present-day Greece may not come as a surprise. Mysticism and meditation existed in the Orthodox circles long before yoga, feng shui, reiki and New Age spirituality made their appearance in the country. But what also needs to be emphasized is the fact that spiritual charisma in contemporary Greece is not a privilege of the Orthodox virtuosi; vernacular religious practitioners can claim it too.

And here lies the uniqueness of the relationship between religion and spirituality in the Greek context. In the Western socio-cultural context, denominational religion and individualized spirituality are perceived and practised in antithetical terms and can hardly co-exist (see Shimazono 1999; Knoblauch 2003; Stark, Hamberg and Miller 2005; Knoblauch 2008). In Greece, however, judging from my ethnographic research at least, the boundaries between the two appear not only softened but almost collapsed. Religion and spirituality are amalgamated in people's everyday spiritual practices. Self-proclaimed atheists do not entirely cut their bond with Orthodoxy. Orthodox devotees are often open to and incorporate New Age ideologies in their lives. The appearance of this exogenous and globalized New Age spirituality and the spiritual synthesis between Orthodox and New Age practices has come to stay.

In order to capture this synthesis and its reference to both Orthodox and New Age ideologies, the term 'spiritual' is employed with reference to both Orthodox Christian religion and New Age spirituality. Although I have found it analytically useful to use the term spirituality as synonymous to an exogenous and thus non-Orthodox form of spirituality, it does not mean I wish to neglect the spiritual character of Orthodoxy. This is where the term 'spiritual' comes into the picture. Whereas 'spirituality' refers specifically to New Age-oriented practices, 'spiritual' refers to Orthodox religion and New Age spirituality, therefore addressing and acknowledging the spiritual character of both. Therefore, the term 'spiritual' in this book is neither employed as the opposite of the 'religious' nor exclusively connected with New Age spirituality. When I talk about the 'spiritual landscape of contemporary Greece', or the fact that my interlocutors are 'spiritually creative', and when I use other equivalent expressions, the terms 'spiritual' and 'spiritually' stand for both New Age spirituality and Orthodox Christian religion. In this book, the terms 'spiritual' and 'spiritually' serve as an analytical tool and rhetoric, which portrays the spiritual character of both Orthodox Christian and New Age practices; it portrays their mutual interaction and amalgamation in Crete and northern Greece.

Evil eye research in Greece

Most of the well-known Greek folklorists included the evil eye in their studies of Greek tradition. Politis approached the evil eye as a folk superstition and a social survival that belonged to a Greek past. Megas taxonomized it as a magical act and Loukatos as folk medicine (Veikou 1998: 81–2). Hardie's (1925) West Macedonian evil eye study can be considered a link between folkloric and anthropological approaches towards the evil eye. She mainly focused on the healing aspect of the practice, seeing the ritual healing of *ksematiasma* as an 'old wives' remedy'. Ultimately, her mainly descriptive analysis remained closer to a folklore study rather than an anthropological contribution. A few monographs and articles, written mainly by non-Greek anthropologists who chose Greece as their ethnographic locus, are the only anthropological studies that adopted the evil eye as part of their analysis, albeit briefly in most cases.

Campbell's (1964) study of the Sarakatsanoi people is probably the first anthropological work that attempts to interpret the evil eye in social terms. In his study, the Sarakatsanoi attribute evil eye affliction to the devil. High social status and honour provoke envy, which in turn sets off the evil eye while turning people away from God. The evil eye is attributed to emotional interaction by Blum and Blum (1965, 1970). Their research in a rural environment around Attica showed that the evil eye works as a form of social control: the poor use it as a tool to prevent others from earning too much wealth and consequently to keep a social balance in their community. Dionisopoulos-Mass' article (1976) is based on ethnographic research she conducted in a Greek-island 'peasant village' (1976: 42), where gossip, social criticism and envy prevail. She offers an extended and engaging analysis of evil eye amulets and healing practices. However, she fails to establish a convincing argument. She claims that the ideology of the village is rooted in three powers that constitute the structural elements of a social continuum: the evil eye, gossip and magic (1976: 43). According to her analysis, the evil eye performs a social function (1976: 60) and, together with gossip and magic, it constructs a regulated system of social control.

This idea that the evil eye is a practice of social control is also adopted by Hirschon (1998 [1989]: 181). Lykiardopoulos' (1981) 'exhaustive study' of the evil eye as a folk belief makes the argument that it is a form of social communication and is cast intentionally. Du Boulay (1974) places the belief in the context of religious ideology, and so does Stewart (1991), who draws a parallel between baptism, exorcism and spells such as the evil eye ritual healing; Hart (1992), who argues that evil eye belief and Christian faith are not separated; and Danforth (1989), for whom the evil eye, just like firewalking, constitutes a religious idiom of ritual healing. Dubisch (1986) connects it with gender identity, asserting that, through its practice, women gain power and authority. Kenna (1995) looks at the evil eye in relation to Greek hospitality and asserts that the latter prevents the former from occurring. Chryssanthopoulou (1993, 1999, 2008) demonstrates how Castellorizian migrants in Perth, Australia, use the evil eye as a sociocultural indicator of their ethnic identity.

Using data from Rhodes and Crete, Herzfeld (1981) argues that the evil eye forms a symbol, a feature of larger symbolic systems; the signs around the evil eye's socio-cultural surroundings are the ones that matter the most (1981: 560–1). Herzfeld eliminated the usefulness of the evil eye as an analytic category, at least until enough local studies are conducted and enough data collected (1981: 561; see also Galt 1982: 664, 668). In another article (Herzfeld 1986), he places particular emphasis on issues of illness (as a text) and healing (as the reading of the text). At the end, his analysis is led to the conclusion that, through the textual, performative and embodied evil eye practice, social disorder is symbolically re-established.

Veikou's book, published in 1998, deserves special attention, since it is the most recent and thorough work on the evil eye in Greece. Based on fieldwork she conducted in the Macedonian community of Neo Kastro between 1989 and 1992, this is the only anthropological monograph that actually positions the evil eye at the centre of ethnographic analysis. Her ethnographic data are rich, and she touches the research subject from multiple socio-cultural angles, offering a wealth of theoretical directions and analytic interpretations. According to Veikou (1998: 16), her study concerns a local example of an indigenous variation of the evil eye, inside a peripheral Mediterranean rural community. With the theories of social constructivism, practice and symbolic interaction filling her analytical suitcase (1998: 20), her aims are as follows: to look into the community's history and everyday social life for these associations that make evil eye existence justifiable and reasonable (1998: 16); to investigate the cultural meaning of a system of relationships as they are expressed through the belief in the evil eye and the healing practice of *ksematiasma* (1998); to examine how a cultural form of visual perception, that of *matiasma* (evil eye affliction), is transformed into a significant code of communicational strategy (1998: 15, 27); and to focus on questions of identity construction through visual contact and social interaction (1998: 205). The contribution of her study, as she puts it, rests on the fact that the evil eye, 'apart from being a cultural form, a symbolic system, a structural social element and a psychological idiom, it is also a type of visual perception and a code of communication: a strategy people use in order to construct their social relationships and their personal identity' (1998: 20).

Unfortunately, her approach appears to end up more rigid than that. The idea of social control dominates throughout Veikou's analysis. A controlling gaze 'punishes those who violate the social values' (1998: 128) and exercises its authority on people – as it happens in the case of Hrisoula, one of Veikou's interlocutors. Hrisoula enjoys social power both inside and outside her familial space. She comes from a wealthy family. She takes care of the financial situation of her own family. She prefers to do her shopping in the nearby city of Kavala and not in Neo Kastro, possibly, as Veikou explains, because she wants to highlight her high economic and social status. Her shopping excursions are for Hrisoula a way to project her social superiority, and a way to attract the evil eye. Whenever she goes to Kavala, she makes sure people in the community know about it. When she returns, she visibly shows off to her friends and her co-villagers. As Hrisoula told the anthropologist, she is given the evil eye every single time she returns from Kavala, and wonders why this is so. Veikou asserts that Hrisoula provokes the evil eye. She knows that she 'has to' feel evil eyed, because she has behaved against the social norms and she is going to be punished. According to Veikou's main argument, which is depicted in Hrisoula's ethnographic example, the evil eye is a form of visual communication, which constructs social relationships and identities inside the community. It is approached as a communicative strategy of controlling identities, in an attempt to safeguard the coherence of the community (Veikou 1998: 193) and to keep the relationship between society and its individuals balanced – a relationship, where ultimately society is presented as having the upper hand (Veikou 1998: 18–25, 147–8, 199).

In general terms, Veikou affirms that, through people's visual interaction, the community is in charge. The evil eye practice forms a social tool, which the community uses so as to impose its priority over the individual and to maintain its harmony. It is a social strategy which defines the boundaries of acceptable agency, forcing individuals not to exceed the common social standards, and prevents deviating behaviour and social differentiation. Social subjects are subsequently disempowered, constantly constrained and continuously liable to the community. Veikou follows a structuralist, anti-practice approach. She sees the evil eye as a closed system, where the community, not the action of individuals, is in charge. As far as her analysis is concerned, the evil eye is a social structure, not a practice: people's agency and cultural creativity bear no power to stir up their socio-cultural surroundings.

As described above, the Greek evil eye was treated by folklorists as a superstition which, as a survival from the past, did not occupy an active social position in present-day Greece. Anthropological approaches, on the one hand, did not fully explore the multiple dynamics it entails. On the other hand, they analysed the evil eye as a power of social control, ultimately implying that people lacked social power and agency and were subordinated to the absolute authority of the community/society. My approach takes a different analytical route. The evil eye practice is not treated here as social power that renders people passive and inactive. The evil eye practice, as explored in this book, is about people who dare to act, to make changes, to become not just simple observers of but dynamic participants in their socio-cultural environment. It is about people who become socially empowered by practising creatively.

Creativity has been defined as 'activity that produces something new through the recombination and transformation of existing cultural practices or forms' (Liep 2001: 2). It is linked to both space and time (Hastrup 2001: 32) and to human agency 'as the capacity to respond imaginatively to new experiences – and thereby to find the ontologically new' (Hastrup 2001: 43). My approach, consequently, rests on the insistence that the Greek evil eye constitutes a culturally dynamic process, where social subjects act; challenge their current socio-cultural settings, relations and identities; gain power; and where, ultimately, they creatively practise. Evil eye practitioners are active agents. They transmit, get attacked by and cure the evil eye. In doing so, they develop strategies to move with and around it. And by actively practising the evil eye in their everyday life, Greeks demonstrate agency and creativity, challenge their identities, and socio-culturally act in a dynamic field of interpersonal interactions. It is those moments of creative agency at a perceptual, ritual, performative, material and discursive level, as practised by people in Crete and northern Greece during their everyday lives, which have brought contemporary religion and spirituality to a crossroads. It is these of moments of creative agency as practised in the Greek evil eye that make up the core of this book.

Fieldwork and its methods

Urban and rural: Transgressing spaces

With only very few anthropological exceptions, the evil eye has been almost exclusively studied within the locality of rural Greek communities. As Hirschon (1998 [1989]: 233) points out, 'In Greece, the folk-urban continuum has too often been applied as the folk-urban divide. In this rural emphasis, what constitutes posited "tradition" is implicitly located in the countryside, the city being seen as the locus of inevitable, radical, and rapid social change where any "traditional" practices are only curious remnants, soon to pass into oblivion.' I chose Rethymno, a town in Crete, and Thessaloniki, the second largest city of Greece, as my fieldsites, because I wanted to escape the folk-urban divide as well as the stereotype, cultivated by both Greeks and ethnographers, that the evil eye is only practised by female villagers in rural 'traditional' environments. This methodological choice allowed me to observe the socio-cultural mobility of the evil eye inside an environment which, for a change, was not rural. At the same time, however, it led to the ethnographic realization that rural and urban spaces are not separated but intertwined.

Migration from rural to urban environments has thrived in Greece in the last few decades. Crete and northern Greece have not been exempted from the process. Former residents of rural communities have moved to Rethymno and Thessaloniki, in search of opportunities and the lifestyle an urban space can offer. Rethymno and Thessaloniki are not inherently urban spaces. People circulate between the urban and the rural to visit relatives and friends. The urban and the rural spatial domains drop their fences and defences. They share 'borderlands', 'physical spaces that suggest something in-between, a contact zone, an area where discontinuities become somewhat blurred' (Herzfeld 2001: 141). As Massey (1994: 5) argues, 'The particularity of place is constructed not by placing boundaries around it and defining its identity through counter-position to the other which lies beyond, but through the specificity of the mix of links and interconnections to that "beyond". Places viewed this way are open and porous.'

In my research, 'that beyond' is the rural environment. Although my fieldwork was conducted in two urban sites, Rethymno and Thessaloniki kept their spatial boundaries open to a communication with the rural. Through the evil eye practice, the boundaries between urban and rural space are crossed, and this is mainly accomplished through the ritual healing of *ksematiasma*. Often, my interlocutors would call their relatives and friends who live in a village and asked them to perform the ritual healing. Other times, they would leave their cities and pay their relatives a visit to have the evil eye removed in person. The healing of *ksematiasma* thus creates a socio-cultural link between the urban and the rural. My urban fieldwork overcame the stereotype that the evil eye is a folk belief, confined within the spatiality of villages. The evil eye is practised actively and creatively in both Rethymno and Thessaloniki. Yet, since social phenomena and spaces consist of social relations that are never still but dynamic (Massey 1994: 2), the evil eye follows the actions of its practitioners in the social arena. It pervades both urban and rural space, creating a fluid two-way communication between them through a web of social relatedness.

Fieldsites

Located between Chania and Heraklion, Rethymno is the third largest town of the island of Crete in southern Greece. According to the General Secretariat of the National Statistical Service of Greece, it is inhabited by approximately 40,000 residents.[4] Its economy relies heavily on tourism. From around the middle of June till the beginning of October, tourists from all over Greece, Europe and the United States swarm the Old Town and its shops, cafeterias, taverns and sights.

Fortezza Castle, Krini Rimondi, Megali Porta, the mosques, the lighthouse in the port and the beautiful narrow alleys constitute some of the main tourist attractions. Rethymno is divided into two parts: the Old Town, with its narrow paved streets, the houses with the beautiful architecture, the shops, and the tourist rush; and the New Town, which is not clearly separated from the Old Town, apart from one major street, which perhaps serves as an open spatial boundary. The New Town mainly consists of supermarkets, professional offices and blocks of flats that climb up the hills which surround the town.

Crete was ruled by the Venetians from 1210 to 1669. In 1645, however, Turkish armies attacked and invaded the island. Rethymno fell into their hands by the end of 1646 (Herzfeld 1991: 17), and it was liberated from Turkish domination and became part of the Greek state in 1912 (Herzfeld 1991: 19). As Herzfeld (1991) points out in his ethnographically rich book about Rethymno, the Old Town still embraces reminders of its former invaders. Many of its locations maintain their Italian names, and its buildings, with their Venetian architecture, are legally protected as a national conservation area of historical 'monumentalism' (1991: 47). At the same time, a mosque stands erect in the very heart of the Old Town, clearly constituting a historical clue. A mosque was also located close to my fieldwork residence, a small studio flat in the new part of the town. Every day, throughout my Rethymniot stay, I crossed the street boundary between the New and the Old Town to wander around the narrow streets of the Old Town (see Figure 2). Apart from a few cases, where I visited people in their New Town houses or they came to mine for a discussion, fieldwork was predominantly conducted in the Old Town. And, without realizing it, I had set a spatial boundary between my personal and my professional self, between home and research. This separation was essential to acquire a – symbolic as well as actual – distance from the field.

With a population of more than a million in its metropolis and about 300 and 70,000 in the municipality, Thessaloniki deserves its characterization as the co-capital of Greece. Thessaloniki is spatially understood as constituted by the city centre, with all its shops, cafés, bars and offices, and by its different residential zones spread out around the east, north and west of the centre (see Figure 3). I lived in the eastern part of the city, which is considered a socioeconomically lower-middle- and middle-class area. Although I spent a lot of research time around the centre, walking many hours per day trying to find shops with evil eye objects displayed in their windows, an equal amount of fieldwork was conducted in my neighbourhood. My fieldsite in Thessaloniki was not defined by territorial stability. Namely, fieldwork was not restricted in one part of the city. Instead, I

Figure 2 A typical Rethymniot alley.

kept moving around various parts of Thessaloniki. This ethnographic spatial fluidity enriched the research with a variety of perspectives.

Multi-sited fieldwork has been defined as a 'circulation of cultural meanings, objects and identities in diffuse time-space; this mobile ethnography takes unexpected trajectories in tracing a cultural formation across and within multiple sites of activity' (Marcus 1995: 96). I chose to conduct my fieldwork on two sites.

Figure 3 Aristotelous Square.

Yet, its subfields were multiple. I pursued social meanings, objects, performances and people in a multiplicity of spatialities. And by moving geographically (from Crete to northern Greece, from Rethymno to Thessaloniki), spatially (among different locations inside my fieldsites) and socio-culturally (in between the evil eye, Orthodox, New Age and other healing, ritualistic, spiritual practices and discourses), I kept the boundaries of the 'field' open (Gupta and Ferguson 1997). My choice of a dual-sited fieldwork stemmed primarily from three factors: first, the need for a comparative approach towards the Greek evil eye phenomenon, which has so far been studied in strictly localized terms; second, the need for diversity, which can lead to vibrant ethnographic itineraries; third, the geographic position and cultural distinctiveness: a town in the far south and a city in the northern part of Greece sharpen the potential for comparison and diversity in the research, and offer two urban environments for a study that aims to shift the many stereotypes concerning the practice of the evil eye.

Rethymniots refer to the evil eye as *ftharmos*, diverging from the common terminological term *mati*, which is utilized almost exclusively by mainland Greeks, Thessalonikans included.[5] The Church of Crete jurisdictionally belongs to the Patriarchate of Constantinople and is not under the authority of the Church of Greece. Thessaloniki is part of the autocephalous Church of Greece, and its citizens are well known for their religious devotion. Rethymno is an urban town.

Thessaloniki is an urban city. I had never been to Crete; yet, the many years of my love for Cretan music and consequently Cretan culture had established a sense of familiarity. Thessaloniki was connected with my experience to visits to medical doctors, a few shopping excursions and kin-related weddings/baptisms; it is less than two hours away from my home town, with which it also shares social commonalities; it is close to being a cultural home.

Spiritual diversities between my two fieldsites have made themselves present in terms of belief, practice and ritual healing performances. Both Rethymno and Thessaloniki render a rural-versus-urban demarcation unnecessary. The culturally alien locus of Rethymno offered familial warmth and the reasonably familiar site of Thessaloniki occasional frost. In any case, my pre-fieldwork assumptions have been replaced by post-research ethnographic factuality. Southern and northern Greece, Rethymno and Thessaloniki, are creatively diverse in people's everyday practices, actions and perceptions. Simultaneously, my comparative approach has indicated that, especially when it comes to the evil eye, my freshly discovered (Rethymniot) and my newly re-discovered (Thessalonikan) ethnographic homes are socio-culturally related.

Doing anthropology 'at home'

Going back to my country of origin to carry out fieldwork, and choosing a research theme with which I had already been quite well acquainted, has not been an undemanding ethnographic undertaking. 'Native anthropology', or 'anthropology at home', has been heavily criticized:

> There is no way one can speak from a native and an anthropological position simultaneously. It is logically impossible to speak from an internal and external position simultaneously (…). The native anthropologist cannot possibly incorporate objectivity. Without a doubt, native anthropology is a contradiction in terms.
>
> (Hastrup 1998: 358–9)

Hastrup (1998) argues that knowledge production is based on objectification. In order to produce knowledge, anthropology needs to occupy a position of otherness. According to her, an indigenous anthropologist can never become an ultimate 'other'; hence, s/he can never entirely achieve objectivity – knowledge production through the path of indigenous anthropology is doomed to fail. It is probably all too easy to dismiss anthropology at home on the grounds that it is non-objective, illogical and unable to distinguish between indigenous/local and ethnographic discourses. But as Latour (1993 [1991]: 7) has pointed out, 'It is because they remain incapable of studying themselves that ethnographers are so critical, and so distant, when they go off to the tropics to study others.'

Anthropologists at home have indeed been accused of not immersing themselves in 'real' ethnography, since they do not seek the exotic and the culturally distant. A polarization is thus constructed between 'native' and 'real' anthropologists. Yet, this paradigm goes back to the era of colonization, when 'natives were genuine natives (whether they liked it or not) and the observer's objectivity in the scientific research of Other societies posed no problem' (Narayan 1993: 672). Contemporary anthropology is supposed to have escaped its colonial past. However, when adherents of the discipline argue in favour of an objective scientific research of the indigenous and exotic other, while simultaneously arguing against indigenous anthropology, it appears as if the colonizing impulse in anthropology has never been eliminated.

The most methodologically complicated issue when it comes to native anthropology seems to concern the unique relationship between the 'self' and the 'other'. The ability of the anthropologist at home to separate his/her native self from the cultural other, in order to keep a certain degree of ethnographic distance between him/her and the field, is distrusted. The fact that the 'self' and the 'other' are part of a familiar cultural space has been characterized as an oxymoron (Gefou-Madianou 1993: 46). It is not an easy ethnographic mission to study an 'other' who is also a 'self'. Certainly, some form of 'otherness' has to be looked for inside the familiar (Gefou-Madianou 1998: 381). It is required by the native anthropologist to own the capacity to administer the double, most likely 'schizophrenic', identity of being both a cultural insider and an outsider, of belonging to 'us' and to 'them'. But this thin line between the personal and the professional is not experienced only by anthropologists who study 'at home'. Once an anthropologist, whose field is located very far away from home, familiarizes him/herself with the socio-cultural environment and the people s/he studies, his/her positioning and manipulation of the line boundary do not differ much from those of his/her native colleague.

Auto-ethnography, or who am 'I'?

Panourgia's (1995) ethnography about death rituals in Athens is a vivid example of a deeply involved anthropologist who has studied 'at home' and who describes her ethnographic journey in an autobiographical and confessional way. Panourgia based her research on her own family in Athens. She narrated deaths of individuals who belonged to her family. She even ethnographically dealt with the death of relatives who were close and very dear to her. At the end, she manages to talk not only about the continual alterations in her family's social and emotional bonds, but also about how death leads to identity constructions and negotiations in the Greek capital. And in the process of doing that, she does not hesitate to reveal her own deeper personal feelings, while casting the analytical eye of the anthropologist on herself and her family. Her ethnography has received criticism. It has been regarded as too personal, and too autobiographical. Nevertheless, Panourgia has managed to creatively mix her personal and her professional 'I' in such a way that the reader feels she can understand her ethnography 'from the inside'. Hers is an anthropological experiment of what an auto-ethnography can look like.

> Auto-ethnography synthesizes both a postmodern ethnography, in which the realist conventions and objective observer position of standard ethnography have been called into question, and a postmodern autobiography, in which the notion of the coherent, individual self has been similarly called into question. The term has a double sense – referring either to the ethnography of one's own group or to autobiographical writing that has ethnographic interest.
> (Reed-Danahay 1997: 2)

And, sometimes, it incorporates both senses. Auto-ethnography considerably blurs the boundaries between the ethnographic 'I' and the individual 'I', especially in cases where the anthropologist relies heavily on autobiographical experiences in the process of participating in and making ethnography. Reflexivity prevails, and the objective anthropological eye is replaced by the ethnographer's personal I (Marcus 1998: 88). However, an auto-ethnographer should not be treated with academic disbelief. Ethnographic autobiographical writing is not about self-narcissism, but about self-awareness (Okely 1992: 2).

My own ethnography, up to a certain degree at least, can be categorized as auto-anthropology, or auto-ethnography. I went to a field that was culturally familiar and I was well acquainted with the socio-cultural practice I was about to study. My evil eye autobiography followed me to the field. I could compare my interlocutors' experiences to my own. I was able to devise my research methodology, having already been somewhat aware of the sensitivities and difficulties entailed in the practice. I had to constantly deal with two selves who were either battling or cooperating. I explicitly participated during my fieldwork as much as I observed. Or, perhaps, I observed through and while participating.

When Favret-Saada (1980) went to the Bocage in France to conduct her research on witchcraft, she realized that the only way she could actually be let into the community was if she began to participate actively in its everyday rhetoric. In the Bocage, witchcraft is practised through the use of words. A person sends bad words to another one and bewitches her. Words are also used for reversing the results of witchcraft. Favret-Saada was thought to be an unwitcher because she was not afraid to talk about witchcraft; she did not hesitate to engage it in her discourse. The anthropologist, therefore, was accepted as a powerful unwitcher. She also became a client of an unwitcher herself. Favret-Saada's ethnography indicates how an auto-ethnographic piece of research, where the anthropologist becomes intimately entangled with her core theme of study, can successfully combine personal and professional facets of the anthropologist's self, while simultaneously offering an insightful account of reflexively rich and methodologically powerful ethnography.

Like Favret-Saada, I was intimately and actively involved in my main focus of study. I was accused of casting the evil eye. I was afflicted by people's negative gazes and feelings while I was in the field and I gradually learned how to become an evil eye healer. Until the age of eighteen, the (threat of) the evil eye had been well established in my everyday life. My encounter with anthropology during the years of my undergraduate studies resulted in my dismissal of the evil eye as a socio-cultural construct. Occasionally, I had to be healed from its effects; yet, I had decided to do my best to exclude it from my personal life and only keep a professional relationship with it. I commenced my fieldwork, therefore, while carrying – in my personal and anthropological suitcase – years of evil eye affliction and a recent realization that I should treat the practice simply as the socio-cultural phenomenon I was about to study. Of course, my ethnography wiped away all the initial preconceptions and pulled me into a context of active participation and identity reconfiguration.

But this book is not about my autobiography. It is about what and how the individuals I have met in my fieldsites experience, practise, live and negotiate with the evil eye. This is their autobiography, as channelled through the ethnographer. Of course, the personal and the ethnographic 'I' of the anthropologist is involved in the lives of her interlocutors. Autobiographic narratives of my ethnographic experience and of my fifteen months of continuous living among people in Crete and northern Greece are included in the text. Rethymniots and Thessalonikans decided to let me actively participate in their everyday practices, discourses and lives, and that fact has had its implications in the research. My own beliefs and feelings have influenced my behaviour as to how I have approached the field, individuals and social situations.

What has mostly determined the ethnographic outcome is the multiplicity of roles my interlocutors attributed to my 'I'. They did not distinguish between my being Greek and knowledgeable about the evil eye, and my being an anthropologist. As far as they were concerned, I had chosen to be among them; therefore, I should also go through various everyday challenges and engage with the dynamics of everyday life, no matter how unpredictable they would prove to be. The 'I' as used in the book is not (intended as) authoritative. It is the 'I' of being aware that the ethnography presented here required my participation in all aspects of the evil eye practice. It is the 'I' of recognition that sometimes my past experiences with the practice and my native identity resulted in an insufficient ability to approach ethnographic situations with anthropological clarity. It is, ultimately, the 'I' of the anthropologist who, during fieldwork, became an evil eye giver, an evil eye sufferer and an evil eye healer.

A stereotype follows the native anthropologist and certainly I could not escape it. Sometimes out of concern, other times out of negative suspicion, I was asked the reason why I chose Greece as a fieldwork locus; how I could deal with going back to such a familiar culture to do research; how I would prevent myself from getting ethnographically bored; and why I did not grab the opportunity to fly off to a remote and fascinating ethnographic site well outside Europe. At the same time, my fieldwork was considered an easily borne task. Before leaving for the field, I felt quite a few times a silent criticism for returning home. After going back to the academic environment, this feeling persisted. I had to deal with the fact that my research would be undermined at times, simply because I had not separated my 'self' from the 'other' as much as the unofficial rules of the discipline 'demand'.

Drawing on a stereotype, people might think that a native anthropologist finds all the doors open; interlocutors are easily reached and generously offer information; no obstacles have to be jumped on the way; fieldwork runs easily and smoothly. But anthropology at home is not easy, and it is not smooth. It is as challenging, rewarding, difficult, demanding and unpredictable as any ethnography can be. Of course, the fact that the language spoken in the field and my native language was one and the same made the research easier – I had to neither spend time developing linguistic skills, nor lose time trying to linguistically interpret my data. I had extensive previous knowledge of the subject under study, which meant that I was able to deeply recognize and efficiently taxonomize my data. Still, I was a stranger, and, on many occasions, I was treated as one. Crete was culturally unfamiliar to me. Apart from the language (although Cretans are renowned for their distinct dialect), when I arrived at Rethymno I was a cultural infant, absorbing everything as a new-born. Thessaloniki was supposed to be an almost native place for me. Yet, although the city and its people approached me as a fellow northern Greek, I was socio-culturally feeling more at home in Rethymno than in Thessaloniki. I went through all the stages of dealing with the 'other': unfamiliarity, excitement at the prospect of approaching the unknown, cultural intimacy, gradual loss of the initial ethnographic enthusiasm, identification with the natives, taking the field as a matter of course, absorption in everyday life.

Rethymno and Thessaloniki had the advantage of being inhabited by some friends and relatives. I was promised by all of them that I was going to be introduced to all of their acquaintances, something that made me happy because the 'snowballing method' (Bernard 2002: 185) would work efficiently. Very few ended up keeping that promise. During her fieldwork in Kokkinia, Hirschon (2008: 198) observed how verbal threats and promises were never followed through into action. This dissociation of stated intention from performed action, as adopted by Greeks, could be attributed to an attempt to avoid obligation and debt[6] (2008: 192), to 'a cultural premium placed on personal autonomy/ independence, the reluctance to accept the obligation to follow through a stated intention, and a consequent lack of accountability' (2008: 198). Perhaps my friends did not want to initiate a relationship of obligation and debt between us. Perhaps they did not want to play the role of a middle-person and be held responsible for a potentially negative outcome of my interviews with their social contacts. The fact is that my friends' reluctance to materialize their promises meant that social webs were not easily created, leaving me to face a proper struggle in my attempts to approach interlocutors.

When I found them, it was not always an open-access offer of knowledge. My Greek nationality closed a free information flow on some occasions: my interlocutors presumed that my Greek upbringing had granted me all the knowledge I need with regard to the evil eye – 'you know all these things, there is not anything more I can tell you', is the phrase I came to dread – therefore why should they repeat what I already knew? As for trust, I was never accused of being a spy, but I was suspected of being a witch or some kind of a mystic. And, perhaps more out of insecurity than out of mistrust, I was constantly being refused the use of a voice recorder, despite my reassurance that people's identities were totally safe and not to be disclosed. I complied. If recording was seen as a hostile anthropological activity, I was not going to turn my interlocutors into enemies. My memory and my hand would have to work extra shifts instead.

I did not confront more ethnographic struggles than any other anthropologist would have. It does not matter whether one is native or not. The challenges she needs to face in the field are potentially alike. The ethnographic data one brings back to her academic home go through processes of suspicions, uncertainties, newly developed friendships, unique relationships, emotions and – especially – people. Instead of being concerned with whether the anthropologist at home does 'real' or 'authentic' ethnography, and whether s/he manipulates the self-ness and the other-ness 'properly', we, native and non-indigenous anthropologists, must focus on our 'positionality', keeping in mind that our identities, representations and truths are multiple, partially controlled and constantly re-negotiated (Bakalaki 1997: 518). We must focus our attention on what is really important. And this is nothing other than the quality of our relationships with the people we first study and later represent in our texts (Narayan 1993: 672).

Contextualizing ethnography

The ethnographic data in this book come from two periods of ethnographic fieldwork, with a relatively large gap between them. The primary period of research was conducted from the summer of 2005 to the end of 2006 and lasted one and half years for the needs of my doctoral thesis. The main focus of this research period was the evil eye and most of the interlocutors quoted in the book were initially encountered then. Between 2012 and 2019, and for the needs of my postdoctoral research project on the relationship between Christianity and New Age spirituality in southern Europe, part of which was conducted in Greece, I had the opportunity to revisit my fieldsites and the theme of my thesis, that of the evil eye, during frequent Greek ethnographic visits. Although the theme of my study had changed, the frequency with which the evil eye appeared during these visits surprised me.

In parallel to my New Age research, then, I re-approached many of my old interlocutors, some of whom I managed to see in person and many of whom I contacted via online means. I also revisited my old fieldsites a few times and I got to observe in person how the gap of those six years without any specific ethnographic observation and participation reshaped the evil eye practice, my interlocutors' attitude and my own anthropologically reflexive approach to it. The only certain ethnographic observation I was able to make had to do with the changing relationship between the evil eye and New Age spirituality:

during the primary period of my fieldwork, New Age spirituality was making its appearance more timidly and less forcefully in the practice of the evil eye; however, during the second, longer and more dispersed period of fieldwork, the connection between the evil eye and New Age spiritual practices had clearly become stronger, with people not hesitating and/or being afraid to mention New Age any longer, as it was – and is – an active part of vernacular religious practice.

The ethnographic data come from the approximately 120 in-depth, mainly semi-structured and unstructured, interviews and open discussions I conducted during both periods of field research – eighty during the primary period and forty in the more recent one, in addition to many interviews I re-conducted with older interlocutors. Characterizations such as 'Rethymniots and Thessalonikans', 'people in Rethymno and Thessaloniki', 'people in Crete and northern Greece', 'Greeks' and 'my interlocutors' in the book refer particularly to those hundred and twenty interlocutors: on their beliefs, practices, discourses, knowledge, observations, allegations, convictions, everyday life, vernacular religiosity, without any attempt to claim that the argument offered in this book is and should be considered as a generalized presumption with regard to the current Greek religious context. The analysis draws specifically on my interlocutors' practices, discourses and observations and their encounters with the sacred through a vernacular religious practice, which depict a moment of spiritual creativity in present-day Greece. At the same time, the main argument is furthermore based on my own anthropological participation in and observation of Rethymniot and Thessalonikan everyday life for over a decade of ethnographic visits to Greece, which have allowed me to draw a broader picture of analytic anthropological interpretations and conclusions.

I talked to a relatively equal number of shop owners, civil servants, artists, teachers, pensioners, students, housewives and young professionals. They are mainly educated, since most of my interlocutors have graduated from high school, and a large number of them are in the process of obtaining or have already obtained university degrees. They also seem to lead a relatively comfortable life. Variations do occur. There are some Rethymniot and Thessalonikan interlocutors who, although financially comfortable, only just managed to finish primary school. Others have obtained a university degree, but their financial situation resembles that of a working-class person. With these factors in mind, it can be maintained that my interlocutors generally belong to a middle class, which, however, is not homogeneous but consists of multiple internal levels of social, economic and educational deviation. Whenever the class issue is raised in the book, those levels of deviation will be taken into consideration and analysed appropriately. In terms of age, the youngest of my interlocutors are in their early/mid-twenties and the oldest in their late sixties/early seventies. Again, deviations are present and general social categorizations based on the age parameter are difficult to assert. For example, one could assume that older people are more religiously observant than younger people and reject New Age spirituality. This in many ways has proven to be a valid argument. However, I encountered quite a few young people who attend church liturgies every Sunday, and older people who decorate their house by following the feng shui rules. Rethymniot and Thessalonikan social stances are dynamic, varying and are determined by age only up to a certain degree.

Except for ten individuals whom I already knew before going to the field, I happened to encounter the rest of my interlocutors in the course of fieldwork. The only criterion that determined my choice was the desire to keep the range of my interlocutors open. Namely, I wanted and managed to speak with both men and women of diverse ages, occupations and levels of education. Although the evil eye was the main topic of research, I did not only (want to) talk with individuals who believed in it. I did not therefore select my interlocutors on the sole basis of their belief in the evil eye. Nor did I select them on the sole basis of their belief in Orthodoxy, or their involvement with New Age spirituality. I sought to collect opinions from as large a variety of positions as I could find: believers, sceptics, scientists, clerics, young, old, male, female, ritual experts, evil eye sufferers, students and professionals. The boundaries of my evil eye research were never rigid and ordained. Even in the case of evil eye and New Age shop owners and my own friends, who I knew had something to say about the research topic, the outcome of our discussion and their views were often surprising. My field research was thus based on a broad sample of Rethymniots and Thessalonikans to expose a wide array of views on the subject of study.

People in Crete and people in northern Greece share a common socio-cultural path: they practice the evil eye in dynamic and creative ways. For many years, the evil eye was perceived as a superstition and regarded as a rural phenomenon which was only worthy of the attention of folklorists. My research among Rethymniots and Thessalonikans revealed that the evil eye practice has left such opinions behind. My interlocutors engage their senses, perception, their bodies, New Age spirituality, energy and religion in their practices, beliefs and utterances about the evil eye. Through this engagement, they display their ability to improvise socio-culturally (Hallam and Ingold 2007: 19) and to be 'imaginatively creative' (Hastrup 2001: 41). It is their creative agency of performance and of imagination – that is, the creative and innovative ways in which they practise the evil eye through ritual action and embodiment, as well as through rhetoric and imagination – which has created a novel and dynamic spiritual stream in contemporary Greece.

2

The New Age of Greek religiosity: Orthodox Christianity and beyond

Yiannis is a young Thessalonikan in his early thirties, who has characterized himself as a *papadopaidi* (priest's boy), because he has been involved with religion and helping the local priest during Sunday mass in his neighbourhood ever since he was a child. When I first talked to him during my Thessalonikan fieldwork back in 2006, he believed in the evil eye and explained it as a form of energy exchange between people, which could only be removed through Orthodox prayers by a priest. Back then, Yiannis did not really believe in alternative forms of healing and contemporary spiritual practices. More than a decade later, Yiannis has encountered New Age spirituality through his girlfriend, who practises reiki and yoga, while decorating her room with feng shui objects and believing in negative energy and the need to keep it away via energy crystals and evil eye amulets.

In 2019, I had the opportunity to meet with both and discuss again their views on religion, spirituality and healing and what changed during all these years that had passed since our last interview. Yiannis is now married to his then girlfriend and they have a child together. She continues to be open to contemporary spiritual influences and alternative healing and she believes in the power of the evil eye and in energy, while keeping a typical relationship with her denominational religious belonging. Yiannis still defines himself as a keen Christian Orthodox believer; he very often asks his grandmother and mother to perform the ritual against the evil eye for him and his young son, and always wears *komposhinia* (religious rosary beads) from various monasteries he frequently visits as a spiritual protection. Yet, he does not go to Sunday liturgies with the same frequency he used to since, as he has told me, his close relationship to Orthodox Christianity has changed: Yiannis has grown more and more sceptical with regard to the authoritative role of priests in particular and of the Greek Orthodox Church in general. As he notes:

I don't want to be part of all these games of religion. Priests want to impose their power on us, they want to be in charge of our religion, my belief, your belief. They think that because they are part of the Orthodox Church they can control everyone. And the Orthodox Church wants to control everyone too. But I won't stop being a Christian, this is part of who I am.

In our recent encounter, Yiannis declared that he has now warmed up to non-Orthodox religious beliefs and he is open to try any kind of alternative therapies (see Figure 4). It is still his wife who consistently practises yoga, feng shui and reiki more than he does, but his plan is to follow her footsteps and try 'these New Age things that appeal so much to my wife, and the rest of the world, in Thessaloniki these have become so popular, so people must know something, right?' Both Yiannis and his wife want their son to grow up as an Orthodox Christian, while providing him with the freedom of choice to be open to other religious traditions and alternative spiritual practices.

In present-day Greece, Orthodox Christianity continues to be regarded as the legally recognized denominational religion of the country, where Orthodoxy's penetration in Greek culture is still actively observed. Furthermore, the popularly used concept of 'Helleno-Orthodoxy' (Molokotos-Liederman 2004) indicates an attempt to create a nationalistic link between Greek ethnic and socio-cultural

Figure 4 Feng shui and Orthodox Christianity at home.

identity and Orthodox Christianity. In recent years, however, the contemporary Greek religiosity appears to be diverting away from the exclusivity of Orthodoxy and has opened up to alternative forms of religious expression, which belong to the so-called New Age spirituality. Namely, contemporary religiosity in Greece is slowly yet steadily reaching a new age of religious pluralism, where Orthodox religion and New Age spirituality cross each other's paths and multiply interact; as a result, a novel form of an interactive religiosity is creatively practised in the contemporary Greek religious landscape. In the rest of the chapter, Orthodox Christian religion and New Age spirituality will be contextualized separately, and their interactive relationship in the contemporary Greek religious landscape will be further analysed.

Orthodox Christianity in contemporary Greece

Despite the existence of other religions, at least as far as my field experience has allowed me to observe, Orthodoxy in the twenty-first-century Greece possesses a central status. According to Article 3 of the 1975 Greek Constitution, 'the prevailing religion of Greece is that of the Eastern Orthodox Church of Christ, under the autocephalous Church of Greece, united in doctrine to the Ecumenical Patriarchate of Constantinople' (Alivizatos 1999: 25; Molokotos-Liederman 2004: 404–5). The status of Orthodoxy as the *epikratousa thriskeia* (prevailing religion) of Greece should not come as a surprise. Orthodox Christianity and Hellenism, as it has been claimed by many historians and other intellectuals, share an intimate bond. The concept of 'Helleno-Orthodoxy' has been used to represent a historic and socio-cultural continuity of ancient Greece, through Byzantium, to modern Greece (Molokotos-Liederman 2004: 404). As Molokotos-Liederman (2004) accurately observes:

> Orthodoxy lends itself historically to nationalism, and it is with this in mind that the Church of Greece continues to justify its legitimacy in Greek society ... Helleno-Orthodoxy is a body of thought which holds together the national unity of Greece both institutionally and culturally ... Helleno-Orthodoxy resonated in various aspects of contemporary Greek public life, including Church-state relations, civil/religious celebrations, popular religiosity, rites of passage and the education system.

Indeed, Orthodoxy's penetration in Greek culture commences from central – as far as one's socio-cultural education is at stake – social units, such as the family and the school. Children who belong to Orthodox Christian, and not necessarily devoted, families, learn from a very young age to go to church every Sunday; they get entangled with the Orthodox sacraments and are considerably influenced and led, through a process of catechism, to believe that Christianity in its Orthodox version is the best and the only 'true' religion of all. Religious education is taught systematically, both at primary and secondary educational levels, and it is predominantly about Orthodoxy with only scarce references to other world religions or even other denominations of Christianity. Even so, some educational material on world religions is usually placed at the very end of the schoolbooks, and most of the time is never covered at the end of the school year. Consequently, although the Constitution forbids proselytism even in favour of the prevailing religion (Alivizatos 1999: 27), an everyday favouritism for Orthodoxy evidently takes place, both institutionally and informally.

Public invocations that focus on the inseparable bond between Orthodoxy and Greek identity had already commenced in the 1980s, when certain intellectuals, artists and priests, the founders of what is nowadays called 'neo-Orthodoxy',[1] began to publicly denounce Western culture and its ideals and values. They argued that Western modernity can only lead to socio-cultural erosion and identity loss, and that only Orthodoxy could protect Greeks from the dangers of the West. 'Using the media in a particularly skilful fashion, they have advanced a populist interpretation that blends Greek nationalism, anti-western attitudes, anti-modernism, and Orthodoxy' (Roudometof 2005: 91). Neo-Orthodox thinkers themselves have not accepted the term 'neo-Orthodoxy', for, according to Christos Yannaras (one of the acknowledged leaders of this movement), their aim is not to invent new Orthodoxy, but to go back to the authentic roots of Orthodox tradition (Makrides 1998: 142). Some neo-Orthodox intellectuals still appear on Greek television shows from time to time, where they are asked to comment upon current socio-political affairs. However, neo-Orthodox ideology has considerably lost its influence in present-day Greece, and, as a consequence, the public discourse of its representatives has in turn lost its weight.

The Ecumenical Patriarchate of Constantinople, as perhaps the oldest Orthodox Christian religious organ, is considered to be the core of Orthodoxy. Throughout its early history, the Ecumenical Patriarchate successfully played its role as the 'Centre of Orthodoxy'. With the genesis of independent nations in the Balkans, and the subsequent creation of autocephalous Churches – including the Church of Greece, which became a self-governing Church in 1833 – the Patriarchate lost its initial authority and glory, although it still held the primacy of the Orthodox faith. Until today, and in spite of the occasional controversies with the Greek Orthodox Church, it remains the imagined mother of Orthodox Christianity.[2]

After the end of the Greek War of Independence, the autocephalous Church of Greece was created and was placed under the authority of the state (Molokotos-Liederman 2004: 404). At present, it belongs to and is controlled by the Ministry of National Education and Religious Affairs, but governed by its own Holy Synod, headed by the Archbishop of Athens and by the Bishops of the geographic prefectures of Greece. Together with the Church of England, and the Churches in Scandinavian countries, the Greek Orthodox Church holds a place among the established Churches in Europe (Alivizatos 1999: 26; cf. Hart 1992: 20). A clarification needs to be made at this point: to talk about a unified Greek Orthodox Church is imprecise. One of the reasons why I chose my two fieldsites is their distinct religious character, as far as Church manifestations are concerned. Thessaloniki belongs to the Church of Greece, which at the time of the main period of my ethnographic research (2005–6) was powerfully led by the (now deceased) Archbishop Christodoulos, substituted in recent years by the more moderate Archbishop Ieronymos. Thessaloniki is proud of its central participatory role in the affairs that the Church of Greece has to manage, and its current Bishop Anthimos, who has served in the same position since 2004, has frequently expressed his negative opinion against New Age spiritual practices. It is also renowned as a city full of religiously devoted citizens. Crete, on the other hand, is a different story. As is clarified on the official website of the Archiepiscopate of Crete, the Church of Crete is semi-autonomous,[3] and is dependent on the Ecumenical Patriarchate of Constantinople and not on the Church of Greece.[4] The Archbishop of the Church of Crete is elected by the Patriarchate of Constantinople. Still, it does not escape state control, as it too finds itself under the authority of the Ministry of Religious Affairs.

The Orthodox Church, therefore, is not an analytically uncomplicated designation. It is the legislative, doctrinal organ of Orthodox Christianity in Greece, and although its discourse does not come without variations, it still reproduces the 'official' religious ideology of Orthodox Christianity in Greece. This 'official' attitude has been largely expressed by the Archbishop of the Church of Greece, Christodoulos: a very dynamic figure whose influence spread all over the country during his official position in the Greek Orthodox Archbishopric; and as far as my ethnographic research has indicated, at least, during various conversations I have had with both Orthodox priests and believers in my field visits to Greece between 2011 and 2019, the aftermath of his religious authority continues to date.[5] The denominational Orthodox discourse is also expressed by the 'official' representatives of the Greek Orthodox Church; I do not include lay people as part of the Church discourse since, although they belong to the Church and they largely constitute it, the Church I am analytically employing (with a capital 'C') is different from the vernacular notion of a church as congregation or local groups of believers. When my interlocutors use the term, the context remains the same, for they refer to Church as their religious doctrinal organ of Orthodoxy. Yet, regardless of who the leader of the Orthodox Church is, the evil eye is written in the ecclesiastic holy books (books of gospel, prayer and saints books and so on) and is accepted by both the Church of Greece and the Church of Crete and their representatives.

Greece began to acquire national and religious homogeneity after the compulsory exchange of populations between Greece and Turkey following the 1923 Lausanne Convention (Hirschon 2009: 3). In this new homogenized national and religious context, the predominance of Orthodoxy in Greece became apparent. However, following the Schengen Agreement, Greece faced a religious pluralization, 'as the forced and voluntary migration generated by the disintegration of Yugoslavia and, more recently, the regional integration of Southeastern Europe, have intensified the growth in religious and ethnic minorities within the last decade to about 10 per cent of Greece's total population' (Prodromou 2004b: 477). Furthermore, contemporary Greek society includes a range of religious non-Orthodox minorities, including the Old Calendarists, Muslims, Roman Catholics, Jews, Evangelical Protestants and Jehovah's Witnesses (Prodromou 2004b: 477). And although Orthodoxy has not ceased to be the official and dominant religion of the country, such a religious pluralism, albeit seemingly inconspicuous, has changed the religious map in contemporary Greece, challenging the monopoly of Orthodox Christianity.

Of course, the existence of other religions in the country, the immigration flow and the opening of the Greek national and socio-cultural boundaries to heterogeneous influences contributed to the subsequent openness of boundaries in the spiritual landscape of contemporary Greece. Furthermore, the socialist political party of PASOK, which governed Greece for a period of almost twenty-five years, and lost power shortly before I began my fieldwork,[6] took large steps towards Greece's 'Europeanization' and modernization, and urged social innovations and intra-cultural convergences. The spiritual renovation which I observed while studying the evil eye in Rethymno and Thessaloniki has been very much a long-term by-product of this political and socio-cultural boundary-opening. The Church, of course, fought and continues to fight against such modernization and Europeanization tendencies; yet, Orthodoxy could not avoid being influenced by these tendencies and acknowledge, at least, the existence of other spiritual globalized influences in the context of contemporary Greek religiosity.

Religion in urban life

The study of urban Greek religion is, peculiarly enough, limited. Hirschon's *Heirs of the Greek Catastrophe* (1998 [1989]) was the first full ethnography of an urban setting in Greece, being also the first ethnography that focused analytically and eloquently on urban religion in the Greek context. When Hirschon began her research, she had reservations with regard to how important religion would and could be in an urban locality. As she (1998 [1989]: 192) noted:

> Among my unexamined assumptions before setting out was that religion would probably have little importance since this was a fully urban locality inhabited by people whose origins were also primarily urban. My error lay in accepting uncritically a deeply entrenched model of urban life as secular, marked by the diminished importance of religious institutions and the disintegration of family structure, among other things.

When I began my fieldwork in the urban localities of Rethymno and Thessaloniki, I too had reservations concerning the degree to which religion would possess a central role in vernacular practice. The scholarly idea that ties secularization and urban life together, namely that 'god is dead' (Bruce 2002), was prevalent in my ethnographic mind when I began my fieldwork. Having chosen to study the evil eye in two urban environments out of an ethnographic need to escape the stereotype of previous folklorist and anthropological works that approached the evil eye as a rural superstition, I was worried that people would feed on their hypothetical and potential urban secularized tendencies and, as a consequence, dismiss the evil eye, drawing on its close relationship to religion; up to a certain degree, I did come across such tendencies. Furthermore, I was uncertain what an urban spiritual cosmos would be like and whether the evil eye would be part of this cosmos.

In his article focusing on a religious festival in the urban locality of St Marina, in the Athenian municipality of Ilioupoli, Vozikas (2009) has not only offered an important contribution to the study of urban religion in Greece but, equally essentially, argues for an urban environment and Greek spiritual field that lack rigidity and are open to external rural influences. Vozikas (2009: 65) has suggested that 'thanks to the late development and incomplete urbanization of Greece, the inhabitants of the locality retain the basic structural elements from their rural cultural capital'. The locality of St Marina is mainly inhabited by people who migrated to Athens from rural environments. The migrants wanted to transform their new locality into a familiar place and develop its distinct character. Their first act was to build a church that was dedicated to St Marina and was founded in the same year that the community, which was named after its protector saint, was officially recognized (2009: 67). The residents of St Marina celebrate all the major religious festival of Orthodoxy (2009: 69); yet, the most important and popular one is that of their patron saint, St Marina (2009: 70). As Vozikas (2009: 72) explains, paraphrasing one of the most well-known folklorists, Megas, 'the religious *panegyri* [festival] is an important event for the community to which the church belongs, the reason being that in traditional culture, Greek rural communities are identified with their church and the protecting saint of the village to whom the church is dedicated'. Consequently, people in St Marina incorporate rural elements in celebrating their religious festival in their urban locality, collapsing the supposing boundary between the urban and the rural, and rendering the separation between the sacred and the profane obsolete.

After extensively studying everyday religious life and death among Greek refugees from Asia Minor in Kokkinia, an area of Piraeus, Hirschon (1998 [1989]: 194) concluded that the separation between the sacred and the secular was not relevant for that locality. Although for those *Mikrasiates* (people from Asia Minor) church attendance did not constitute the focal element of their religious life (1998 [1989]: 194), their affiliation to Orthodox Christianity was a vital part of their identity. Religion and the Church formed a core aspect of the refugees' everyday practices, and it 'embodied community life in social as well as in spiritual terms. The church also provided a concrete point of orientation where specific links with their past life could be expressed and experienced' (1998 [1989]: 195). Furthermore, religious rituals – in Sunday liturgies, Soul Saturdays, Easter, Christmas, marriages, funerals, baptisms, pilgrimage (1998 [1989]: 195–32) – were an inseparable part of the refugees' everyday life. As Hirschon (1998 [1989]: 195) concluded, 'in essence, this worldview can be characterized as religious for it is based on the notion of continuous interaction between the human and divine realms'.

In the urban localities I studied, religion appears to possess an equally important position to the one Hirschon observed in Kokkinia. More often than not, Rethymniots and Thessalonikans participate in everyday religious rituals. They habitually attend church liturgies on Sundays, at weddings, funerals, baptisms, and on Christmas and Easter. They venerate icons in the small shrines scattered around the urban landscape, they cross themselves when they pass outside churches, they pray in front of the household *eikonostasi* (icon stand, see Figure 5). Of course, my interlocutors' everyday religious performances vary according to their age, gender and degree of religious adherence. Generally speaking, however, religious acts constitute part of the Rethymniot and Thessalonikan everyday life in an urban context. As Hirschon (2009: 3–4) rightly

Figure 5 Household icon stand.

observes: 'Greece is reckoned to be a nation with a high degree of religiosity. This is revealed in the observance of religious practices of various kinds and, even though church attendance may not have been high, it is the interweaving of the religious with so many aspects of daily life that strikes the outsider.' What I observed during my field research was that a separation between the sacred and the secular cannot be applied in the Rethymniot and Thessalonikan social life.

> Christianity tries to provide an exact definition of the dogma, to its last detail, so that they make it into a booklet of how our world is functioning and what is the right or wrong thing to believe. Whereas, in the Koran for instance, I have heard that it does not have anything to do with how the world functions, things are much simpler ... but Christianity, at least the Orthodox one, is an attempt to explain the world, it determines the powers of good, the powers of evil etc. And it can accuse you of cooperation with evil spirits, demons and I do not know what else, as in the case of the evil eye.

The above quote comes from Dionisis, a thirty-year-old man in Rethymno. He presents an image of Orthodoxy as a strictly dogmatic and rigid religion – a controlling force of social behaviour and practice. Compared to other world religions, he feels that Orthodoxy is not as oriented towards freedom as it should be. It aims at inflicting its own dogma upon people – whether they like it or not. During our interview, Dionisis stated that he no longer believes in religion, compared to what he thought when he was a child when his mother used to take him to church liturgies every Sunday. He thinks that 'this whole religion idea is a human creation' and the more he learns about it and compares Orthodox Christianity with world religions, the more he regards it as a socially constructed institution. Religion for him has ended up becoming a social regulator of human behaviour in Greece, for one has to adopt its rules so as not to become socially isolated. The Greek religious system, according to Dionisis, is a mere power game. Religion in Greece, he asserts, is trapped inside an ambivalent labyrinth of authority imposed upon its devotees, of conflicts between the Patriarchate and the Church of Greece, of lack of interaction among the multi-faith communities that exist in the country. For all these reasons Dionisis refuses to participate in a religion, the integrity of which he seriously disputes, although he still practises the evil eye and has also begun to turn his attention towards New Age spirituality.

Many of my younger Rethymniot and Thessalonikan interlocutors share Dionisis' views and treat Orthodoxy and its doctrine with suspicion. The majority of the 'moderately religious' young men and women whom I have spoken to, and who are aged from their twenties to their late thirties, have admitted their faith in Orthodoxy. At the same time (and this is why they characterize themselves as moderately religious), they have told me that they do not keep up with going to church every Sunday or performing any other 'religious duties', like fasting or confessing, regularly. 'I do not go to church to sit in liturgies. If I walk in front of a church I may light a candle', a mid-twenties Thessalonikan woman stated. It is true that, amongst younger people, church attendance has been dropping quite steadily. Frequently, they hold on to their faith, or they invoke their faith when they are in need. Most of them have, at some point, encountered the practice of the evil eye. They are also open to other spiritual paths, as they have made clear, and they practise yoga, follow the feng shui rules in house decoration, do reiki, own New Age objects and believe in the existence of some kind of energy that can influence personal interactions.

I have also encountered a small number of young Rethymniots and Thessalonikans who have consciously cut their bonds with the Church. Those individuals have declared themselves atheists and refuse to adopt any religious practices, usually regarding the evil eye as such, and thus banning it from their lives. They express anti-clerical sentiments and distrust towards the Church, a stance that is also adopted by some religiously devout informants in both Rethymno and Thessaloniki. Such distrusting attitudes have possibly been triggered by and 'exacerbated after 2005, following scandalous revelations. Multiple accusations of financial mismanagement, homosexuality and links related to corruption in the judiciary rocked the Church of Greece' (Hirschon 2009: 6). These young Rethymniots and Thessalonikans have found an alternative way to express their spiritual quests. As they explained to me, they are open to spiritual practices that do not have to do with Orthodoxy. Rather, they are keen on following a godless spirituality of a New Age orientation, immersing themselves in practices such as yoga, reiki and crystal healing. For those who belong to this social group, church attendance is off limits, apart from occasional weddings and baptisms that they need to attend. They usually believe in the evil eye as a form of energy exchange between humans and regard the ritual healing against the evil eye as a spiritual type of alternative therapy.

On the other hand, in general, older people attend church liturgies frequently. A woman in Thessaloniki commented on her grandmother's attitude: 'My grandma goes [to church] every Sunday ... all elderly people do. When they reach an age where death seems closer, they all run to church.' Most of the older women whom I encountered in my fieldsites, who are between sixty-five and eighty years old, have declared their adherence to Orthodoxy. They go to church every Sunday, they fast, they receive Holy Communion and many of them are popular evil eye healers. As Hirschon (1998 [1989]: 139–40) notes, in Yerania, a Greek neighbourhood of Piraeus, Attica, it is the housewives who were responsible for the everyday religious activities of the household. They would take care of the household religious icons, light the oil lamp that was suspended in front of the *eikonostasi* (icon stand) and, generally, they were 'responsible for maintaining the stock of holy substances, the spiritual resources of the household used in protecting members of the family'. My older female informants, both in Rethymno and Thessaloniki, act equivalently, performing the same tasks, and assuming responsibility for the spiritual health of their families. Older men are more sceptical towards religion; yet, although they do not adopt the paradigm of their wives, they follow them to church liturgies every Sunday and frequently ask for the ritual healing against the evil eye to be performed on them.

Of course, there are always exceptions. In a conversation with Matina, an older woman in northern Greece, who is a devoted believer, as is her son, who lives with her, I asked whether she performs the ritual healing against the evil eye (*ksematiasma*). The moment the word *ksematiasma* came out of my mouth, she looked wary; she gazed towards her son, who was at that moment occupied with a task just a few metres away from us, and she asked me to keep my voice down, because her son 'does not want to hear a word about *mati*. He is too attached to religion'. Her comment was ethnographically interesting. As far as I had understood, her devotion to religion was as strong as her son's. Yet, she created a differentiation between her Orthodox adherence and the adherence of her son, which she finds overwhelming. Although she is a strong believer in Orthodox Christianity, she is open to practices, such as the evil eye, that escape the rigidity of doctrinally defined religious boundaries. Her son, however, is 'too attached to religion', he strictly follows what the Orthodox Christian dogma preaches and lay *ksematiasma* is not included in the official Orthodox ideology. His mother does not approve of his degree of Orthodox observance and thinks that her son acts at an exaggerated level of piety.

It has been argued that 'the Orthodox Church is considered being in the category of parochial traditionalism and is seen as a major static anti-acculturation force that is impeding modernization and secularization' (Makrides and Molokotos-Liederman 2004: 462). One could invoke such an approach to explain why church attendance is popular among elderly Greeks, whereas it declines among the younger generation. Such an analysis goes back to the well-explored dichotomy between tradition and modernity: old people follow traditional ways of living (including church going), whereas young people, being modern and secular, pursue a different lifestyle from their predecessors.

Yet, as it can be observed in Matina's case above, such a schema does not – always – apply to my ethnographic findings and analysis. In the course of my Greek fieldwork I met older individuals who refused to go to church and did not go along with the Church ideology and young people who attended church liturgies and whose relationship to Christianity was impeccable. All those individuals can be 'modern', 'traditional' and/or 'secular'. Labelling them as 'traditional' or as 'modern' according to their age would only create a stereotypical view on how religion is practised in contemporary Greece. Church/church is a matter of cultural practice, not an issue of stereotyping. The frequency of churchgoing depends on individual attitude and having faith does not imply frequent visits to church (cf. Dubisch 1995: 58). Besides, as Dubisch (1995: 60) argues: 'Even those who consider themselves devout Orthodox Christians do not necessarily demonstrate reverence for the church and its functionaries.'

The urban landscape of both Thessaloniki and Rethymno is dominated by church buildings at a – perhaps surprisingly – density. In Thessaloniki, many churches stay open during the whole day, giving to people the chance to go and visit, pray and light a candle: a common Orthodox vernacular practice of communicating with the sacred and asking for spiritual protection. Other church buildings only open on Sundays and on special occasions – weddings, funerals and baptisms-but, as an alternative, one can find small shrines at the entrance of some church buildings, which consist of a saint's icon – usually the protector of the particular church – a square of sand, where one can light a candle and a locked box where people can contribute their money (see Figure 6). Many of my interlocutors in northern Greece, both young and old, who have a relatively good relationship with Orthodoxy, have told me that when they pass in front of a church, they feel guilty and cannot just ignore it; so, they almost always stop in order to light a candle, kiss the icons and deposit some money. On the other hand, the shrines, as plenty of Thessalonikans I talked to have observed, are not there only for the believers' benefit and in order to offer them a chance to express their spiritual desire. As Kostas, a young male Thessalonikan, put it, 'the Church is not so naïve', explaining that, 'even though it keeps some of its church buildings closed on weekdays, it has these little shrines outside in the street, to make people guilty and make them go and deposit their money and light a candle; it is all about making profit'.

In Rethymno, the situation is somewhat different. Vernacular practices of religious adherence were not so obvious during my fieldwork there. Occasionally, I would see people, mainly elderly women and men, entering a church to light a candle. But Rethymniots, perhaps due to a lack of spiritual guilt enforced by the

Figure 6 Church small shrine for lighting a candle.

Church and since finding a small shrine in the town centre was not an easy task, seemed much more relaxed in that respect. Furthermore, the priests were usually nowhere to be seen around the church spatial periphery; yet, I was constantly bumping into them during my town walks. Rethymniot priests sipped coffee in local *kafeneia* (coffee-shops) and café-bars, loosely mixed with the lay crowd. They accompanied their wives for shopping clothes. In some cases, they were not even wearing the black robe of priesthood, having replaced it with black trousers and a long black shirt on top. Priesthood in Rethymno collapses the stereotypes regarding how a priest should behave, look and how he should express his beliefs or handle the evil eye practice. In Rethymno, the representatives of the 'official'

Church ideology are free to act, believe and practise, in the same way the actors of the 'unofficial' lay religious ideology are free to react, disbelieve and perform.

This religious freedom that both lay people and priests appear to enjoy in Rethymno has partly to do with the fact that the Church of Crete belongs to the Patriarchate of Constantinople, and not the Church of Greece. Many Rethymniots, young and old, men and women, have criticized the Church of Greece for being too strict, especially when it has to do with vernacular religious practices, such as the evil eye. As Manos, a seventy-year-old Rethymniot remarked:

> Let them (the official representatives of the Church of Greece) talk. They don't govern us. We are Orthodox too, ok. But we practise our religion however we want in our everyday lives. And we believe in evil eyes and the twelve Gods of Olympus, and everything.

This statement that my older informant has made captures the ambiguity that Orthodoxy faces in present-day Greece, and it is both Rethymniots and Thessalonikans who emphasize the fact that they feel the need to practise their religion freely and without doctrinal conventions and/or exaggerations. Orthodoxy has been part of my interlocutors' everyday lives since they were small children and has influenced their vernacular religious practices and social discourses. Orthodox Christianity in Rethymno and Thessaloniki is lived and acted as a popular part of Greek everyday life. When Greeks refer to *thriskeia* (religion) during their everyday lives, what they usually have in mind is the predominant Greek religion and the way in which it is believed, practised and manifested. Sometimes they incorporate the evil eye in their understanding of *thriskeia*. Other times they separate it from *thriskeia*, viewing it as a practice that relates more to the spiritual than the religious. Most of the time, however, they recognize that, through the evil eye practice, the boundaries between what is conceived as religion and what is perceived as spirituality are demarcated. Cretans and northern Greeks treat the evil eye in a variety of ways. Although they might not be conscious of it, even when they deny it, my interlocutors are entangled with and influenced by Orthodox Christian mysticism. Every day that passes by enriches them with new intellectual and practical modes of confronting Orthodoxy and the evil eye. It provides them with enough apparatus to establish links among the three: to choose and/or discard one, some, all or none of them from their belief and/or performance(s), and to go along a route where New Age spirituality joins their path.

The New Age of Greek religiosity

With particular reference to the last decade (2009–19), Orthodox Christianity in Greece has faced a challenge both at an official and unofficial level, due to two recent factors that have resulted in the transformation of the Greek socioeconomic, political and cultural context. First, the socioeconomic and political crisis, which has affected most southern European countries, including Greece, has resulted in increasing distrust towards the Church and its representatives: at the level of vernacular religious practice at least, and as far as my fieldwork has allowed me to observe, negative discourses regarding the role of the Church in such challenging times are heard these days even by the most faithful Orthodox adherents. The second factor is related to the most recent transnational influx of both refugees and migrants from different cultural and religious backgrounds, which has resulted in a pluralization of the contemporary socio-cultural, political and, consequently, religious Greek landscape.[7] These two factors have in turn affected the status of Greek Orthodox Christianity in various manners. Perhaps one of the most important influences is the fact that, amidst the dangerous rise of extreme right-wing political parties within the context of the Greek crisis (Kirtsoglou 2013), Orthodox Christian discourses have been utilized by those parties as a tool to create a neo-populist association between religious and national(istic) Greek identity. Following this paradigm, there are many Greeks who have opted to adopt a nationalistic approach when it comes to their religious identity and treat their religiosity as uniquely and exclusively Orthodox. Moreover, in the context of the socioeconomic crisis, the Greek Orthodox Church has developed welfare programmes in order to help the financially challenged (Molokotos-Liederman 2016: 35–8) and, as a result, has regained some of its lost respect and authority among those who had lost their faith and/or criticized it, reclaiming thus its central position within Greek vernacular religious life more dynamically. Despite the improvement of Orthodox Christianity's religious and social authority, there is still a large part of the Greek population that has chosen willingly to distant itself from the imagined exclusivity of its Orthodox Christian roots and be more sensitive to multicultural and global spiritual influences of a New Age character.

Orthodoxy and mysticism

Such an amalgamation of Orthodox and New Age elements may not come as a surprise, however, taking into consideration the fact that Orthodoxy has a long tradition of mysticism in its circles. Mysticism, the 'personal experience of the divine mysteries' and theology, 'the dogma affirmed by the Church', support and complete each other in the Eastern Church tradition (Lossky 2005: 8). 'Spirituality and dogma, mysticism and theology, are inseparably linked in the life of the Church' (Lossky 2005: 14). Perhaps the most well-known practice of Orthodox mysticism is the so-called 'Hesychast method of prayer' (Ware 1997 [1963]: 65). The Hesychast method of praying, whose name originates from the Greek word *hesychia*, which means stillness and designates a prayer of silence, stripped of imagery and discursive thinking, began in Thessaloniki in the fourteenth century (Ware 1997 [1963]: 64). It is based on the continuous reciting of the Jesus Prayer ('Lord Jesus Christ, Son of God, have mercy on me'), while one regulates one's breathing and adopts a particular bodily posture, namely chin resting on the chest and eyes fixed on the place of the heart (Ware 1997 [1963]: 65).

The Hesychasts claimed that they could see the Divine and Uncreated Light of God with their eyes; consequently, they were accused of gross materialism, since it was considered impossible for someone to see God's essence with his bodily eyes (Ware 1997 [1963]: 66). St Gregory Palamas, the Bishop of Thessaloniki, came to the Hesychasts' rescue. He defended the use of bodily exercises in prayer, arguing that placing emphasis on the body during their praying did not make the Hesychasts gross materialists; it simply indicated their faithfulness to the Biblical doctrine of the body and soul unity in a person. Palamas also accepted the Hesychast capability of experiencing the essence of God through prayer by developing a distinction between the essence and the energies of God (Ware 1997 [1963]: 67), namely, between the nature or inner being of God and his energies, operations or acts of power (Ware 1995: 22). Hesychasm remained popular throughout the centuries, especially on Mount Athos which, in the eighteenth century, served as the locus of a movement of spiritual renewal. The members of the movement, known as Kollyvades, advocated a rejection of Western Enlightenment and a return to the true roots of Orthodox Christianity, which would result in the regeneration of the Greek nation (Ware 1997 [1963]: 99, 100). One of the most prominent effects of the Athonite spiritual renewal was the publication of the *Philokalia*, an anthology of ascetic and mystical texts, which was published in Venice in 1782 by leading members of the Kollyvades movement. The *Philokalia* was intended for both ascetic monks and lay people and was devoted to the practice of the Jesus Prayer (Ware 1997 [1963]: 100).

Greeks paid more attention to the *Philokalia* from the 1950s onwards. The *Philokalia* 'has acted as a spiritual "time bomb", for the "true age of *Philokalia*" has been not the late eighteenth but the late twentieth century' (Ware 1997 [1963]). Indeed, the so-called neo-Orthodox movement emerged in the late twentieth century and was supported by intellectuals, artists and theologians who aimed to revive a more authentic Orthodox tradition (Molokotos-Liederman 2004: 405–6). This movement revived the Kollyvades' spiritual renewal by espousing the continuation of ancient Greek culture and Christianity, in the unity of the Greek nation and Orthodoxy, and in strongly supporting the idea that Orthodoxy forms the main source of Greek ethnic identity (Pachis 2004: 353). Although neo-Orthodoxy became popular and reached its heyday in the 1990s, it is today receding (Pachis 2004).

Orthodoxy, therefore, has a long history of incorporating mysticism in its circles and is by no means a stranger to processes of spiritual creativity and renewal. Despite the fact that mysticism is not foreign to Orthodoxy, New Age spirituality is. Nevertheless, one can observe certain commonalities between Orthodox and New Age mysticism. For instance, the specific bodily stance and the repetitive manner in the reciting of the Jesus Prayer are not so different from yoga practice, during which certain bodily postures need to be adopted, while repetitive mantras are usually recited. Furthermore, the concept of energy is part of Orthodoxy, in the form of the 'energies of God'. Energy is also a very popular idiom in New Age spirituality, and even Orthodox adherents who have dismissed energy in the past use it extensively nowadays when they talk about the evil eye and their religious activities. Yet, the meaning which my interlocutors have attributed to energy is not related to the Orthodox 'energies of God' but is directly linked to New Age interpretations of the concept.

Living religion as New Age

According to the most commonly offered and popularly adopted discourse, the evil eye is transmitted through the exchange of electromagnetic energy or electromagnetic waves – the two terms are used alternatively and hold the same meaning. As most of my interlocutors have clarified, energy is an invisible power or life-force, which can be scientifically measured and is existent in our everyday world. Like electronic devices, such as mobile phones or radios, individuals are able to exchange electromagnetic energy through immediate or distant contact. Every person possesses a certain amount of energy in his/her own self. If this energy is negative, or excessively positive, evil eye affliction is likely to occur. If it is positive, it can be used for healing purposes, as in the ritual therapy against the evil eye.

Energy, as Brown (1997: 90) maintains, is

> the perfect organizing concept, because it is both all-encompassing and ambiguous. Like the spirit world itself, energy is everywhere yet difficult to see. Each of us has experienced energy in palpably physical forms: sound, vibrations, light, heat, gravity. By bridging scientific and spiritual approaches to the world, energy offers a way to bring everything together in a grand synthesis.

Energy, a concept that is primarily and directly linked to New Age spiritual ideologies, has invaded the everyday Greek discourse about religion, spirituality and vernacular religiosity. Doing yoga and reiki, burning sage and *palo santo* wood sticks, tarot reading, spiritual therapies, placing energy crystals around the house, using feng shui objects, doing meditation and reading mind–body–spirit books, aura cleansing, wearing jewellery beads that are believed to possess mystical qualities constitute only few of the practices or performative acts that indicate the recurring popularity of New Age spirituality in northern Greece and Crete.

In this continuously changing Greek religious landscape, where New Age spirituality is becoming more and more popular, what appears to characterize primarily the presence of New Age practices is indeed the concept of energy. According to the majority of Cretans and northern Greeks I spoke to, for example, feng shui is employed so that all the negative energy can be eliminated from their houses and their selves. Reiki is equivalently performed as a healing method which utilizes positive energy. And yoga is practised in order to dispose of negative energy and be open to receive positive energy back. At the same time, having a priest perform a house blessing can throw negative energy away from one's house. Going to a church liturgy or reciting a prayer at home can fill someone with positive energy too. The widespread use of the concept of energy in present-day Greece is symptomatic not only of the popularity New Age ideologies have gained in the country, but also of how these new forms of spirituality have already begun to establish a steady bond with the practice of the evil eye.

New Age has been defined as 'a broad cultural ideology, which privileges holistic medicine, intuitive sciences like astrology and tarot, ecological and antinuclear political issues, and alternative therapies, medicines and philosophers' (Luhrmann 1989: 30). As Heelas (1996) argues, New Age is mostly about individuality and the spiritual development of the self. So does Brown (1997: vii), who defines New Age as 'a diffuse social movement of people committed to pushing the boundaries of the self and bringing spirituality into everyday life'. But perhaps the most useful – for my argument, but also generally speaking – scholarly definition and description of New Age, since it furthermore encompasses ethnographically the practices I have found in the field, is the following by Sutcliffe and Gilhus (2013: 3):

> The expression 'new age' has been used in the academy since the mid-1980s to describe a sometimes bewildering variety of 'holistic' or 'mind body spirit' phenomena, including astrology, tarot and other kinds of divination; practices of possession, channelling and mediumship; magical ideas about multiple 'bodies', and occult ideas about hidden anatomies; body practices like yoga, tai chi and ch'i kung; popular psychotherapies and counselling ideologies; and forms of healing positioned as either 'alternative' or 'complementary' to biomedical healthcare, from Reiki to homeopathy.

Judging by its definitions above, New Age appears to be an unbounded field of spiritual pursuits, which can involve a large variety of practices, and it is hence difficult to define. There are many scholars in the field of social sciences (see, among others, Hanegraaf 1996; Heelas 1996; Sutcliffe and Bowman 2000; Sutcliffe 2003; Heelas and Woodhead 2005; Kemp and Lewis 2007; Wood 2007; Sutcliffe and Gilhus 2013; Fedele and Knibbe 2013) who have offered elaborate and often critical analyses on the phenomenon of New Age historically, sociologically, anthropologically and ethnographically, in the context of contemporary spirituality. Taking into consideration the multiple challenging views on New Age, the main position of this book is in agreement with Sutcliffe and Gilhus (2013: 1) that '"New Age" is among the most deputed of categories in the study of religion in terms of agreeing content and boundaries (…) studying "new age spiritualities" tantalizingly reproduces issues central to defining and theorizing religion in general', following their suggestion that 'we need a model of religion that comprises new age phenomena, either as part of the old model of religion in such a way as to expand its parameters, or as part of a fresh prototype' (2013: 2–3).

Although there is a lack of bibliographic resources with regard to the history of New Age in Greece, drawing on testimonials of interlocutors who have been proven to take part in the Greek New Age movement since its beginning, it appears to have been initiated, as in most countries in the world, in the 1960s. Yet, it was not until almost a decade later, when a mystical movement, whose participants adopted the term 'occultists', was established. Around that time, *Pyrinos Kosmos*, an esoteric publishing company, was born. *Pyrinos Kosmos* is presently the most well-known esoteric bookshop in the Greek capital of Athens;

yet, it ships its merchandising – including New Age books and spiritual material objects, such as energy crystals and tarot decks – to customers around Greece and there are many of my interlocutors, especially in northern Greece, who buy online their mind–body–spirit books from that source.

Terminologically speaking, there is no term that captures effectively the multiple connotations of New Age in contemporary Greece. Although an exact translation of the New Age term exists (*Nea Epohi*) and has more or less the same meaning as its English equivalent, it has not really caught on as a popular term. My interlocutors in Crete and northern Greece have not used *Nea Epohi* to refer to New Age practices. Instead, they have talked about mysticism (*mystikismos*), the supernatural (*yperfysiko*) and *parathriskeftika* phenomena (phenomena outside/ beyond religion). Many of them are aware of the term New Age and use it to characterize themselves as 'New Agers', but most times such statement involves a certain tone of sarcasm, since they too are aware of the criticism and difficulty the term frequently entails. Ethnographically and analytically speaking, New Age spirituality here refers to a large variety of practices that my interlocutors are engaged with during their everyday life, which range from yoga, feng shui and reiki to alternative therapies and from reading mind–body–spirit books and meditating to using tarot cards and energetic crystals to cleanse the negative energy of homes and embodied selves. Their acts of combining Orthodox and New Age spiritual practices, namely their acts of spiritual pluralism during everyday life, are performed spontaneously, and any attempt to terminologically and analytically restrict them would prove misleading. I have therefore decided to use the term New Age in order to refer to those practices, material objects and ideologies that can be conceptualized as New Age according to the scholarly definitions of the term offered above, based primarily on the conceptualizations and performances of those non-Orthodox spiritual pathways my interlocutors popularly follow in the course of their vernacular religious practice.

By arguing for a novel spiritual pluralism and the emergence of an exogenous New Age spirituality in contemporary Greece, there is no intention to underemphasize Orthodoxy's spiritual role, nor is it claimed that spiritual renewal and creativity in Greece bear no relation to Orthodoxy. The novelty about the process of spiritual synthesis I have observed ethnographically during my evil eye fieldwork has to do with the creativity with which people in my fieldsites amalgamate Orthodoxy and New Age spirituality during their everyday lives. Such a synthesis of Orthodox Christian and New Age ideologies and practices has made its appearance very recently in the contemporary Greek religious landscape, as part of a response to global trends, socio-political influences and the recent socioeconomic crisis, where religion is 'lived' in novel creative ways.

As Ammerman (2014: 190) argues:

> Lived religion does often happen on the margins between orthodox prescriptions and innovative experiences, but religion does not have to be marginal to be "lived". (…) Looking for lived religion does mean that we look for the material, embodied aspects of religion as they occur in everyday life, in addition to listening for how people explain themselves. It includes both the experiences of the body and the mind.

Lived religion is approached here as a multiplicity of religious discourses and practices, be it 'official' religious denominations or 'alternative' spiritual movements, which are creatively amalgamated at the level of vernacular performance and, as a result, produce an open, pluralistic and fluid religiosity. Furthermore, according to McGuire (2008: 12), the term 'lived religion' is useful for 'distinguishing the actual experience of religious persons from the prescribed religion of institutionally defined beliefs and practices'. Following McGuire, religion is approached in the book as 'lived in a particular time and cultural setting' (2008), where a creative 'patchwork' (Ammerman 2014: 193) of mixing different spiritual traditions is woven in everyday life, demarcating the boundaries between official and unofficial religious ideologies and practices, while creating new forms of belief and ritual action. As Ammerman (2014) explains: 'The lived religion we are likely to find will almost inevitably be a patchwork. People looking for a new meditation technique or a possible spiritual pilgrimage can Google their way to the latest religious practices. (…) The mixing and hybridity of religion as it crosses borders means that pure categories tied to location and tradition are disappearing fast.' What follows is an attempt to analyse how religiosity is lived pluralistically and creatively in two quotidian Greek socio-cultural settings through the practice of the evil eye, more specifically. The objective is to demonstrate how vernacular religiosity and spiritual creativity go hand in hand within this field of an everyday religious belief and ritual performance, where New Age spirituality co-inhabits a space along with Orthodox Christianity, having become an active part of vernacular religiosity.

3

Matiasma: The energetic interplay of senses and emotions

People's negative energy often influences me. You feel that there is something negative about a person and, by being in close touch with him, you become negative and moody yourself or you get a headache… and, do not forget, moodiness and headaches are the basic symptoms of matiasma.

The above opinion comes from Eva, a thirty-seven-year-old woman in Thessaloniki. She is a believer in the evil eye and a non-devout Orthodox Christian. She thinks that negative energy invades her body, spirit and soul when she becomes evil eyed, when she sits in close proximity to people who are evil eyed and withhold negative energy in their physical bodies, or when she enters in touch with individuals who carry negative feelings and energy within their soul. Energy and the way in which it is communicated between people seem to be for Eva, and for the majority of the Greeks I have spoken to in both Crete and northern Greece, the principal reason why the evil eye is present in their lives.

According to most of my Rethymniot and Thessalonikan interlocutors, energy is a non-determined, non-specified and non-religious force, and its channelling constitutes the primary reason why *matiasma* (evil eye affliction) occurs. Channelling usually refers to 'the use of altered states of consciousness to contact spirits – or to experience spiritual energy captured from other times and dimensions' (Brown 1997: viii). A spiritual field of inter-communicating energies triggers the evil eye, and people's bodies, spirits and souls are possessed by its energetic power. People in Rethymno and Thessaloniki do not adopt the Church explanation as far as energy channelling in *matiasma* is concerned. Namely, they do not believe that energy emanates from a particular doctrinally enshrined force that is the devil. On the contrary, they adopt a concept of energy that is part of a New Age discourse and regard it as a force that is ambient in the cosmos, without being colonized by a particular religion.

While I was discussing the multiple ways in which the evil eye can affect people with Mina, a young female Thessalonikan, I could feel that she was hesitating to express her opinion fully. She proceeded to reveal that the subject of conscious energy channelling in the process of *matiasma* was making her uncomfortable because, as she explained, it touches 'mystical powers' and their manipulation and thus escapes Orthodox grounds. Mina, being an Orthodox Christian, was not certain whether such a mixture of ideas and practices was 'right'. In her own words:

> I usually avoid thinking bad of others. But I became really angry with this particular person. For all the bad things he did to me, I strongly wished he would fail in all aspects of his life. I believe that this curse came back to me. I think that if you cannot manipulate the negative energy you want to send, then do not do it. Since then, I try to avoid any bad thoughts because I feel I can send negative energy. And it can come back to me, like a boomerang. Or it can reach its destination, in which case I'll regret sending it anyway, since I honestly do not want to do any harm. [Handling this ability of channelling] is a matter of reaching a certain level of spirituality. And by spirituality I mean the sacred, the Orthodox Church, or Buddhism ... generally, it exists as a form of energy ... and I was an amateur. I should have *acted* differently. That is, if I really meant to send bad energy to him it would have happened, I think. But I regretted sending this bad energy. And I sent it so quickly that it did not have time to find its target and bounced back, like a boomerang. At the end, it was my life that sucked, due to this whole process of channelling.

Energy and its channelling are welcomed and supported by Orthodox adherents and practitioners of New Age spirituality – who many times coincide – alike. Even when it evokes a certain amount of uncertainty, as in the case of Mina, the synthesis of Orthodoxy and New Age spirituality is part of Rethymniot and Thessalonikan everyday life. I have met a large number of Rethymniots and Thessalonikans who are both Christian and evil eye practitioners, while simultaneously being open to ideas of energy channelling and New Age spirituality. These are predominantly younger women and men, aged approximately between twenty-five and forty-five, who have graduated from university. Yet, older interlocutors of mine, especially women who are devoted to Orthodoxy, are also keen on accepting energy channelling as part of their evil eye discourse and their lives in general, by talking about the continuous exchange of electromagnetic waves and energy between people. The concept of energy brings religion and spirituality closer together.

Energy has thus become a central part of the everyday discourse of Greeks, even the more religious ones. It is considered to be channelled through everyday sensory communication; it is this energetic interplay of senses and emotions that causes the evil eye. At the same time, doing yoga, burning sage and placing New Age crystals and feng shui objects around the house can protect from evil energy and the evil eye. Keeping religious icons and/or having a priest perform a house blessing can also remove negative energy away from one's household and reduce the possibility of *matiasma* (see Figure 7). Ultimately, the widespread use of the concept of energy in present-day Greece is symptomatic of the popularity New Age ideologies have gained in the country and is currently adopted both by individuals who follow a more denominational religious path and by others who are more inclined to move towards new spiritual itineraries.

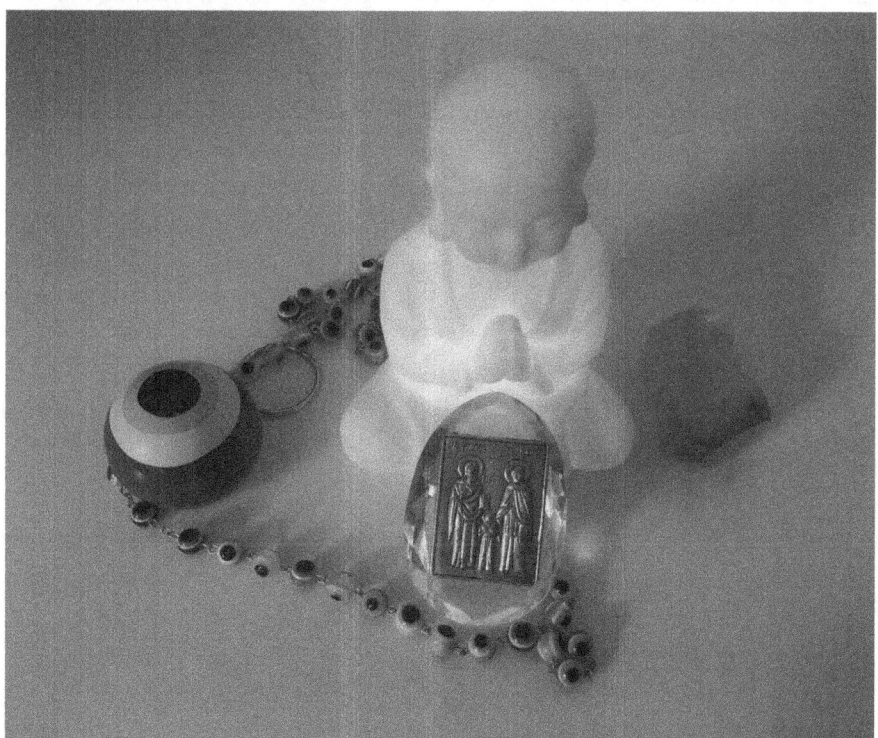

Figure 7 New Age and Orthodox household items for positive energy.

Symptoms of evil eye affliction

Matiasma always results in bodily symptoms that affect one's physical body, sensory perception and sociability. The evil eye power shows its presence by possessing the human body. The outcome of the imposed bodily distress varies. Headaches, dizziness, stomach upsets, eye-related problems, a general state of weakness, or a perceptive awkwardness: in combination or as standalone inflictions, these constitute the most commonly developed ill-symptoms one experiences when possessed by the evil eye. By feeling the evil eye effects on their body, Rethymniots and Thessalonikans become more aware of their spirituality. They know that the bodily symptoms they feel do not originate from physical/biological causality but are of an emotional, energetic and/or spiritual nature. Yet, the spiritual affliction is somatically expressed and physically worn in the form of an illness.[1]

A symptom that is actually, linguistically and symbolically related to the evil eye is the one that affects the sensory organ of the eyes. For instance, in Thessaloniki, a woman saw my interlocutor's pair of glasses, she admired them, and, within hours, the glasses were broken. Furthermore, *matiasma* causes a headache, which usually begins to be felt around the eye area. An evil-eyed person can feel his/her eyes burning. Heaviness develops around them. Or s/he can have distorted vision. Eleni told me that when she is evil eyed she does not see very well, and her vision gets 'all fuzzy'. When he is *matiasmenos* (evil eyed), Giorgos' vision is also blurred. Kaiti feels hazy, as if she does not communicate with the environment 100 per cent and she cannot see very clearly. Chrissa experiences the evil eye as a feeling of being perceptually lost. So does Maria:

> I feel as if I am not present here. If you ask me to perform a task, I will not be able to understand what you are talking about. I feel I am one step behind. It is as if I have entered another dimension from which I observe the present one. As if I cannot observe the present. As if I cannot be here. The phone rings, I answer, I listen to what they say, but I do not remember anything afterwards.

Mati attacks people's sensory perception. An evil-eyed person enters another dimension, as Maria indicated, a state of embodied isolation both from others and from oneself. One's own body feels different, is unrecognizable, alien, suffering from an awkward perception. This isolating feeling can be depicted in one of the most popular evil eye symptoms: *kommara*. *Kommara* semantically derives from the Greek verb *kovo*, which means 'to cut'. Thessalonikans mainly, and Rethymniots to a lesser degree, use the term as a way to describe the somatic feelings the evil eye inflicts upon them: they feel as if their bodily parts are cut from their body. Sleepiness, extreme tiredness, weakness, lack of ability to stand, stillness, lack of energy, deficiency in bodily power are included in *kommara* and contribute to the feeling of a numbed, senseless body. Together with its literal meaning, *kommara* signifies that, by feeling somatically cut, one is also cut from any form of social activity. Having to deal with a body that is possessed by the evil eye, people experience socio-somatic disconnection and isolation.

At other times, this perceptive and social estrangement grows out of a painful bodily awareness. Headaches and serious stomach upsets constitute the second most common symptom of evil eye affliction. Almost every Rethymniot and Thessalonikan I spoke to has characterized this headache as unique: it is not a migraine, it is not stress, it is not fatigue and it is not related to any other form of physical illness; it is the evil eye headache. The way in which it is embodied varies. It can be felt like a stick on the head, as a pain in the temples, or a peripheral pain in the back side of the skull, like someone is putting enormous pressure on your brain. It can be accompanied by dizziness, a general nauseous feeling, or by a loud sound inside the head, as if someone is playing drums inside one's brain.

The symptoms my interlocutors feel when possessed by the evil eye are powerful. A cultural uneasiness is expressed through the medium of the body. Yet, 'the body is not passively scripted with cultural codes, but actors are always already on the stage, within the terms of the performance' (Butler 1990: 277). Even in the state of embodied and social isolation, individuals do not cease to be culturally active. Their somatic condition expresses the social performances which are staged between their attackers and themselves. Those who attack with and those who are attacked by the evil eye are actors in a cultural play. They act and interact, confronting their social relationships in a process that results in power acquisition through energetic embodiment and sensory interaction.

Senses, spaces and the evil eye

The senses are 'bearers and shapers of culture' (Howes 1991b: 3). They carry all those distinct, detailed and sensitive qualities that allow people to grasp intensely the cultural ambience that surrounds them. Rethymniots and Thessalonikans approach perception and the sensory with a fresh cultural light. In the process of giving and receiving the evil eye, they negotiate their individual and collective sensory and emotional perceptions creatively and powerfully. Simultaneously, they express something distinct about the way in which they experience their socio-cultural surroundings. By actively handling the evil eye, while introducing new dimensions – such as the idea of the 'good eye' or energy – to it, and by employing both Christian and New Age spiritual ideologies, not only do they culturally transform and reconstruct the practice, but they also act against social inflexibility.

Greek everyday social life, including quotidian living in Rethymno and Thessaloniki, is principally based on social and sensory interactions within the neighbourhood. 'What other people will say' is, according to my interlocutors, a popular Greek principle around which many Greeks build their lives, being careful not to say or do anything that may attract the neighbours' attention and, as a result, cause the evil eye. This is not to say that Rethymniot and Thessalonikan everyday life is under constant social control. Given the spatial organization of Greek neighbourhoods, where physical and social distance is at times inevitable, social curiosity arises and with that, evil eye affliction may occur. Rethymniots and Thessalonikans are indeed socially curious. They are interested in knowing everything with regard to how their acquaintances lead their lives: who is having a relationship with whom; why their next-door neighbour is coming home so late at night; who is that person sitting on the balcony facing their veranda. But it is not only the close spatial proximity that matters. Curiosity is also expressed towards complete strangers: someone who is dressed up in a fashionable way is looked over; beautiful women and handsome men attract attention; the smell of an expensive perfume is noticed; the compatibility of couples walking in the streets is talked about. Gazes, eavesdropping, the smell of what a neighbour cooks, the taste of freshly made cakes and meals, the touch of a friend's newly bought blouse: a sensory interplay occurs continuously during everyday social communication. Envy and/or admiration reach the cultural surface and, as a result, the evil eye is generated. Such a stir of emotions, which results in evil eye affliction, can also arise without the bodily mediation of and response to the senses. Gossiping or simply thinking about someone is equally capable of causing *matiasma*. In such an event, the power of one's spiritual energy affects another person's body from a distance. A spiritual interaction hence takes place, feelings are exchanged and the evil eye is bodily perceived and felt via this form of channelling.

The smell of jasmine constitutes a strong characteristic of the town of Rethymno; it colonizes verandas, gardens, streets and its distinct smell resembles Rethymniots themselves: fulfilling and persistent, strong yet discreet. Rethymniot identity is connected with the jasmine aroma, and, as the locals have proudly admitted, its persistent scent adds to the beauty and distinctiveness of their town. Hearing constitutes another important sense in Cretan culture. Expressions such as 'I hear what you mean' or 'can you hear the garlic in the food?' are very common (cf. Classen 1990: 722). Furthermore, Rethymniots are loud. They are lively, high-spirited and full of energy and passion. Their local dialect, accompanied by a distinct – to a foreign ear – pronunciation, addresses their high tones during quotidian social exchange in a dynamic way. Strolling around the town, one's sense of hearing is fed by Cretan discussions in the streets, shops, markets and playgrounds (see Figure 8). During the summer, the main sound that occupies the streets is the buzzing multi-linguistic voice of tourists.

Figure 8 Social proximity in the Old Town of Rethymno.

With winter's arrival, the noise of tourism is replaced by social silence, and the sound moves indoors. Additionally, Rethymniots are not afraid to look at people straight in the eyes; they constantly observe social movement and cast glances on whoever passes by. They do not hesitate to stare if something or someone catches their attention. From playful to curious, from friendly to disliking and from flirty to judgemental, these penetrating gazes hold a central position in the everyday interplay of social inquisitiveness and cultural action and can result in evil eye affliction.

In Thessaloniki, visual communication is equally strong. The city centre is a zone where glances and social critiques are exchanged. Thessalonikans are notorious for taking extensive care of the way they present themselves in the social arena. They almost never exit their front door without being bodily adorned in an elegant way. The city high streets are full of women and men with stylish clothes and carefully presented appearance. The large number of cafes around the pier intensifies gazing. The residents of Thessaloniki are well known for the habit of spending their afternoons sipping frappe coffee by the *paralia* (seaside) of the city, while enjoying the sea views and the sight of people passing by (see Figure 9). Flirty stares and gossipy comments are very common if not

Figure 9 The *paralia* of Thessaloniki.

compulsory activities, during which the danger of giving and receiving the evil eye is always present. At the same time, the spatial field of the neighbourhood is full of sensory curiosity. Noises, smells, gazes and tastes all intermingle in Thessalonikans' everyday neighbourly life. The sound of a police car, fire brigade or ambulance siren, people's murmuring in the streets, mumbled voices penetrating the apartments' walls provoke auditory nosiness. Watching what the neighbour in the opposite veranda is preoccupied with is a rather ordinary visual activity. The smell of food cooked by female neighbours raises comments as far as their ability to behave as 'proper housewives' is concerned and so does the invitation for a coffee to a friend's or social contact's house, where one's capability as a host can trigger gossip and the evil eye.

Both Rethymno and Thessaloniki are therefore vividly sensory places, where a variety of sensory interactions occurs on a daily basis. Eyes, ears, mouths, noses are fed by observations, conversations, aromas, noises, awakening the senses, alerting the sensory organs, provoking in many cases the evil eye. Everyday life can be conceived as a sensorial field of glances, sounds and talks, where the evil eye is caused while people interact with each other visually, verbally and aurally. The evil eye can thus be considered as a collective medium of sensory communication (Seremetakis 1994: 6), where people use their senses to confront one another and socio-culturally interact with each other. The neighbourhood, more specifically, constitutes a social space where sensory interaction becomes penetrating. During the spring and summer months, more commonly, when social interactions intensify and everyday practices move outside the household, gazing, eavesdropping and gossiping about the neighbours shape everyday life. As a result of this intense sensory and social communication, the neighbourhood is a site where *matiasma* occurs consistently. Frequently, the way in which one presents oneself inside the neighbourhood is often determined by social expectations and anxiety over 'what people will say'. People in Rethymno and Thessaloniki are aware of the fact that their neighbours can potentially see, hear, smell, judge and gossip about them whenever they exit their home. They are also aware that this social circulation can trigger the evil eye. There are plenty of times, however, when a person is afflicted by the evil eye outside his/her familiar neighbourhood domain. In that case, the evil eye power acts anonymously and without the mediation of sensory perception. This latter form of affliction is quite common and is mainly a consequence of living in an urban environment.

In the urban localities I studied, evil eye affliction can be the result of social proximity and in many cases a personal matter, since it can be triggered by and at the same time against friends, relatives, acquaintances and other social contacts. Yet, compared to a rural space, such proximity is more difficult to achieve, especially in Thessaloniki where the faster – compared to a village or town – rhythms of people's everyday life cannot be easily followed by neighbours. Furthermore, during their quotidian urban wanderings, Rethymniots and Thessalonikans encounter a plethora of strangers, each of whom can potentially be an evil eye giver. And here lies the difference between a rural and an urban locus as far as the transmission of the evil eye is concerned. In Rethymno and Thessaloniki the evil eye is cast within but also beyond the boundaries of the spatially and socially familiar. More often than not, my interlocutors have attributed their evil eye affliction to strangers rather than to members of their social circle. The evil eye giver becomes de-personalized. The urban space inside which the evil eye acts turns out to be large, multiple, porous and anonymous. *Matiasma* in my urban fieldwork loci is not (or not merely) an indication of conflicts between particular individuals who live within a bounded community. Instead, it demonstrates how the evil eye acts in a multiplicity of spatialities and social circumstances, where a certain level of social intimacy between the potential evil eye giver and the potential evil eye recipient is not necessarily required.

Mati and *Glossofagia*: Gaze meetings and mouth feedings

Visual communication is predominantly held responsible for evil eye transmission. Anthropological analyses that have dealt with the evil eye thus far have primarily attributed it to the act of seeing. Western culture is a visualist culture, where sensing habitually mostly equals seeing and this visual domination is linguistically expressed in the use of words like 'worldview' and phrases like 'I see what you mean' (Classen 1990: 722). Anthropologists usually make the same mistake: when studying cultures that deviate from the visualistic model, they translate these cultures' senses into a visual sensory model (Classen 1990). When researching a practice where the sense of vision occupies a central position, the anthropologist must 'redefine [her] orientation to sight, for anthropologists must learn to assess critically their own gazes' (Stoller 1989: 9). Following this paradigm while conducting my own research on the evil eye, I too had to be careful not to impose my own sensorial preconceptions on the ethnographic field and on the analysis; after all, I had grown up believing that the evil eye is principally cast through the eyes. Although my ethnographic evidence argued for a sensory egalitarianism, there existed the danger of overemphasizing the visual. Instead, before highlighting the equal role of the sensory in the evil eye practice, together with discovering and recognizing that the evil eye goes beyond the 'eye' in perceptual terms, I allowed my ethnographic self to sense and feel and not to just see the field, but approach, experience and interpret it multi-sensorially.[2]

'Your own brother can give you the evil eye, if he looks at you intensely in the eyes', Thanasis, a thirty-five-year-old man from Thessaloniki told me one day, as we sat and sipped coffee. He went on to explain to me how he is afraid of intense gazes because he is very susceptible to the evil eye; for Thanasis, the solution is to avoid looking people directly in the eyes so that he can somehow protect himself against evil energy through gaze exchange. Vasilis, a young Thessalonikan, has an aunt who is well known for her negative energy, evil gaze and her ability to cast the evil eye. Whenever he meets her, Vasilis tries hard not to look at her directly in the eyes; in this way, he believes he can escape *matiasma*. In Greece, members of kin and friends are very often responsible for transmitting the evil eye, since the more intimate one is with others, the more penetrative the gaze grows to be. In general, the importance of vision and the power of the gaze have been highlighted by plenty of my interlocutors in Thessaloniki and Rethymno. But it is not only the individuals of one's immediate environment that may be held responsible for sending their gaze and afflicting a person. Vision is a crucial sense, as I was told in the field, because the eyes are the mirror of the soul. Consequently, it does not simply matter whether a person is a relative, a friend or a complete stranger. According to my interlocutors, every person can express himself/herself through visual communication, the outcome of which depends on whether s/he has a good or a bad soul. If a person's soul is filled with negativity and evilness, then, in the words of Eleni, a Rethymniot woman, 'she can fix her gaze on you; her eyes inhabit your being, and immediately inflict the evil eye upon you'.

While Chrissa, a Thessalonikan middle-aged woman, was on her way to the post-office, she felt someone's eyes piercing her back. She turned to look who it was and saw three older men standing on the opposite side of the street, staring at her with intensity. '*Me matiasan*' (they gave me the evil eye), she told me, 'and after a second I tripped, fell down on the pavement and suffered from a very bad injury'. It has become apparent from the various narratives I have collected from Rethymniots and Thessalonikans that the act of gazing is linked extensively to evil eye affliction. *Mati* is caused when people look at each other during everyday social contact. Besides, the word *mati* itself holds a symbolic rhetorical position. *Mati* in Greek means 'eye'. A visual communication is therefore indicated linguistically. The eye's significance as a biological organ is present. Evil eye power is practised. And when *mati* becomes a synonym of *matiasma*, the sensory organ escapes its biological connotations and becomes a means of cultural action.

Veikou (1998: 40) argues that vision is 'the most sociable of all the senses, as visual exchange goes beyond the biological limits of a simple sensory function, and is transformed into a culturally determined form of transmitting ideas, values and symbolisms which are familiar and important to the particular society'. I agree only to the point where the visual part of the evil eye goes beyond its biological characteristics and becomes a socio-cultural practice. But Veikou's statement entails the idea of visualism, that is, of the 'reduction of all experience to the representational means available to only one sensory medium, that of sight' (Herzfeld 2001: 35). Social life in a visualist culture (Classen 1990: 722), where the Western canons of aesthetics produce a visual reductionism (Howes 1991b: 11), might opt for an emphasis on vision's supremacy. Nevertheless, the evil eye, in spite of its linguistic intimacy with the visual, initiates the stimulation of multi-sensory communication. Sight is located as high in the evil eye sensory hierarchy as hearing, smell, taste and touch.

When I asked Tania, a young female interlocutor of mine in Thessaloniki, whether *glossofagia* (being eaten by tongue), namely the *matiasma* caused by gossiping, can be regarded as *mati*, the answer I received was positive. 'But why is it called *mati*?' I insisted.

> It is what I told you. It is one thing to see something, to see this bag for instance, admire it, and after a moment the bag is destroyed because coffee is spilled all over it. This is something direct. It is another thing when *glossofagia* takes place. *Glossofagia* is when I do not see you; I just sit down with my friends and we eat you with our tongues; and you can be home and cut yourself with a knife.

Apart from the eye, the tongue can also be considered dangerous (Harding 1975: 302; Hirschon 1993 [1978]: 68). Gossip is regarded as 'a means of release from the boredom of the routinized and restricted existence' (Cowan 1991: 185). Actually, gossip is more than a simple activity of everyday routine. People are engaged in social encounters, they talk, criticize, establish verbal interactions and negotiate meaning by reaffirming social narratives. Hence, they are actual participants (Harding 1975: 298), who possess the empowered ability to judge others' performances, practices and to impose *glossofagia*.

In his research in two rural parishes of Alto Minho, Portugal, Pina-Cabral noticed how the 'evil tongue' (*má lingua*) and the act of 'speaking or saying evil' (*falar mal* or *dizer mal*) resulted in the transmission of the evil eye and in the disruption of social relationships (Pina-Cabral 1986: 178). Women in Portugal were considered as 'gossip-mongers', who exercise 'evil will' because of their jealousy and who, through their gossip, harm other people (Pina-Cabral 1986). Women in Greece are also thought to have an 'evil tongue', and the content of their gossip can potentially jeopardize social relationships and harm people (Hirschon 1993 [1978]: 68–9). During my fieldwork, the image of women as carriers of an 'evil tongue', which can transmit the evil eye, was occasionally painted. However, men were also accused of gossiping. Actually, the majority of the Rethymniots and Thessalonikans I spoke to did not differentiate gossipers according to their gender and were not aware of whether the social actors of *glossofagia* were men or women.

Marina, a thirty-four-year-old woman in Rethymno, secured her entry to university by studying entirely on her own.[3] But people got really envious because of that, and they 'ate her with their tongue', '*me glossofagan*' as she told me. By eating Marina with their tongue, and by subsequently giving her the evil eye and inflicting somatic symptoms of illness on her, people, according to Marina, controlled her emotional state. As she pointed out, she was ecstatic about her success; however, feeling evil eyed all the time did not leave her enough space to feel as happy and to celebrate as much as she wanted. A social authority was imposed upon her. The evil tongue has evil consequences. 'Being eaten by tongue' can be regarded as a 'metaphor of power' (Gilsenan 1996: xiii). If *koutsompolio*, gossip that is, is defined as 'information exchange through face-to-face interaction', as well as 'informal communication passed about persons' (Handelman 1973: 211), then it is easily asserted that 'gossiping indicates and establishes intimacies among informants that confer authority in everyday life' (Van Vleet 2003: 494).

A small factory which produces milk is situated very close to my interlocutor Ksenia's hometown, near Thessaloniki. Given the predominance of the large Greek factories as far as milk production is concerned, this small business was very successful; all its animals were producing milk, which was bought by big companies like Mevgal, Fage and Delta.[4] But people were gossiping, wondering where the owner of the small factory got the money to build it, if he won the lottery or if he was simply a fraud. They 'ate the business with their tongue', as Ksenia put it, and after a while the production started deteriorating, the animals got sick, and, at the end, the factory closed. 'This is *glossofagia*', Ksenia continued. 'People talk and talk and talk. As a result, they send evil energy from time to time. The effects of this transmission can take up to one, two, three years to be seen.'

A distinction is made here between *mati* and *glossofagia*. *Mati*, being caused by direct contact, as I have been told, has immediate symptoms. *Glossofagia*, being an indirect form of communication, has indirect results, which require their time to develop. Still, people in my fieldsites are not strictly consistent in their statements. Most of them connect *mati* with embodied symptoms and *glossofagia* with the more general way of unsuccessful living. For example, if Maria, a mid-twenties female Thessalonikan, feels the evil eye symptoms on her body, without having left her home at all, she will not think that she is evil eyed. '*Glossofagia* is not about the body', as she has argued. But if someone starts suffering from a very serious disease, she might then consider the possibility of *glossofagia*.

> *Glossofagia* does not result in a symptom, in a headache, the way *mati* does. I think *glossofagia* is stronger. It will affect your home, your family, your health, your job, it can be everywhere. If I trip in the street, it means that someone gave me the evil eye because he looked at me. But if my new house burns down because it is beautiful and everyone admires it, it is *glossofagia*. If my family suddenly starts quarrelling, it is *glossofagia*, not *mati*.

Glossofagia does act as *mati*. Plenty of my interlocutors have felt the symptoms of *glossofagia* on their body. But while producing evil eye symptoms of illness at a personal level, on people's bodies that is, it can also affect their general wellbeing and attack certain aspects of their lives in addition to or other than their embodied selves. Both *mati* and *glossofagia* have negative consequences on individuals, constituting a politics of identity interaction in everyday sensory contact. Through this form of direct and indirect communication individuals have the chance to act, to exercise power, to threaten their fellow subjects' identities, to affect theirs as well and to mobilize their social relationships and cultural surroundings.

Gkantemia: Evil eye and bad luck

My interlocutor's husband is a Cretan army officer in his early forties, a nice and open-minded man, as my interlocutor described him. One New Year's Eve, his little daughter wanted to have the *vasilopita* (New Year's Eve cake)[5] cut before the arrival of the New Year. My interlocutor satisfied her daughter's wish without consulting her husband first, who at the time of the request was in the bathroom. When he came back and saw the *vasilopita* sitting on the table all sliced up, he became really angry and the couple had a huge fight. The husband thought that cutting the *vasilopita* before the change of the year meant that *gkantemia* (bad luck, misfortune) had been brought into their household and something very bad would happen to the family in the course of the next year. A couple of months after this incident, my interlocutor's father-in-law died; her husband has been blaming his wife for the death of his father ever since.

Gkantemia is the Greek word that semantically expresses both bad luck and misfortune, and there are many Greeks that connect it with the idea of giving the evil eye. It is rhetorically used to characterize almost every bad event that occurs during everyday life. Spilling your milk on the table is *gkantemia*, falling down while walking on the street can be regarded as *gkantemia*, missing the bus or the train might also be *gkantemia*. As Nikos, a Thessalonikan man, explains:

> *Gkantemia* is many things. For example, I have to go to the bank, and I do not know that today the buses are on strike. It is getting late, so I decide to take a taxi; and then the taxi breaks down and I never reach the bank at the end ... I think *gkantemia* is a matter of coincidences and incidences.

While in Thessaloniki, I became good friends with a woman who, from the very beginning of our friendship, warned me that she suffered from *gkantemia*. Every other day, Aleksandra called me and always had a fresh story to narrate of another bad-luck incident that had happened to her in the meantime. From one particular point onwards, however, the situation reversed. I started suffering from small everyday misfortunes, and I was the one who had *gkantemia* episodes to narrate, whereas Aleksandra's everyday bad luck seemed to have subsided. My friend got worried. She felt guilty, since she was convinced that she had in some strange way transferred her *gkantemia* to me. How else could my suddenly acquired bad luck be explained? Admittedly, this explanation had also crossed my mind; yet, I had immediately dismissed it. A few weeks later, Aleksandra's *gkantemia* came back to her, mine almost vanished, and the negotiation of our social relationship went back to normal.

One day she accused me in a friendly yet persistent way of having given her the evil eye. Aleksandra has admitted that *gkantemia* is an inherent characteristic of her personality, which she has learned to live with and has come to view with a sense of humour. I wondered, therefore, why she did not interpret the incidents between us with an analogous sense of humour, viewing them as part of her own *gkantemia*, instead of pointing to my ability to give her the evil eye. Her accusation placed our relationship on a different level of interaction. I was not just a friend; I was also a potential threat. Aleksandra has stamped herself with the quality of *gkantemia*, which she does not clearly distinguish from the evil eye. Yet, in her attempt to explain certain personal misfortunes, she appears capable of handling them both alternatively, depending on social strategies and the handling of everyday discourses.

'You carry bad luck; others give you the evil eye ... actually, bad luck is part of both *mati* and *glossofagia* ... yes, [the evil eye] can be bad luck, *gkantemia* as we say. Besides, people do exorcize bad luck with Christian blessings.' As the words of my Rethymniot male interlocutor indicate, *gkantemia* resembles *glossofagia*, since they can both result in continuous and possibly long-lasting misfortune. The boundaries between the evil eye and *gkantemia* are slippery, and one can easily be confused with the other as they frequently share the same symptoms and explanations. Yet, *gkantemia* is not an evil eye as such, and the disparity between the two rests on who actually triggers the suffering. Apart from some rare cases of *auto-matiasma* (self-imposed evil eye), the recipient of the evil eye differs from the sender. *Gkantemia* is a self-imposed and inherent state. And, unlike *matiasma*, the one who suffers from *gkantemia* cannot inflict his/her bad luck upon others.

It is one thing to admit that you suffer from *gkantemia*, which, as analysed above, is predominantly a self-imposed situation; it is another to acknowledge that you can cast the evil eye, that is, to confess that you can consciously – though not intentionally – affect people in a negative way, no matter how smooth this influence is. When she looks at children playing in the street, they almost always fall and hurt themselves. Apart from giving the evil eye to children she finds adorable, Margarita, a Rethymniot in her late twenties, has admitted that when she intensively looks at people walking in the street they often trip. A middle-aged woman in Thessaloniki once saw a pot of beautiful flowers at a relative's house; a couple of hours later the flowers died. She knows that she can give the evil eye, and every time she sees something she likes she spits on it in order to prevent evil eye transmittance. A man who owns a shop in the Old Town of Rethymno has told me: 'There have been many times when I see young women passing in front of my shop; the minute I look at them they trip and fall down. The others tell me that I've got the evil eye.'

It is not an easy task nor is it desirable for someone to admit that s/he can actually cast the evil eye. It means that s/he is aware of the power to harm his/her fellow human beings, even if unintentionally and even if the consequences are not significant. By recognizing their power, those few who have admitted their *matiasma* ability enter an ambivalent status of social insecurity. There is a high chance that others may become afraid of and cut any social links with them as a result, out of fear of receiving the evil eye. From their part, my interlocutors try their best not to provoke *matiasma*, usually by taking preventive measures, like spitting or avoiding over-admiring an item which belongs to another person.

It was an evening in late May, about three months after I first moved to Thessaloniki. I was waiting for Aleksandra, my friend who suffers from *gkantemia*, so that we would walk together to the café where another friend was waiting for us. When she arrived, I noticed she was wearing a new pair of trousers, and I told her how much I liked them and how lovely they looked on her. We arrived at the café and placed our orders. A few minutes later, the waiter brought us glasses of water. While he was leaving them on the table, he slipped, and one of the glasses targeted my friend's trousers, leaving them and her soaked. Some days later Aleksandra called me, and our discussion ended up with the event in the café. Half-joking half-serious, she stated that what had happened was my fault: by admiring her trousers, I had given her the evil eye. In our next coffee meeting, Aleksandra and I decided to test my evil eye abilities: I should choose another material possession of hers which I liked, and we would check whether I could really cause *matiasma* or not. Her necklace became our scapegoat. I proceeded with mumbling words of admiration towards the necklace, which, if I truly had the ability to cause *matiasma*, should get damaged soon. We did not have to wait long. Three days later my friend called me saying that the necklace was cut in half but it could be fixed; therefore, my evil eye was not too strong.

'God, this *mati* of yours!' Andreas told me, half-joking, half serious, while we were relaxing in his Thessalonikan flat. I had met a friend of his who was related to a woman that, from what he had told me, seemed to be taking advantage of him. I had then told Andreas that his friend should not really be with her. Two weeks later, Andreas' friend broke up with his girlfriend. Andreas, who had already known about the trousers incident, was convinced that my *mati* was responsible for the separation. One warm evening, during a brief return to Crete for ethnographic purposes a few years ago, a close friend and I were getting ready to go out for a drink in the Old Town. I watched her while she put her shoes on, while thinking how great they looked and that I should buy a similar pair soon. I told her. Minutes later, the sole of one of her sandals was partly detached from the rest of the shoe. Marianthi turned around and told me that I probably caused that with my evil eye. We glued the sole back to the shoe. Then she mentioned that the particular sandal had caused the same trouble before and I needn't worry too much about what had happened. Yet, I had to be concerned. I was struck with the realization that I most likely possessed the power of giving the evil eye, which was an upsetting prospect and the only role in the evil eye interplay I had not yet acquired.

When Aleksandra first accused me of giving her the evil eye, I took serious offence. 'How could she say a thing like that? No envy stands between friends; besides, I am a good person. How is it possible to act in an evil manner?' I kept thinking repeatedly. When my social insecurity faded, however, and my anthropological self came to the rescue, I realized that the accusations against me were ethnographically fruitful. It meant that I had dived deep into my evil eye investigation and gained the right to intimacy. My interlocutors had empowered and at the same time criticized me. They had let me into their everyday world, by feeling free to get suspicious about me the same way they get suspicious about their neighbours, friends and people they meet in the street. Besides, my evil eye might not have been so evil after all.

Kalo Mati: Disarming evil

During a discussion with Fani, a woman in her late thirties who owned a shop in the Old Town of Rethymno, I was introduced to the idea of the 'good eye' versus the 'evil eye'. A client had come into her shop, paid her compliments, and after that Fani had developed symptoms of *matiasma*. But, as Fani explained, her client had good intentions; he told her everything out of admiration and good will. Hence, his eye was good, not evil. The majority of my interlocutors have had a pretty strong opinion formed with regard to what the 'good eye' (*kalo mati*) is and whether it exists or not. A fair number of them do believe in the good eye. They are keen on the idea that someone can cause ill-symptoms on someone else because s/he has seen or talked about a person with positive feelings, good thoughts and admiration.

'I have heard people saying "oh, this person gave you the evil eye out of her excessive love". Relatives, friends, your partner, they can all give you the evil eye. And this is the so-called *kalo mati*, because I do not suppose a person who loves you can ever treat you in an evil way.' Following the statement of Vasilis, a middle-aged Thessalonikan's statement, one could argue that people hesitate to accuse their beloved ones of transmitting the evil eye; the concept of the 'good eye', therefore, offers a somewhat better alternative. Perhaps *kalo mati* grants social security: connecting someone with the good eye instead of the evil eye would not cause unwanted personal and social relationship disruption. *Kalo mati* is something different from *kako mati* (evil eye), although it provokes bad – but not evil – symptomatology. It is, then, perhaps, partly *matiasma*; and it means well.

I was having a discussion with two Cretan women on the *kalo mati* theme, when one of them suddenly came to the realization that she is a carrier of *kalo mati*. She then told us that when she intensively looks at people in the street, they usually fall down. One time she was staring at a waiter who only seconds later lost his balance and broke several glasses of drinks as a result. She insisted, however, that these were not evil eye incidents, since she has never felt any form of envy towards the people she is looking at, and does not hold any negative feelings inside her; her eye could not but be good. The good eye lets individuals admit that they hold the power to influence others, without the danger of getting socially stigmatized. *Kalo mati* constitutes a new cultural category. Despite my close engagement with the evil eye for many years, I had never met anyone who would talk about the evil eye in positive terms. The good eye is indicative of the fact that the evil eye in Greece is not marginalized. On the contrary, it is socially existent and culturally persistent. People think and act about it in creative ways. They transform its meaning by introducing new terminological categories. *Kalo mati* infuses the evil eye with a renewed cultural plausibility. It is devised by Rethymniots and Thessalonikans as a means to negotiate their social relationships with others. It is a creative discourse of their social action.

Lastly, and perhaps most importantly, the recent appearance of *kalo mati* in the everyday discourse of Greeks is indicative of the New Age influence in the evil eye practice. New Age ideology is largely established on the principle that New Age practices are positive and a path to self-fulfilment. *Kalo mati* is based on the idea that positive energy is heavily circulated between people. It is true that, according to New Age beliefs and practices, the circulation of positive energy results in healing, not in bodily symptoms of illness as happens in the case of the good eye. Yet, *kalo mati* can help people realize their social behaviour in relation to their fellow human beings, alter it so that they can avoid *mati* and subsequently enter a process of self-fulfilment. *Kalo mati* is ultimately an indication that the evil eye is being transformed through its contact with New Age ideology.

Vaskania: Good and evil in the official church discourse

Vaskania is the 'official' term used in the context of Orthodox Christianity to define the evil eye. It derives etymologically from the ancient Greek verb *vaskaino*, which means 'to look at someone with envy'. In the words of Father Ioannis, a Thessalonikan priest: '*Vaskania* is provoked by satanic powers; it is the devil's work.' The Orthodox Church, its priests and its religious devotees may show tolerance towards *mati* and *matiasma*. Yet, they understand the evil eye through its concept of *vaskania*, in other words as a phenomenon involving the devil. In popular understanding, however, the devil may or may not be involved in evil eye afflictions; these may be caused purely by the power of certain individuals or certain emotional states through a process of energy exchange.

When it comes to *vaskania*, there seems to be a polarization between 'doctrinal' and 'practical/local' religion, that is between 'a religion as textual, theological precept of official church, and the one as practiced at a particular time and place as part of a given community' (Stewart 1991: 11). But *vaskania* is practical too. It is not only perceived and practised by the official church representatives. Lay people utilize it rhetorically and do not make a sharp, or usually any, distinction between *vaskania* and *mati*. As Antigoni, a young woman in Rethymno, told me: 'Look, my mum, who is quite religious, accepts what the Orthodox Church accepts, namely that *vaskania* exists. There is this special prayer which the priest reads in order to get rid of this thing.'

Dionisopoulos-Mass (1976: 51) points to a distinction between *matiasma* and *vaskania*, where the latter is a 'stronger, intentional, malicious power to harm people's health, and requires the intervention of a priest'. Yet, this distinction is nothing but a game of rhetoric – a game which I was inevitably involved in ethnographically. I had paid a visit to the only ecclesiastic bookshop of Rethymno and, after unsuccessfully browsing through the religious books in my attempt to find *vaskania* reading material, I asked the man in charge, who seemed a devoted Christian, if he believed in *vaskania*. His reply was: '*Mati* is accepted by Orthodoxy.' His response surprised me. I had used the word *vaskania* because I was inside this particular bookshop, owned by the Bishopric of Rethymno, where I felt I should use a term which would sound 'religiously appropriate'. But the man did not follow my discourse. He preferred, instead, to utilize the local accustomed terminology. The evil eye entails *vaskania* as part of its 'Orthodox' interpretative idiom; accordingly, *vaskania* consists of evilness, since is directly linked to the devil's evil energy.

The popularity that *vaskania* enjoys has partly to do with the Greek educational system. While in Crete, I went to the house of a very religious elderly woman to conduct an interview with her. She greeted my arrival by handing me a piece of paper: a prayer against *vaskania*, which she had photocopied from the state-provided book used in the Greek high school course on 'Religion'. I felt quite surprised and guilty, since I had no recollection of being taught anything about *vaskania* when I was in high school. The following day I asked my mother to search my old school books, find the one on religion, and immediately post it to Rethymno. So she did. The relevant part was dug out of my old book. It represented the evil eye as *vaskania*, strictly following Orthodoxy's socio-cultural interpretation. This should not have come as a surprise; the book was written by theologians. According to my high school book, which, although modified, is used to the present day as an official form of religious education, *vaskania* is equalled to telepathy (*tilepatheia*), envisioning (*enorasi*) and firewalking (*pyrovasia*). Altogether, they are squeezed under the general title 'other contemporary New Age phenomena and movements'. One of the central means of Greek socialization, that is the Greek educational system, reproduces the official Church discourse, when it comes to the evil eye. The most interesting aspect of the categorization mentioned above and somewhat surprisingly is that it is the official ecclesiastic term of *vaskania*, instead of that of the evil eye, the one equated with the New Age, non-religious, phenomena.

Spirit possession

Eleftheria, a middle-aged woman in Thessaloniki, has emphasized the intensity with which she experiences the evil eye. She feels as if she is possessed by a foreign power, a perceptual state where she has no control over her body and actions. 'It is like someone penetrating your being, as if you somatically hold someone else's negative energy.' Ranging from atheists to religious Orthodox adherents, my Rethymniot and Thessalonikan interlocutors share the belief that the evil eye occurs when one has his/her body possessed by someone else's energy. 'The Church thinks that *matiasma* is something that comes from the devil. But lay people are not so stuck with the assumption that the devil possesses you; they think that *mati* is negative energy, but something humanely negative,' Sotiris, a Rethymniot man in his thirties, explains.

Orthodoxy, the Church and its devotees disagree with the lay perception of evil eye possession. According to the official ecclesiastic texts and the Fathers of the Greek Orthodox Church, *vaskania* is a demonic energy, connected with the evilness of the devil, and can result in serious personal damage (Dickie 1995; Hristodoulou 2003: 66). The devil is regarded as the personification of evil in the context of the Orthodox Christian tradition (Stewart 1991: 141). Every form of evil, including the evil eye, which touches Orthodox grounds, is attributed to the power of the devil by the Greek Orthodox Church. Consequently, there are two basic interpretations regarding what triggers the evil eye in Rethymno and Thessaloniki. The first one comes from lay people, the majority of whom argue that the evil eye is predominantly the result of energy transmission between people and is thus of a human nature. The second explanation comes from the Church, which claims that evil eye possession is the work of the devil. Although the Church eagerly rejects the lay interpretation of evil eye possession, people are open to the idea that evil eye possession can also be of a spiritual character.

According to Danforth (1989), who has conducted his fieldwork in a northern Greek community, focusing his research on *Anastenaria*, a possession ritual performed in the Macedonia region, *Anastenarides*, the ritual practitioners, usually women and/or individuals whose social status is low, get possessed by the spirit of St Constantine and walk on burning coals without getting burned. For the *Anastenarides*, spirit possession serves as an idiom of religious expression, which enables them to solve problems of illness and sociability, by reinforcing their status inside the community and gaining respect from their co-villagers (1989: 5). What the evil eye shares with *Anastenaria* is the establishment of a link between social – mainly gendered – disempowerment and spirit possession. Through their act of possession, people become socially active, earning an authority they had not enjoyed thus far. By letting a spiritual power control their body, they in turn control their social positioning. They become active cultural agents. Besides, both Lewis (1966: 312) and Boddy (1988: 13) have observed that spirit possession has close analogies to the evil eye. Indeed, possession by the evil eye forms a religious idiom of social interaction. It is also true that socially deprived individuals are in many cases accused of casting *mati*. Yet, those possessed are usually the ones who are looked upon. Whether possessing or being possessed, Rethymniots and Thessalonikans, the ones who I spoke to at least, belong to both sexes, and most of them are lower middle and middle class. In the evil eye case, the social deprivation/gendered empowerment model of theorizing possession would have to be reversed: deprivation is not a characteristic of the individuals who become possessed; instead, the ones who possess others through their evil eye power are those who are seeking out a spiritual route to social authority.

Discussing the problem of where *mati* comes from with a man in Thessaloniki, he expressed the opinion that the power which results in *matiasma* is not self-existent but it must come from some kind of source. In his words: 'Yes, if the evil eye is some sort of power, then how could it be directed? Not by itself, that's for sure. Someone must lead it, because as a power it couldn't have an opinion and an attitude, someone has to guide it.' Giorgos brings up a crucial point: the agency of the evil eye power. The evil eye is not a reified force, existent to its own avail. It does not arrive, ready to attack, out of nowhere; instead, it is directed by someone. The question is whether this someone is the devil, a demon, a spirit, a person or a form of energy. As already mentioned, Orthodoxy ascribes the evil eye to the devil – to a supernatural force. On the other hand, the non-ecclesiastic line of approach opts for a natural justification: humans are the holders of the power. The problem of agency resurfaces.

Drawing on his research in Valletta, the capital of Malta, during the early 1990s, Mitchell maintains that there are two sources of evil in Malta: the 'strong' evil (which is associated with the devil) and the 'weaker' evil (which is associated with the evil eye (*ghajn*)) (Mitchell 2001: 77). As the anthropologist explains, Malta is situated 'both inside and outside European modernity. Catholicism is used as a means of legitimising the calls for accession to Europe, but also a means of resisting it. Because Malta is Catholic, so the argument goes, it belongs to Europe' (Mitchell 2001: 80). In the context of both ecclesiastic and lay discourse, the devil represents the 'correct version of Catholic "tradition"', which, however, is also considered to be rational, whereas the non-Catholic belief in the *ghajn* represents the 'incorrect or non-standard "tradition" of the superstitious', rendering the evil eye '"irrationally" traditional' (Mitchell 2001: 80). In addition, as Mitchell (2001: 81) argues, the power of the devil originates outside the body but is a felt power, bodily experienced by people. On the other hand, the power of the *ghajn* is located inside the person and is attributed to human agency; yet, even though it originates within the body, the evil eye is not somatically experienced by the Maltese (Mitchell 2001).

Mitchell's (2001: 77) important assertion is that, up to a certain degree at least, this mutual agreement between lay and official Catholic interpretations is the result of the influence the Catholic Church exercises upon people's everyday life in Malta. He points out that in the early-1990s Malta 'the *ghajn* was becoming a thing of the past, the power of the Devil was expanding'. The decline of the evil eye in Malta can too be attributed to the power the Catholic Church exercised on people, and which, subsequently, rendered the devil an orthodox belief and the evil eye a superstition (Mitchell 2001: 97). The *ghajn* was 'discouraged by the Church, and disapproved of in an everyday context, where discourses on modernity and education prevailed, as well as those on Catholicism' (Mitchell 2001: 98).

The evil eye in Greece is felt by the human body, which develops symptoms of illness. Unlike the Maltese, most of my Rethymniot and Thessalonikan interlocutors attributed evil eye possession to human agency rather than to the agency of the devil, without however excluding the latter. Furthermore, the Maltese ecclesiastic and lay discourses seem to agree with one another, since they both render the evil eye 'irrationally traditional' and superstitious, whereas the devil belongs to the Catholic 'rational tradition'. According to my ethnographic observations, this is not the case in the Greek evil eye. Although the Orthodox Church in Greece has influenced and continues to influence its adherents' opinion about the devil and the evil eye, there seems to be a separation between ecclesiastic and vernacular discourses when it comes to explanations concerning evil eye possession and who is the active force behind it. In my interlocutors' opinion, the agency of evil eye possession most likely belongs to people, not the devil as the Church supports. At the same time, however, people in Rethymno and Thessaloniki do not exclude the possibility that the devil possesses people's bodies and, as a result, one is afflicted by the evil eye. In this sense, they adopt the official ecclesiastic ideology; yet, they are also open to and strongly support the idea that the evil eye is caused by energy exchange between human – and not supernatural – beings. My interlocutors amalgamate official and unofficial beliefs and create their own vernacular religious discursive devices in order to explain evil eye possession.

The Greek *exotiká* that Stewart (1991) has studied in Naxos are closely linked to the Christian devil, being considered as dangerous spirits that can cause illness and destruction but are not recognized by Orthodox Christianity as such. Yet, as Stewart (1991) demonstrates, *exotiká*, namely demonic supernatural beings, fairies and spirits, possess an ambiguous position between doctrinal and popular religious belief and bring the two closer together. The Orthodox Church does not accept the existence of *exotiká*. Although they could be categorized as the devil or demons (fallen angels), such a categorization is dismissed from a theological point of view (Stewart 1991: 148). Naxiotes, however, believe that *exotiká* masquerade as the devil or demons. There are stories of priests who have encountered *exotiká* (Stewart 1991: 97–8), as there are stories of lay people who have encountered saints (Stewart 1991: 96–7). Consequently, although 'according to the Orthodox Church the *exotiká* are nonstandard beliefs, constitutive of superstitiousness, such a proscription does not make sense at the village level, where the *exotiká* are perceived to be manifestations of the devil' (Stewart 1991: 99).

'From what I can understand, the evil eye is like a mini demonic possession. People get sick, not from natural causes, like a cold or a virus or something, but from other reasons ... maybe it is these electromagnetic waves we were talking about earlier.' Nikos, a Rethymniot in his thirties, manages to capture the ambiguity of possession in the evil eye practice. *Matiasma* is a form of demonic possession. At the same time, it can also be the result of energy exchange between people, a possession caused by human beings. Unlike *exotiká*, the role which the Christian devil plays in *vaskania* is recognized by the Church, and the devil and the evil eye belong to the same cosmology. Yet, as explained in detail earlier, *vaskania* constitutes only one restricted part of *matiasma*, representing the doctrinal, theological viewpoint as far as the evil eye is concerned. Like Naxiotes, people in Rethymno and Thessaloniki combine doctrinal and popular religious beliefs in their everyday practice. Ranging from atheists to religious devotees, my Rethymniot and Thessalonikan interlocutors share the belief that *matiasma* occurs due to possession by the devil and/or possession by someone else's energy. The very same individuals may espouse New Age-influenced views (the evil-eyed person is possessed by someone's energy) and Orthodox-influenced views (the evil-eyed person is possessed by a demon or the devil) simultaneously. In such syntheses of lay and doctrinal belief, religion and spirituality interact creatively at the level of vernacular religious practice.

Extra-sensory perception, mysticism and the evil eye

During our conversation on whether he believes in the evil eye or not, Antonis, a middle-aged Cretan man, observed that there are two kinds of belief in the world: belief in good and belief in evil. Then, he went on to talk about miracles that Christ performed; about magicians and miracles mentioned in the Old and New Testament; and about the existence of magic and shamanism in various tribes in Africa. Morton Smith (1977) famously argued in his book *'Jesus the Magician: Charlatan or Son of God?'* that Jesus thought of himself as a magician. In a hermeneutical way, when Antonis equates Christ with an African shaman, he ethnographically expresses a viewpoint that has already been theoretically made. As Brian Morris argues (2006: 23):

> The most famous shaman or spirit-medium in history was, of course, Jesus of Nazareth, although many Christians and even some anthropologists seem to baulk at the idea. From the New Testament record, it is evident that Jesus had visionary experiences, believed himself to be possessed by god the father and interpreted illness and misfortunes as being due to unclean spirits and devils.

It has been asserted that magic is a modernist religion, since 'it challenges the validity of religious dogmatism, authoritative symbology, and intellectual analysis' (Luhrmann 1989: 336). There is definitely a very intimate relationship between them. The evil eye practice belongs to neither and simultaneously to both. It inhabits a space in between them, touching both, but hesitating to choose. Besides, if the boundaries between religion and magic are blurred, there is no need to make a choice of belonging. And as Despina, a young interlocutor of mine in Rethymno, has affirmed, while talking about the evil eye process, 'Everything that has to do with the evil eye can be resolved with the magic of religion.'

In one of the few books that have been published on the theme of the development of Greek magic from antiquity to contemporary Greece (Petropoulos 2008b), the section with regard to contemporary Greek magic is primarily dedicated to the evil eye practice. For the potential reader, then, a specific image is created that magic and the evil eye are tightly connected in the context of contemporary Greek culture. In the introduction of the section on modern Greek magic, Petropoulos writes:

> It is scarcely surprising that this section features three chapters that deal with the evil eye from different angles, for it is demonstrably one of the most ancient – and therefore more durable – and widespread aspects of magic in the Greek-speaking world. Whatever its derivation, this belief is clearly a 'pagan way of looking at the world', and its continuance in modern Greek society attests how slowly well-entrenched cultural habits change over time.
>
> (Petropoulos 2008a: 85)

Though my ethnography would not support that magic and the evil eye are almost synonymous in contemporary Greece, what my study has revealed is a close relationship between the two. When Petropoulos characterizes the belief in the evil eye as a 'pagan way of looking at the world', he is not exactly missing the point. However, I disagree with his portrayal of the evil eye as a cultural habit which has barely changed over the years. On the contrary, the affinity with paganism that Petropoulos describes does not indicate a return to the past but, instead, a dynamic present of contemporary Greek religiosity that leans towards New Age globalized influences. Based on my interlocutors' insistence that the evil eye holds a close relationship with the mystical, the spiritual and the supernatural, it appears that its practice is equated to the type of mysticism and extra-sensory communications that are commonly found in spiritual practices of a New Age orientation.

Giannis is a Rethymniot in his fifties, who strongly believes that the evil eye is directly linked to the supernatural, as they both have a powerful influence that we cannot thoroughly comprehend but only speculate its origins. Giannis specified that he regards the evil eye as very similar to certain peculiar supernatural incidents he has recently experienced. As he said, he had predicted that his sister was going to give birth on her birthday, and that the child was going to be a girl, which turned out to become a reality. The second incident had to do with his deceased grandfather. Giannis' cousin dreamed of their grandfather, who was persistently asking to have his glasses placed with him in the coffin, specifying that they had been dropped near a particular bush during his funeral. The day after the dream, Giannis and his cousin went back to the cemetery to search for their grandfather's glasses. They found them lying in the exact spot indicated in the dream, and they placed them in their grandfather's grave, accomplishing his wish.

Despina is Giannis' colleague, whom I interviewed together with him. Once Giannis finished narrating his 'supernatural and spiritual', as he characterized them, experiences, Despina immediately took over the narrative, agreeing with him that the evil eye is supernatural and has to do with 'mysterious and mystic powers that affect us'. She then began to tell us about an incident that happened during another funeral, that of her father-in-law. After the funeral, Despina explained to us, the close family of the deceased returned to his home. Since it was a warm day, they opened the window to let some air in. Suddenly, a butterfly came through. It was large – her father-in-law was 'chubby', Despina clarified. The butterfly fluttered around and sat on his favourite sofa and on all the places he used to sit. It stayed in the house for the whole day until it died, late in the evening. Despina's daughter was saddened by the butterfly's death, but she was told that she should not be feeling badly: this butterfly was her grandfather's spirit, which came for a last visit to say goodbye to her and to everyone else. Both the butterfly and her grandfather would now be looking after them from heaven.

Giannis and Despina are only two of many of my Rethymniot and Thessalonikan interlocutors who have lived extra-sensory experiences, which they have found similar to evil eye affliction. Those individuals place the evil eye in the realm of *yperfysiko* (supernatural), considering it a phenomenon that is beyond the five senses schema. At the same time, they believe that the evil eye is both a natural phenomenon, which involves sensory perception, and a supernatural one, which involves spiritual powers. They perceive their supernatural experiences and their engagement with spirits as physical phenomena, and as such approach *matiasma* too.

Elena is another young Rethymniot who believes in the existence of a 'reality of spirits' (Turner 1993). As she has told me, when she feels the evil eye on her body, and then she has it removed by her mother with the mediation of the spiritual, she has the same sensation as she had when she was only ten years old, during a spiritual experience involving her grandfather. One day, she and her brothers saw their deceased grandfather. He was wearing his usual clothes, and he looked very much alive. Elena and her brothers, however, did not experience their grandfather's presence simultaneously. Each of them saw him in a different place, and at a different time of the day. 'And, you know, we all thought we were hallucinating. We did not talk about what happened till many years later, I think it was last year or something. That was a supernatural experience none of us is ever going to forget!'

Elena explained that she was scared because she did not know whether the person she saw was really her grandfather. In his study of supernatural experiences in Malta, Mitchell (1997) argues that the memory of feelings plays a crucial role in the process of how people believe and how they articulate their religion in relation to their supernatural experiences. Religious belief creates supernatural experiences that are explained a priori. 'These experiences present the believer with ready-made memories, which act as a blue print or a reference point for people's subsequent experiences' (Mitchell 1997: 81). Elena's experience with her grandfather has shaped her current approach to religion, spirituality and the supernatural. Every time she and her mother participate in a ritual healing against the evil eye, she has the same sensation of communicating with the spiritual and sacred world, 'just like when I saw my grandfather's spirit'.

> Let's take mobile phones as an example. They transmit radiation that we cannot see since this is happening at another level that we cannot perceive. Imagine bright radiance being transmitted here and there. Something like that happens with the evil eye. Beams of negative energy are exchanged. In essence, there are zones of energy – whether these zones are called energy or supernatural powers – which we cannot perceive, but that does not mean they do not exist.

Manos, a Thessalonikan man in his forties, is a vivid representation of how the evil eye not only escapes visualism but can also be perceived supernaturally. He indicates how sensory perception is both a physical and cultural act (Herzfeld 2001: 240). Like Manos, a large number of Rethymniots and Thessalonikans assert that the evil eye is an invisible, tasteless, non-olfactory, untouchable, inaudible power. At the same time, they narrate incidences where they perceive this power through their social and physical body. But perception, in the evil eye case, does not stop and is not constrained by the five-sense 'scientific' schema. On the contrary, it is dynamic. It travels around the body, the sensory organs, but also around feelings, cultural sensoriums that transcend biological representations, spiritual battles and supernatural powers. The evil eye moves around and beyond the presumptions of positive science, but within Greeks' everyday practised and spiritual life. 'For the objective scientist, phenomena that fall outside the limits of rational and objective sensory perception are dismissed as non-existent' (Petrus 2006: 3). The evil eye is sensed by the sensory organs, is physically experienced and perceived through spiritual communication. Besides, *empeiria*, the Greek term for experience, denotes a human act that is not restrained within the sensory field, but extends beyond physical reality and touches the supernatural. Additionally, empiricism is subjective; and so is perception. The evil eye encounters and is confronted by a perceptual multiplicity of dynamic empiricisms, which are to be found in both the physical and the supernatural spaces of belonging. As Meredith McGuire (1990: 285) has eloquently put it: 'Through our bodies we see, feel, hear, perceive, touch, smell, and we hold our everyday worlds.'

Nektarios is a young Thessalonikan man in his early thirties, who is very religious and believes in the existence of the evil eye. He also strongly believes in the reality of spirits and the communication that occurs between the human and the spirit world. As he confessed during our conversation, he has experienced the presence of his deceased father many times, and he now believes that the spirit of his father is his guardian angel. He has also felt the presence of spirits in other instances, sometimes with his wife, sometimes by himself. He makes a clear distinction between his 'spiritual experiences, that is more like these New Age stuff that you study, more alternative spiritually, not exactly like the evil eye', as he defines them, and his religious belief: if he was to tell his priest-confessor about those spiritual experiences of his, Nektarios has told me, his confessor would have exorcized him, as he would have thought that Nektarios has begun to practise magic. Therefore, he prefers to keep these 'New Age spiritual experiences' to himself, regarding them as 'alternative', which experiences he also considers to be closely linked to his wife's beliefs in energy, the efficacy of alternative healing and 'all these new forms of keeping the evil, including the evil eye, away through feng shui, reiki, and crystals with cleansing power'.

Rethymniots and Thessalonikans have often attributed New Age qualities to *mati*. It is a fact that people in my fieldsites who are closer to the Orthodox Church have often expressed their scepticism towards New Age spirituality, especially because they believe there is a link among the evil eye, New Age, mysticism and magic. A young Cretan man has made the statement:

> I think *mati* is more hidden in Greece due to the existence of mysticism. If someone claims that he knows how to do *ksorkia* (spells), he knows how to deal with *matiasma*, to heal from the evil eye or to cast the evil eye, then he can definitely be accused of being a heretic, an alternative spiritual believer, or as *parekklisiastikos* (one who does not belong to the Church, a New Age practitioner) or whatever. That is why they keep *mati* out of sight.

When I asked Grigoris to explain further what he meant by the term 'mysticism', he drew a picture of a non-Orthodox spiritual field, constructed with elements of New Age and magic. He saw the evil eye as belonging to this non-Orthodox assortment, but he could not really manage to justify the reasons why he thought that. The young Rethymniot had constructed two opposite religious cosmologies in his mind: on the one side stood Orthodox Christianity. On the opposite side stood everything else that Christianity accuses, by labelling it magical and New Age.

Du Boulay (1991) has recognized the existence of a Greek cosmological multiplicity. She argued that Ambeliots, the people in Euboea among whom she did her research in the 1960s, were able to discern two different cosmologies as part of their everyday lives. The one was focused on Orthodox Christianity. The other centred on nature. It was based on a belief that the moon and the sun were part of a metaphysical circle of life, and, as such, they were ritually and spiritually utilized as powerful cosmic forces (Du Boulay 1991: 57–62). Equivalently, many of my interlocutors, both younger and older, men and women, in Rethymno and Thessaloniki, have recognized the existence of two non-antithetical cosmological elements in the evil eye: Orthodoxy, the first one, and New Age mysticism and magic, the other one, do not only co-exist, but interact actively in the evil eye practice.

In an article that focuses on the history of the supernatural in Greece, Stewart (1989) asserts that the supernatural was adopted by upper-class Athenians to serve as an indicator of their special status in the social hierarchy. In the beginning, as Stewart explicates, 'irrational' and 'traditional' beliefs in the supernatural were only sustained by rural, lower-class and mostly non-educated people, and dismissed by their urban, upper-class, educated counterparts. Then, as the rural and uneducated group dispensed its supernatural beliefs in an attempt to merge with the middle class, those beliefs were adopted by the educated, urban, upper-class group instead, which recreated the supernaturalism and adapted it according to its standards. The rural supernatural was joined by Western mysticism. The popularity of books dealing with mysticism and the quest for the supernatural (Stewart 1989: 92) was indicative of the fact that the Athenian elite used the supernatural as a form of cultural capital so as to gain social distinctiveness. As Stewart (1989: 94) notes, upper-class Athenians 'look beyond Greece to the mystical systems of other countries (Asian, African, native American) which have recently been receiving a good deal of popular attention in Europe and the United States ... foreign forms of mysticism have served as a model for re-approaching indigenous supernatural lore'.

Like the Athenian elite mentioned above, Rethymniots and Thessalonikans have re-approached the indigenous supernatural, the evil eye, through a foreign form of mysticism, namely the New Age spirituality. People in Rethymno and Thessaloniki believe that the evil eye has transformed itself in order to be part of the new global trends. Furthermore, my interlocutors maintain that New Age spirituality is adopted by people as a signifier of 'taste' and a 'distinctive' social status (Bourdieu 1984). Rather than adopting New Age spirituality as a way to reinforce their middle-class status, Rethymniots and Thessalonikans believe that such an adoption of global trends can constitute a personal marker of their status as citizens of the world. The blending of the indigenous supernatural with foreign forms of mysticism in everyday practice has created a syncretic spiritual field, which can point to their knowledge of foreign trends, as well as their ability to transform these trends culturally and ritually, and make them their own.

4

Ksematiasma: Healing, power, performance

Irene, a female interlocutor of mine in northern Greece, who comes from a small town near Thessaloniki, has developed her own ritualism when it comes to *ksematiasma* (ritual healing against the evil eye). One afternoon, as we were discussing about the evil eye and its bodily symptomatology, I asked her to perform the ritual healing on me. She accepted. She made the sign of the cross on my forehead, kept murmuring a prayer and then we both began to yawn. So far, nothing out of the evil eye performative ordinary had caught my ethnographic attention. She reached the end of the healing ritual and then, all of sudden, exceeding my ritual expectations – I had witnessed the performance of a large number and forms of rituals over more than twenty years, after all, therefore I almost always (thought I) knew the ritual process and what to expect – she clapped her hands once. I was surprised and my personal and ethnographic curiosity was noticeably raised. She stated that I had lots of evil eye on me, we yawned for a few minutes to make sure we would totally get rid of it and then, not being able to keep my inquisitiveness down any longer, I asked her why she had clapped her hands at the end of her ritual performance. She explained that it had to do with reiki.[1] Clapping her hands after performing the *ksematiasma* would help the negative energy of the evil eye, which she had bodily absorbed as the energy had migrated from my body to hers, disperse into the universe. 'I have developed my own *ksematiasma* technique', Irene joked, adding that she was both a very successful and respected *ksematiastra* and a reiki healing master. She had decided to combine her Christian routes with her reiki training and bring religion and new spirituality closer together creatively into vernacular ritual action.

Marina is an eighty-year-old Rethymniot woman, who is a religious adherent but not dogmatic in her thinking about religion and the evil eye. From the moment we met, however, she made it clear that she feels Christianity is part of her spiritual identity and her religious heritage. She considers the evil eye to be part of Orthodox Christianity, but she does not agree with the main position of the Greek Orthodox Church that the evil eye can only be removed by a priest; after all, she is an excellent evil eye healer, according to all her family, friends and neighbours, having gained recognition and a powerful social status as a result. Succumbing to the religious authority of a priest would deprive her of her ritual healing empowerment.

When I asked her to perform the ritual healing against the evil eye on me, so that I could have a first-hand experience of her detailed ritual performance, she gladly accepted; she used the popular water-and-oil-in-a-coffee-cup version of *ksematiasma* and recited Christian prayers. During the ritual, however, I noticed she had also kept religious icons as well as feng shui objects and energetic crystals close by (see Figure 10). As she explained afterwards, she keeps these

Figure 10 *Ksematiasma* performed alongside Orthodox icons and New Age crystals.

'alternative', as she calls them, 'spiritual things', being influenced by her daughter who has gifted those objects to her and who 'deals with these new spiritual things, to keep any negative energy and evil spirits away, so that we are protected from every corner we can and have our backs covered from all evil'. Although Marina is open to 'these new spiritual things', during our conversation she placed emphasis on the fact that her ritual healing against the evil eye is the Orthodox way to perform it, trying to maintain the 'Greek religious character of the evil eye ritual', as she mentioned, while perceiving her daughter's influence on her ritual performance as 'foreign' to her own culture and religion, and eventually considering it to be a by-product of globalized spiritual interactions.

The cases of Irene and Marina described above are two characteristic examples of the contemporary character of *ksematiasma*, which entails Orthodox Christian as well as New Age discourses in its core performance. In general terms, when a person is possessed by the power of the evil eye, s/he predominantly develops somatic symptoms of illness. A spiritual healing is then performed in order to remove the ill-symptoms and to exorcize the power that has possessed the afflicted individual's body. This predominantly vernacular type of ritual healing used to only involve Christian prayers and religious discourse in the core of it. In recent years, however, as I witnessed in my ethnographic research, even older religious adherents, who are considered stereotypically to dominate in the field of healing against the evil eye, welcome new spiritual influences and adapt their ritual creatively so that new spirituality is included in their performance.

The ritual performance: A sensory path to healing

I put water inside a small coffee cup. I cross it three times, in the name of Holy Trinity. Then, with my finger, I take oil from the *kantili* (oil lamp), which I have already removed from the *eikonostasi* (household altar/icon stand) (see Figure 11).[2] While silently saying a prayer, I drop oil into the water (see Figure 12). If the person is evil eyed, the oil drops directly to the bottom of the cup and dissolves. If not, then it stays on the surface. I do this seven times. Then I cross his forehead and I give him to drink three times. I also do a *ksematiasma* with salt. I put some salt in a napkin, I cross his head with the napkin and the salt three times and I make the shape of the cross on the salt with my finger. I do that seven times and I say my prayer seven times. I give him a bit of salt to eat. Afterwards, I throw most of the salt inside the sink because they say the water takes the evil eye away. I throw some salt in the air – the air must take it too – and the rest behind my back, the evil has to leave from there.

Figure 11 Icon stand and *ksematiasma*.

Figure 12 The most typical ritual of *ksematiasma*.

Ksematiasma falls in the category of ritual healing that draws heavily on Christian symbolism. Numbers three – signifying the Holy Trinity – and seven – denoting the seven sacraments – are repetitively used: the *ksematiastra* (evil eye healer)[3] recites the prayer either three or seven times, she crosses the sufferer's forehead three times and the latter has to drink/eat the ingredients used three times. In Rethymno I was told that *ksematiasma* is much more effective if it is performed by three women whose name is Maria (the equivalent of the English name Mary); a symbolic connection with *Panagia* (Virgin Mary) is present. Furthermore, oil is used because, to quote a middle-aged Thessalonikan, 'Christ sat below the olive tree, he prayed in an olive field, and oil is sacred because we use it in Church'. Water is important 'because we cannot live without it, it is a natural element of nature and of the human organism ... and so is the salt, a basic component of life'. Hence, *ksematiasma* composes a ritual action, during which the participants symbolically communicate with one another without performing entirely consciously or attempting to encode and interpret every detail of the ritual process.

The *ksematiasma* that is performed with the help of the water and oil ingredients seems to prevail in both northern Greece and Crete, with the one which involves the use of salt following closely behind. In Rethymno, and generally in Crete, people additionally perform a unique type of ritual which I had never heard before and neither had my Thessalonikan informants. This form of healing is practised with a towel or a scarf and is very popular among Rethymniots (see Figure 13). Manolis, an elderly Rethymniot man, describes the Cretan ritual:

> You spread a towel on the table. You put your arm on, and you measure the towel, starting from the elbow; on the spot where you touch the towel with your fingers you pour some salt and you make a strong knot. You say the words of *ksematiasma*. If the person is evil eyed, when you look again the salt has moved.

Ksematiasma is a performance of healing. As Laderman and Roseman (1996: 1) argue, all medical encounters are dramatic episodes, where the protagonists play out their respective roles of patients[4] and healers according to their society's expectations. By practising *ksematiasma*, Rethymniots and Thessalonikans enter an everyday 'performance process, a dynamic system of action' (Schechner 1987: 10). They experience a 'social drama', a truly spontaneous unit of human social performance (Turner 1987: 90–2). And spontaneity is a basic characteristic of *ksematiasma*, since every performance is unique, as it shifts according to the demand of the occasion and of the audience (Herzfeld 1981: 219), keeping the 'performative limits open and decentred' (Schechner 1987: 8).

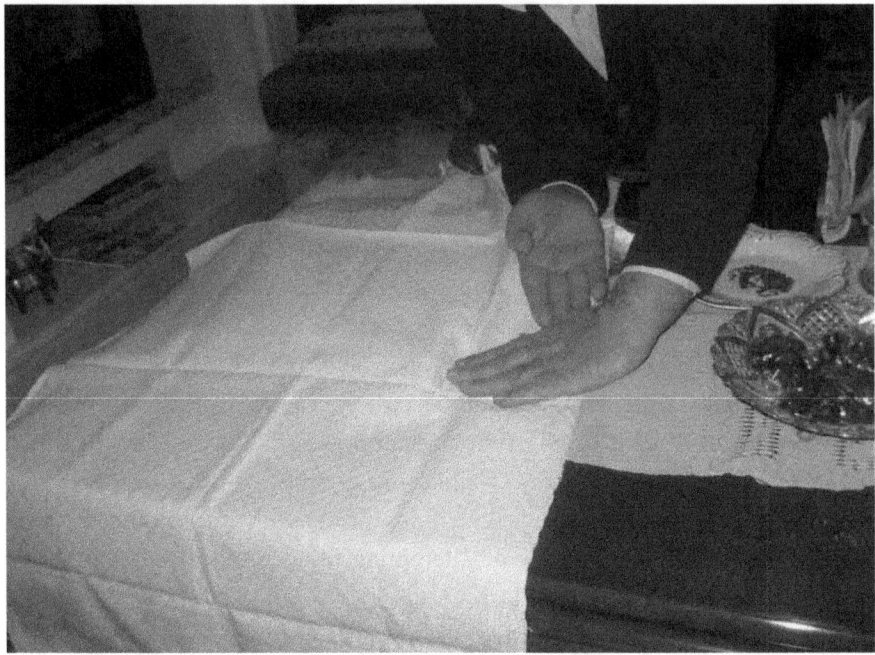

Figure 13 The Cretan *ksematiasma* with the use of a towel.

The notion of performance, as Csordas (1997 [1994]: 91) observes, has gained a central position in the study of religious healing. Cultural performance 'has a power to transform experience and social relations' (1997 [1994]: 92). *Ksematiasma* is a 'paradigm of process' (Schechner 1987: 8), through which people experience, act and transform their selves, and negotiate their social relationships. This experiential and social transformation could not be achieved if the senses did not contribute to the healing performance.

> The ingredients are used because the evil eye person has to taste them ... he tastes the oil, the salt ... and also the crossing I do on the forehead ... it is like a touch ... he feels that the evil eye is removed ... he sees, he wants to see, to feel that the evil eye is removed ... to see that I make the cross on his forehead (see Figure 14), and to hear that I murmur the prayer ... he wants to see me and to listen to me and to taste these ingredients of *ksematiasma*.

The above words, coming from a seventy-year-old female interlocutor of mine in northern Greece who frequently performs the *ksematiasma*, highlight the role of the senses in the healing performance. Areti acknowledges that both she and her patients become engaged in a sensory communication that leads

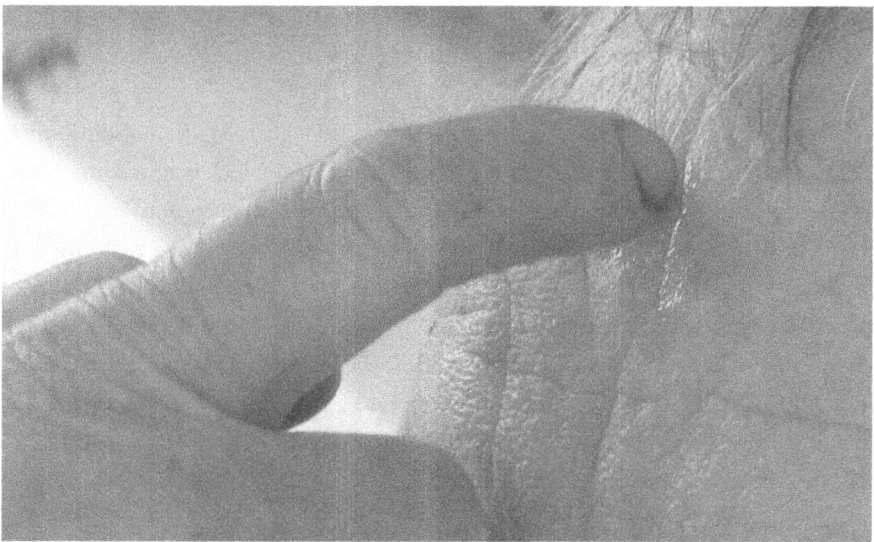

Figure 14 Sensory engagement through touch during the ritual healing.

to healing. By performing the ritual, Areti triggers the patients' senses, changes their sensibilities and makes them feel healthy and perceptually and somatically present in the world.

Drawing on his research among the Yolmo Sherpa in Nepal, Desjarlais (1996) presents a sensory performance of healing that is similar to *ksematiasma*. According to his research, the Yolmo Sherpa lose their spirit – their *bla* – and, as a result, they experience a variety of symptoms that vary from bodily heaviness, lack of energy and of appetite, and the inability to talk and socialize, to troubles in sleeping and proneness to illnesses. In addition, they lose the sense of kinaesthetic attentiveness, or 'presence'; by losing their spirit, their sense of (bodily and perceptual) presence also disappears (Desjarlais 1996: 144–5). Equivalently, when they are possessed by the evil eye, Greeks also enter a process of somatic and social absence. When the evil eye affects my interlocutors' perception, their spiritual and embodied presence is lost. The Yolmo healer tries to successfully heal those who have lost their *bla* and make the spirit return to its owners by changing their feelings and by altering their sensory stimuli and activating their senses (1996: 160). This activation can 'wake up a person, prompt new sensibilities, and so reform the cognitive and perceptual faculties that make up a person' (1996). The evil eye healer needs to stimulate the sufferer's senses in the same way. As a healer in northern Greece observed: 'The evil-eyed person sits somewhere in the room, probably lying down since she does not feel well.

After I finish praying, I take a bit of the water and oil with my finger and I cross her on the forehead. She drinks three times and I throw the rest away ... after a while, she feels well again.'

By stimulating the senses, the healer is able to convert the patient's sensibilities into a healthy embodiment. Besides, as Desjarlais (1996: 159, original emphasis) argues, 'healing transformations take place not within some cognitive domain of brain or heartmind, but within the visceral reaches of the eyes, the ears, the skin, and the tongue. Indeed, the *feeling* of rejuvenation (rather than just its idea or symbolic expression) is essential'. *Ksematiasma* performance activates the senses. Sight, touch, taste and hearing all play a significant role in shifting the suffering body into a fully perceiving and healthy somatic state. When someone is affected by the evil eye, s/he is socially isolated and perceptually absent; s/he has to confront a body that suffers from sensory loss. The return to sensory embodiment requires a *ksematiasma* performance. When the evil-eyed person sees the healer using the ingredients, hears the murmur of the praying, feels the touch on his/her forehead and tastes the water, oil and salt, a transformation takes place. The healer triggers the senses, altering what the sufferer feels. Through the ritual, the feeling of socio-sensory isolation is removed from one's embodied self. The spirit returns from its cultural ostracism. Presence is reclaimed and repossessed.

There are times, however, that the ritual fails. One January afternoon I was invited by Katerina, a female Rethymniot around my age, to have a coffee at her house. While discussing how my research was proceeding, she told me she knows how to perform the ritual healing. We decided to try her performance on me. So, Katerina got a towel, measured it with her hand, starting from her elbow, poured some salt, and at the point where her hand ended, she tied a knot. She silently recited a prayer and then she untangled the knot. There lay the moment of the ritual performance's 'truth'. If the salt had moved, her performance would be regarded as successful. But the salt had stayed put on its initial position. This of course could just have meant that I was not evil eyed. But Katerina interpreted the lack of the salt's movement as a result of her failed performance. It was not that she was not able to perform *ksematiasma*. What she had just done for me, however, was not an actual ritual, but a representation of one. Neither of us had taken her *ksematiasma* seriously, since we knew it was simply a performative test. And our focus on representing, rather than ritually practising, resulted in a non-efficacious enactment.

About five months later and having already situated my ethnographic research in northern Greece, I arranged with a *ksematiastra* to record her performance on video. Again, I was the one who would play the role of the patient. I was in need of the ritual anyway, since I was feeling the evil eye's presence on my body. The *ksematiastra* began crossing me with the golden cross she was wearing on her chest, while murmuring her prayer. I could see she was sceptical and fully aware of the ritual representation that was taking place. Suddenly she began to yawn deeply. She kept murmuring the prayer, and kept yawning, with tears running down from her eyes. When her embodiment subsided, she turned to me and said: 'All jokes aside, you had *mati*.' Sofia was totally conscious of the directed performance we had dived into. Each of us played our healer and patient role respectively, constructing a far-from-spontaneous ritual healing performance. Sofia was very impressed that at the end I was suffering from evil eye affliction and that she did cure me from it. A 'fake' *ksematiasma* had just been transformed into a 'real' one. Contrary to Katerina's case then, the visually represented ritual had an effective outcome. Maybe I was evil eyed, as I felt I was, with Sofia and not with Katerina. Maybe we believed it more in the second case. What matters is that these two cases are indicative of how the ritual can take a multiplicity of forms and be performed in a range of spatialities and temporalities with a variety of individuals involved, even when one of these individuals is the ethnographer herself. It is the participants that make the ritual vigorously active, creative and unique in each and every performance.

In his research about the Catholic Charismatic Renewal, a religious movement that began in 1967 and was initiated by junior faculty and graduate students at Catholic universities, Csordas has shown 'how the rhetoric of transformation achieves its therapeutic purpose by creating a disposition to be healed, evoking experience of the sacred' (Csordas 1997 [1994]: 94). Bearing similarities to the CCR movement, the evil eye ritual performance is successfully therapeutic when the sacred is evoked.

> Whenever I had the *ksematiasma* done for me, my mind would just travel around: to a boy who teased me at school, to a friend who did not call. And I felt so guilty doing that ... I knew, however, that I had to focus my thoughts on God and not on my friends ... otherwise, the ritual would not be right.

Just like Mirto, a woman in Thessaloniki, the majority of Rethymniots and Thessalonikans feel that *ksematiasma* brings them closer to the divine; that it opens a conduit between them and the sacred world. When they stand opposite the ritual healer and listen to her praying murmur, they feel the need to recite a prayer themselves in order to come closer to God and to other spiritual powers. By constructing a 'sacred reality' (Danforth 1989: 55), the path to an efficacious healing appears unhindered.

Ksematiasma does not always require face-to-face ritual communication. In fact, instead of visiting a healer in person, my interlocutors often phone their relatives and friends and ask for a *ksematiasma* at a distance. Sometimes, this is because the healers live outside Rethymno and Thessaloniki, usually in a village or small town in close proximity to my fieldsites. In this case, a communication between the rural and the urban is established. *Ksematiasma* collapses the sociocultural boundaries between them. The ritual performance against the evil eye is influenced by both urban and rural ideologies, which, rather than entering a conflictive relationship, are woven into each other instead. In other cases, both evil eye sufferers and healers may be situated in the same city. Their busy lifestyle schedules, however, do not allow for personal visits and the ritual healing is performed over the phone instead. Long-distance healing is a constituent of an urban lifestyle. Rethymniots and Thessalonikans lead busy everyday lives. As many of them have stated, picking up the phone and calling their healers is much easier, since it saves time for both the afflicted individual and the *ksematiastra*. It also saves social disruption and invasion of the healer's privacy. *Ksematiasma* in person presupposes a visit to the healer's home, who then has to prepare his/her house for the visit, even if s/he is not in the mood to receive visitors. Long-distance healing can be performed without such household concerns and social implications.

I have argued earlier that it is the direct sensory communication during the ritual process that principally covers the ritual with healing efficacy. One might presume, then, that long-distance healing contradicts such an assumption. In the long-distance *ksematiasma*, the sensory ritualistic landscape, though represented and only imagined, is present. The patient might not be there to see, taste, hear and have his/her senses activated. However, s/he can still feel it. For Rethymniots and Thessalonikans, the *ksematiasma* in person is more powerful. But even via telecommunications, the sensory performance effectively works in a more imaginative yet equally immediate ritual way. Healing at a distance is based on energy exchange and a spiritual communication with the sacred, which is thought to be developed independently of spatial proximity and direct contact.

Spiritual healing has to do with the evocation of energy, and 'this is shared between Christian and "New Age" discourses of healing' (Csordas 1997 [1994]: 54). New Age healing embraces manifestations of energy, and so does *ksematiasma*. Long-distance *ksematiasma* is efficacious since a certain amount of energy is transmitted from the healer to the individual suffering from the evil eye. The sufferer may not be physically present; yet, s/he is represented energetically. The positive, sacred, divine energy that is evoked through the ritual reaches him/her from a distance. The ritual imagery is activated: positive energy enters the body, negative energy escapes through the body of the healer and the evil eye is gone. By engaging in direct communication, and/or by channelling at a distance, the healer possesses the power to bring the sacred intimately close to the everyday.

Lay healers and the clergy: Gender and power

'Sometimes we say that a person has the devil inside him', said Alkyoni, a middle-aged woman in Rethymno, drawing on a well-known Greek phrase to describe how the evil eye possesses one's body. When asked to develop her thought further, she told me that *ksematiasma* in everyday life works exactly like exorcism works in the Church: some kind of spirit or power occupies a person; in order to remove the influence of the spirit/power from one's body and energetic field, a ritual performance is needed. He proceeded to explain that the lay performance of *ksematiasma* and the religious exorcism performed officially by a priest are based on the same principles. This is a common belief shared by the majority of Rethymniots and Thessalonikans who are Orthodox believers, yet not fanatic adherents. Devoted Orthodox Christians, on the other hand, usually follow the official Church discourse: being possessed by the evil eye equals being possessed by demons and the devil. For the Orthodox Church, evil eye possession does not exist, unless the devil or one of his demonic substitutes is responsible for it. It does not, hence, come as a surprise that the ritual healing against the evil eye, as performed by lay people, is not recognized by the Church and the clergy. The excerpt below, coming from Leonidas, a forty-year-old Thessalonikan male interlocutor, portrays the vernacular relationship between the Orthodox priests and the lay evil eye healers, as religious authority is claimed and negotiated between them:

> The Church does not accept the ritual because it does not want its own authority – that of the priest in particular – to be transferred to lay believers. It is clearly a matter of power. The Church wants to maintain the dominance of the ritual. It is the king of Orthodox rituals. Do you know any (lay) citizen who can perform baptism? No. Anyone who can perform marriages? No. So, why should anyone perform *ksematiasma*? Therefore, the evil eye is a part of life where lay people have taken up an authority that used to belong to the priest. That is why they [the priests] don't like it; because it is – supposedly – a stolen power. A priest thinks: 'How come *you* have the power to get rid of the evil and of the evil eye? I am the one who has become a priest to be able to do that?'

People in my fieldsites, practitioners of alternative forms of spirituality as well as Orthodox adherents, have argued that if the Church positively acknowledged the lay evil eye healers as powerful enough to perform ritual healings, it would presumably grant them authority in exorcism. But if the Church did that, it would lose its exclusivity as far as the ritualistic authority to expel evil is concerned. And, naturally, as my interlocutors point out, the Church cannot allow such a loss of dominance (cf. Favret-Saada 1980: 97). Therefore, Orthodoxy and the clergy remain intact in their position: *matiasma* equates to demonic possession, and priests are the only legitimated individuals responsible for its exorcism. But, as many interlocutors have also noticed, the exorcistic practices of the clergy do not differ from the performances of lay healers but are equally powerful and ritually effective.

Stirrat (1992) captures the relationship between lay healers and the clergy in his study of possession and exorcism among the Sinhala Catholics in Sri Lanka. As he observes, it is not only the priests who perform exorcisms for the demonically possessed. Lay healers perform exorcisms too, and they do so by using Christian prayers. Although during the nineteenth and twentieth centuries there was a conflictual relationship between lay healers and the clergy, the former continue to be popular among the Sri Lankans (Stirrat 1992: 80). 'Between priest and layperson there was and is a continual dynamic, a continual process of teaching, accommodation and rejection in which forms of religious practice were and continue to be developed, reproduced and transformed' (1992: 196).

'The priest places you under his *petrahili* (stole) and reads you a prayer for *vaskania*', a woman in Thessaloniki explained, adding that when she and her siblings were young, her mother used to take them to church, where the priest would bless them with a prayer against *vaskania*. Going to the local priest and asking him to bless one's children for general protection, or for a specific anti-*vaskania* prayer, is a quite common attitude amongst Thessalonikans and Rethymniots. It is a popular practice for mothers, especially, who feel that a priest's blessing shelters their children from the attacks of demonic forces and exorcizes people's negative energy. At the same time, going to a *ksematiastra* and having the ritual healing performed is equally powerful to the exorcism performed by priests. Many times, the relationship between lay healers and the clergy is conflictive. But, as it happens among the Sinhala Catholics in Sri Lanka, there is a continuous dynamic between priests and lay evil eye healers. The practice of exorcizing evil spirits and evil energy is continually transformed and renegotiated. For people in Rethymno and Thessaloniki exorcism as performed by clergy and *ksematiasma* as performed by lay healers are not that different.

According to most of my interlocutors, *ksematiasma* can be considered a mild form of exorcism. Rethymniot and Thessalonikan healers trust their ability to expel the demonic spirit and evil energy from an evil-eyed person without the intervention of a priest. At the same time, they recognize the authority of the clergy to perform exorcism and *ksematiasma*. Lay healers are Orthodox believers, and they maintain a very good relationship with the Church and the clergy. They always use Christian symbolism in their ritual healing, and the prayers they recite contain strong Christian references. Lay healers visit priests in order to be blessed and sometimes they even ask for a prayer against *vaskania*. There are also times when a priest surrenders his religious authority to the lay healing of a *ksematiastra*, willingly or without their knowledge. Zoi, for example, is a northern Greek in her early sixties, who is a kin Orthodox believer, goes to church every Sunday and is very involved in the religious duties of her church and its priest. She recently narrated an incident to me, which describes eloquently the unmarked ground between lay healers and religious authorities in relation to power negotiation in vernacular religious practice and the evil eye.

> The priest of our church organized an excursion, to go to visit a monastery and spend the day there. We were many women there on the bus, a few men who usually help the priest, and the priest. We went to the monastery, everything went great. Then, on the way back on the bus, the priest began to feel unwell, as if he was going to faint. 'Someone gave him the evil eye', I thought to myself. The bus stopped, he went out with the help of one of the men to get some air, he came back on the bus, still looking pale and feeling bad. 'I will do a *ksematiasma* for him', I decided, 'I don't care what the other women say, I will do it'. So, I started making the sign of the cross and saying a prayer silently. We arrived back safely, he wasn't cured, but at least he never fainted and he managed to go back home safe and sound.

In Zoi's case, the priest never found out that she performed the ritual healing against the evil eye for him; some of her female friends on the bus witnessed her act, however; and it was as if this secret knowledge among lay healers infused Zoi, as well as the women who were present in that moment of healing, with a vernacular spiritual power over the religious authority of the priest. In the course of my research, I have also heard quite a few narratives from healers themselves, as well as other evil eye practitioners, who have described the *ksematiasma* performed by lay healers for priests after the request of the latter. Dispute over the ownership of ritual and spiritual authority continues to make an appearance between Orthodox priests and lay healers. Yet, their interaction is not always conflictual but can also be accommodating. In these performative acts, the hierarchical relationship between Greek priests and lay healers is transformed into a partnership, healing exchange and a joint fight against any form of evil.

Vasiliki, a thirty-year-old woman in Thessaloniki, has pointed out that Church sacraments and lay *ksematiasma* share affinity. 'Do you know what I believe? When too many unfortunate incidents happen in a household, people call the priest and do a blessing to get rid of the evil spirits, right? In essence, *ksematiasma* is a small prayer to get rid of the bad energy from you, that's what I believe.' Nasos, a Cretan in his forties, has expressed a similar opinion: 'There is good and there is evil. House blessings are performed in order to exorcize evil spirits.' Ecclesiastic exorcism and everyday *ksematiasmata* share ritualism, symbols, sacredness, performative engagement, healing results and, above all, a common goal: the expulsion of evil spirits and evil energy. Rethymniots and Thessalonikans, from what I have heard and observed, ask priests to come and bless their house when, to repeat Vasiliki's words, they experience continuous unfortunate incidences or the evil eye. It does not have to be an evil spirit, the devil or some kind of demonic force which, after having invaded their home space, needs to be exorcized. A priest can exorcize negative energy too, in the same way lay individuals exorcize the evil eye and negative energy from the body of their fellow human beings.

'My grandmother knows how to do the *ksematiasma*, you know, being a priest's daughter and all', an interlocutor of mine noted during an interview in Rethymno. I was quite surprised to hear that he presented the priesthood of his great-grandfather as the reason why his grandmother had learned how to take the evil eye away from people ritually. Gerasimos continued to explain that: 'My grandmother learned the *ksematiasma* from her own mother; this goes from mother to daughter, since we are a family of priests.' He went on to clarify that his family has a tradition of priesthood. Apart from his great-grandfather, other members of his kin have also become priests. Yet, the priests in the family have never got to know the words of the *ksematiasma*, since only women are permitted to learn them. At the same time, they have also never expressed any objections towards their female kin's evil eye performances, because they trust that the women use Christian prayers. Although it may be doctrinally illegitimate, speaking in strict Orthodox Christian terms, lay healing is part of Greek vernacular religious reality. Being part of this reality, priests, as shown above, are unlikely to condemn *ksematiasma* openly or at all when lay healers belong to their social circle, since they too recognize the vernacular religious power lay healers enjoy in the(ir) common socio-cultural surroundings.

The prayer that the *ksematiastra* murmurs during the ritual healing is a secret. It can only be transmitted in a verbal exchange between a woman and a man. Should two same-sex individuals try to exchange the knowledge of the prayer, its sacredness and efficacy will be lost. The female to female transmission that Gerasimos described was an ethnographic rarity. Perhaps, however, priesthood comes to legitimize inter-gender evil eye relationships. The male priests of the family do not dispute the ritual practices that the women of their kin perform. Instead, they incorporate and acknowledge them as a fragment of their everyday life. Gerasimos' family illustrates a cultural integration between ecclesiastic and lay healing practices. It shows that priests and lay healers can co-exist without arguing over the ownership of ritual and spiritual authority.

'My neighbour believes very much ... she cleans the church, she takes care of the candles and icons ... my grandma on the other hand is normal, she believes in the good God, in his help, that's all.' While having lunch with Elina in Thessaloniki, she mentioned that there are two women who usually perform the ritual of *ksematiasma* for her: her grandmother and her elderly female neighbour, who is a friend of the family. The stereotypical image of a *ksematiastra* is socially, culturally and imaginatively created to depict a woman of an older age who, besides her religious devotion, offers considerable aid when it comes to religious practicalities, including the healing performance against the evil eye. The elderly female *ksematiastra*, who usually acts religiously under the authority of the community/neighbourhood priest, holds considerable spiritual power and knowledge that can actually symbolically contest the authority of the male priest. At a quotidian level of religious practice, she is considered religiously powerful due to her ability to communicate with the sacred and offer a powerful and empowering ritual performance.

> I learned how to do the *ksematiasma* from my grandmother, who told the prayer to my dad and then he secretly wrote it in a paper and gave it to me. There needs to be some kind of mysticism involved. You know, I somehow believe in God, Jesus etc. but I am also into these alternative spiritual things ... I do yoga, reiki, I have crystals, feng shui amulets in my flat. When people come to my flat to get the evil eye healing, I do it for them, I say all the prayers, the Orthodox ones that my grandmother taught me. But I have pushed my *ksematiasma* a bit further, I always want to have my energetic crystals around, I follow the feng shui rules about where to stand and where the other person stands when I do my *ksematiasma*, I want to have positive energy to communicate with my spirit

guides and my angels while removing someone's evil eye away. Is that wrong? I don't know, but I don't want to play by the rules that the priests tell us, that religion force on us, you know?

Eleni is a Rethymniot woman in her mid-forties, who knows how to perform *ksematiasma* for the last twenty years. We had met during my fieldwork in Rethymno in 2006 and we encountered each other again in 2019, during a visit of mine in Crete. Although she had initially performed her ritual healing against the evil eye following her grandmother's example, she later modified it according to her own vernacular religious path. Eleni is a keen believer in New Age spirituality and she practises regularly yoga, owns New Age items, such as crystals, and follows the feng shui rules in her house. Although she has not cut bonds with Orthodox Christianity, her religious heritage is mostly practised through her ability to perform *ksematiasma*, during which she recites religious prayers and uses Orthodox symbols, such as the cross and icons, during her performance. At some point, as she has told me, Eleni realized she wanted to incorporate in her ritual against the evil eye her new spiritual influences, in order to represent better who she is as an individual. As her description above depicts clearly, she now creatively amalgamates religion and spirituality in her vernacular religious practice of the evil eye and of her life in general, feeling satisfied about freeing herself from the authority of the Church, the local priest and her devoted religious family.

As it is evident in Eleni's case, these days younger women also learn how to perform *ksematiasma*, treating it as an alternative form of spiritual healing. Some are still in touch with their religious heritage of Orthodox Christianity and do not deviate much from the classic *ksematiasma*, others combine new spirituality and Orthodoxy in their practice. Especially in the last decade or more, there seems to be a certain divergence between younger and older generations in terms of vernacular religious practice, which is based on different lifestyle principles, trends and beliefs. Indeed, younger Rethymniots and Thessalonikans show a greater inclination towards New Age spirituality, while their older counterparts appear to be more drawn to Orthodoxy. And women usually prevail in the practice of the ritual healing against the evil eye. Yet, I have also encountered male Orthodox adherents of a young age and some older men who practise New Age spirituality. And as has been seen earlier in the chapter, there are elderly female healers who have become influenced by new spirituality and incorporate it in their practice. In practising *ksematiasma*, people in Rethymno and Thessaloniki raise issues of gender empowerment, especially in relation to the male religious power of the Orthodox priest and the predominantly female power of the *ksematiastra*, while escaping the stereotypical image created for them and proving the fluid character of contemporary Greek vernacular religiosity.

During my fieldwork, I observed ethnographically that the majority of evil eye healers are women and many of my interlocutors also made the point that it is women who are more engaged with the evil eye and its ritualism. I agree with Dubisch (1995: 223) that women's engagement in everyday religious activities should not just be interpreted as socially indicating greater feminine piety. In terms of practising the evil eye, Rethymniots and Thessalonikans should not be stereotyped according to their gender. Both women and men are immersed in the practice. Both men and women cast, heal and openly express their opinions with regard to the evil eye. Perhaps differently, but as cultural equals, female and male individuals participate in everyday spiritual activities. And, through practising the evil eye, they manage their gendered selves and empower their identities. Simultaneously, according to my research at least, it is women who are indeed more engaged with *ksematiasma* and, through such engagement, challenge the religious and often authoritative figure of the Greek Orthodox priest.

The close engagement among gender, power and the evil eye welcomes into the analytic picture the popular discussion with regard to the close relationship between new spirituality and feminine identity. Many social scientists have demonstrated the role that new spiritual practices play in the acquisition of feminine power, emphasizing upon the empowerment of women through the practice of contemporary spirituality (Eller 1993; Herriot 1997; Sointu and Woodhead 2008; Aune 2014; Fedele and Knibbe 2013). Assuming a novel mediating position between Orthodox religion and new spirituality in contemporary Greece, the evil eye, especially in the form of *ksematiasma*, can be approached as a socio-cultural and gender tool of female spi/ritual empowerment. Rethymniot and Thessalonikan women, both the ones who are involved with new spiritual practices and the ones who maintain a position closer to their religious Orthodox routes, express a 'desire to move away from traditional roles ascribed to the feminine' (Sointu and Woodhead 2008: 260), sometimes less intentionally, other times more consciously. Through their ritual performance against the evil eye, and by sometimes incorporating new spiritual symbolisms, discourses and materialities within it, they develop a critique against the patriarchy that is directly linked to Orthodox, hierarchical constructions of authority.[5] At the same time, however, it is important to emphasize that there are many Rethymniot and

Thessalonikan men who also recognize the female spiritual power in the evil eye ritual performance, while expressing their scepticism towards the authoritative role of the Orthodox priests and institutionalized religion. Empowerment through the evil eye spirituality is not simply a female matter, but a gendered tool of fluidifying the boundaries between religion and spirituality in vernacular religious practice.

Mind–body–spirit: Emotion, spirituality and holistic healing

During *ksematiasma* I start yawning and tears run down my face. And if the evil-eyed person is indeed evil eyed I receive a headache from him. Actually, it depends on what he feels. If he feels a headache, his headache comes to me, if he feels *kommara* then my feet are 'cut'. After a while you can see that the evil-eyed person feels well, I feel what he felt, but these symptoms gradually go away. That is, I am like the middle person.

Embodiment plays a vital part in the therapeutic process against the evil eye. As Dimitra, a middle-aged Thessalonikan *ksematiastra*, explains above, the evil eye healer's body acts as a mediator between the suffering body of her patient and the spiritual world. She offers her body as a means to exorcize the evil energy and the evil eye away from the sufferer's body and lead it to a healthy embodiment. This transference of the ill-symptoms between the evil eye healer and patient is very common in the ritual process of *ksematiasma*, serving as a sign of the performance's success.

When an elderly female neighbour visited Chrisoula in her shop in Thessaloniki, she found her in a bad bodily state; someone had given her the evil eye. The elderly woman promised to perform the *ksematiasma* for her sometime in that day. Truly, Chrisoula felt relieved after a while. Two days later, the same neighbour went to Chrisoula's house, where she told her that after performing the healing she became very sick and collapsed into bed feeling sick. 'You mixed up the insides of my body and my soul', she remarked. Chrisoula's elderly neighbour absorbed the symptoms of evil eye illness from Chrisoula's body, and felt what her patient had felt. This embodied exchange between the two parts of the therapeutic communication, where feelings and somatization are interacted and transferred, is far from easy. Yet, such an inter/personal healing process and the somatic sharing of ill-symptoms it involves make the road to therapy more empathetic, emotional and creatively embodied.

When someone tells me that he feels strange and he feels *kommara*, that he has the evil eye and all, I feel it. It is like I receive a wave which he casts right on the top of my eyebrows … I feel an unbelievable heaviness on my forehead, and I want to yawn. I say my prayer, and when I take a big breath I feel I have absorbed his evil eye, I have healed him … For example, I once did the ritual for a colleague of mine. He was in a bad mood; he had an upset stomach etc. Earlier that day I had heard someone gossiping about him. After I did it [the ritual], I spent the rest of the night vomiting like crazy. Namely, I took all of his bad energy away from his body and absorbed it into mine.

For Noula, a Thessalonikan experienced *ksematiastra*, the ritual against the evil eye is a form of relieving the other person of his/her embodied suffering. Noula feels the symptoms of the evil eye sufferer in her own body almost every time, as she has told me. She does not mind going through the ill-embodied state herself, for it is through this bodily transference that she can understand why and how the evil-eyed person is suffering in the exact moment of their therapeutic interaction; this mutual understanding and sharing, according to Noula, 'makes my body feel weak but, what is more important, makes my spirit empowered, gives me the power to feel better what suffering from the evil eye is like, to understand better, and, as a result, heal better'. During *ksematiasma*, the evil-eyed person's body is speaking of its own suffering (Pandolfi 1990: 258). As Pandolfi (1990: 263) has put it, 'Suffering incorporated in the body becomes something that marks what is no longer the biological but the experiential rhythm of life.' When the sensorium of the patient meets the ritualism of the *ksematiastra*, suffering is transformed into a bodily experiential rhythm for both. The evil-eyed individual feels his/her body in distress. During the ritual, the veil that has covered his/her senses is removed, and s/he experiences the sensory and emotional interaction with the ritual healer clearly and efficaciously. The *ksematiastra* in turn experiences an embodiment which does not belong to her. She suffers; her body is captivated by the evil eye power that used to possess her patient's body. This is not an easy embodiment; it is a different one. The healer becomes the patient. She does not only cure the illness; she adopts it on her embodied self. She is willing to get ill in order to cure. And when she finally frees herself from the possession, the ritual is completed and the perceptual abilities of both return to their normal levels of engaging in the world.

In the evil eye healing, *soma* (body) is the human organism (Ingold 2000: 170). At the same time, it perceptually attends to the world (Csordas 1993: 138–9). The symptoms, which are somatically felt after the evil eye affliction, are present on the human body just as it would happen with every other type of biological illness. Then, through an exchanged incorporation between the *ksematiastra* and her patient, they cease to possess one's body. *Pnevma* (spirit) is equally involved. Spiritual energies somatically affect people; spiritual forces are invoked to heal them. The evil eye also affects one's psyche and it is through ritual healing that one's psyche is relieved from the heaviness of the evil eye symptoms. The channelling of positive energy and religious sacredness through Christian prayers and the symbolic performance of Orthodox ritualism, furthermore, leads to healing. As in the case of Charismatic healing that Csordas has studied, the evil eye ritual therapeutic system requires the combination of healing genres into a 'pneumopsychosomatic' synthesis (Csordas 1997 [1994]: 40). *Pnevma* psyche and *soma* encounter each other before and during the *ksematiasma*. Their interaction leads to the habituation of a charismatic world and the creation of a sacred self through healing (1997 [1994]: 24).

> When a *ksematiastra* does her thing, with the cross, the oil, the water, the prayers, I feel she creates a sacred atmosphere. Like when you go to church to have a priest read you a prayer, don't you feel the sacredness of the space and the moment there, in the church? Don't you feel Jesus, the saints, the angels, God, closer by? It is the same when I have someone remove the evil eye from my body. The *ksematiastra* is like a saint to me at that moment, she takes away my illness, but she also cleans somehow my soul, my spirit, my spiritual development, my spiritual growth.

Faidra is a Rethymniot woman in her sixties, with whom I reconnected and re-interviewed while finalizing my research findings in 2019. During our interview back in 2005 she was the first person to have offered the very interesting perspective of the religious charisma of a priest and of an evil eye healer, and the sacredness of their ritual practice. During our second interview, and already being influenced by new spirituality by practising yoga and reiki, she now sees *ksematiasma* as a form of spiritual growth. Charismatic ritual healing corresponds both to biomedical cure, where healing is achieved through a religious communication with the divine, and to contemporary New Age healing, which leads to spiritual growth (Csordas 1997 [1994]: 26). The evil eye ritual healing is charismatic. It administrates Orthodox Christian symbology in its performance. Simultaneously, it encompasses a therapeutic pathway which comprises new forms of spirituality. A multiple ritualism is assembled in the performance of *ksematiasma*; a form of ritualism, the religious and spiritual elements of which make sure that a culturally complicated and dynamically acted charismatic healing is under effective practice.

During *ksematiasma* I enter another sphere of spirituality. The *ksematiastra* communicates with sacred figures of the Orthodox Church, saints etc., by praying to them. I communicate with my spiritual superior self, with my spirit guides, asking them for healing, for assistance. I kind of meditate, if you know what I mean. I don't know if it is right or wrong, as sometimes I feel I should actually be praying, reciting Orthodox prayers, and not do my alternative spiritual stuff. But I can't help it, I feel the Orthodox angels and the spiritual angels are the same, are both here to help, it is just the pathway to them that is different. I don't have the healing charisma of a *ksematiastra*, so when I am evil eyed I can't just meditate and it will go away. No. I need her. But I also think that by my own spiritual travel I do something to reinforce our healing meeting.

Lysandros is a Thessalonikan man in his mid-thirties. He is very involved with new spirituality. His house is full of New Age objects, he meditates almost every day and has tried the majority of New Age activities that are offered in Thessaloniki. He still believes in the power of the ritual healing against the evil eye and, as he has confessed, *ksematiasma* is these days his only means of being in touch with Orthodox Christianity. He does not immediately reject his Christian roots, as many of his friends, who are closely involved in new spirituality, do; instead, he makes an effort to maintain his religious upbringing through continuing to participate in the ritual healing against the evil eye, even if he has transformed the evil eye healing encounter to incorporate his new spirituality creatively.

The majority of my younger interlocutors, up to the age of thirty-five, both in Thessaloniki and Rethymno, are thoroughly involved in everything that is new spirituality-related. From practising yoga and reiki to owning energetic crystals and tarot decks, this is their pathway to encountering spirituality in their own, individual manner, without the obligations and close-mindedness that, as they have told me, feel comes with their denominational religion, namely Orthodox Christianity. Despite their rejection of institutionalized religion, most of them continue to accept *ksematiasma*, separating its practice from what they consider 'official religion', and defining it as a 'vernacular, alternative religio-spiritual expression'. Like Lysandros, they treat the evil eye healing encounters as less religious and more spiritual, which provide them with the opportunity for further spiritual growth and action.

Ksematiasma, especially for the younger generation of my interlocutors, is treated as a form of spi/ritual healing and a spiritual pathway in communicating with the sacred. At the same time, the evil eye healers, whether involved or not in new spirituality, also 'see themselves therein as a channel to the spiritual/transcendent which would allow them a subtle empathetic understanding of the client' (Stöckligt et al. 2015: 7). And whereas in biomedical encounters the healer–patient relationship is based on a duality between the medical doctor and the client, in spiritual healing this relationship shifts to include a third actor in the therapeutic encounter, that of a transcendental source, whether it is religious figures, spiritual entities or the sacred in general. In the evil eye healing encounter, the healer, especially the one involved in new spirituality, often sees himself/herself as a 'channel which allows an intuitive, subtle, or even clairvoyant perception', where the patient is 'felt, seen, and understood by the healer' and is 'spiritually (re)connected' (2015: 5).

> I believe *ksematiasma* works because, you know, there is so much emotion involved in the process. I mean, the *ksematiastra* absorbs all these symptoms you feel when you are evil eyed. She listens to your problems, who you think gave you the evil eye and why. She feels what you feel. Like, literally. Does your doctor do that? Of course not. He doesn't care, doesn't give a damn about how you feel, only treats the symptoms, not the real you. It is a very emotional process for me, I appreciate her so much, she cares, she is there every time I ask her to get rid of the evil eye for me. She truly cares.

A couple of months ago, during an interview I had with Anthimos, a fifty-year-old man in northern Greece, I asked him to describe his relationship to the person who frequently performs *ksematiasma* for him, who is his aunt. As can be seen by his response above, he was very keen to mention that, as far as he is concerned, the most important aspect of evil eye healing is the emotional interaction between the patient and the healer in the process. Anthimos appreciates a lot that his aunt takes time out of her life to perform the ritual healing for him and make her body vulnerable each time to receive his evil eye symptoms and then get rid of them. The majority of my interlocutors have actually emphasized upon the fact that it is crucial for them to experience an emotional understanding on their evil eye healer's part, to feel that their evil eye healer cares about them. It is not just about the fact that the healer's embodiment of the evil eye symptoms shows a great willingness to heal; it is, more generally, about the emotional exchange that occurs in the ritual healing process and the fact that they are treated holistically and not just as objectified bodies.

Along with the embodied transference of ill-symptoms between the healer and the patient in the evil eye therapeutic context, an emotional interaction takes place as well. One of the most important aspects of *ksematiasma*, therefore, is the regulation of a patient's emotional state, which makes the therapy possible.

The evil eye sufferer hands his/her feelings to the *ksematiastra* who, being their recipient, transforms, rearranges and resolves them. The *ksematiastra* does not respond to this emotional exchange by offering an analytical way out. She actually incorporates them, she feels them on her own body and she has no choice but to deal with them directly and instantly. Consequently, emotional and embodied reciprocity is what renders the evil eye ritual healing successful. The evil eye healer does not inhabit the therapeutic space untouched and unaffected by the individuals standing opposite him/her. On the contrary, s/he 'radically empathizes' with them: s/he actually incorporates the feelings of suffering and bodily distress, experiencing the symptoms as felt by the evil eye-afflicted people. Inside this field of 'radical empathy' (Koss-Chioino 2006), evil eye healers 'respond altruistically to persons in distress seeking their help' (2006: 878), and the 'individual differences between healer and sufferer are melded into one field of feeling and experience' (2006: 877).

Altruism and emotional empathy and a holistic approach are some of the most important characteristics in the New Age healing and of the so-called 'holistic health movement' (see Baer 2003), which is directly connected to it.[6] As Poulin and West (2005: 257) put it: 'The New Age movement, characterized by recognizing the depth of our interconnectedness, valuing multiple ways of knowing and healing (...), has created a space for holistic healing to become more accepted and sought after.' Holistic healing gives priority to the balance between the mind, body and spirit (Baer 2003: 235). Being part of the New Age, it seeks to break with official, legitimized establishments, namely biomedicine and official religions (McGuire 1993: 149). And as a spiritual healing movement, it expresses 'the dissatisfaction with the limitations of the compartmentalized, rationalized medicine' (McGuire 1993: 148).

The evil eye healing can be considered to be part of the New Age and the holistic health movement. Although it is closely linked to Orthodox Christianity, these days *ksematiasma* also involves alternative spiritual discourses in its practice, as well as New Age elements of ritualism through the use of New Age material objects and alternative spiritual practices in its performance. At the same time, it shares many of other characteristics of New Age and holistic healing: the radical empathy, the emotional interchange between evil eye healers and patients and the mind–body–spirit idea that permeates it, the spiritual channelling and the alternative communication with the sacred are all indicators of *ksematiasma*'s turn towards new spiritual influences. And in addition to challenging the religious authority of the priest, the authority of the medical doctor is provoked as well, through the efficacy of ritual performance in vernacular religious practice, which offers in turn a criticism against the distant, non-empathetic Greek biomedical system and its 'scientificity'.

After witnessing an evil eye ritual performed by an older woman in northern Greece, her husband, who was also present, commented at the end, with a tone of humour in his voice: 'She is a scientist, better than a doctor!' In Greece, biomedicine is considered as the official, trusted scientific pathway of rationalized medical action, as physicians go through positive-science training before they can become health professionals. Equating a ritual healer with a medical doctor, therefore, might sound peculiar. However, when the evil eye healers admit they feel that they play the role of a doctor, since they make people feel well, and are hence scientists, the constructed parallel has to do more with their social role than their actual training. They are characterized, with or without hints of teasing, as scientists, because they possess knowledge of a realm where not everyone can claim expertise. Although the evil eye is so culturally widespread that everyone can actually claim knowledge of the practice, the efficacy of healing can only be achieved by the few who are deeply involved, have certain spiritual powers and their performative acts of healing are almost always efficacious.

'Judging from the doctors I have met, they reject the evil eye when they hear about it. They do not accept it as a disease. They are very practical scientists. That is, they think mathematically, 1+1=2. If you tell them you are evil eyed, their minds cannot accept it.' This statement, coming from a Rethymniot man, proved to be an ethnographic reality. I did not have the chance to talk to many doctors exactly because of this stereotypical preconception. The few that accepted to talk to me, however, followed quite varied paths. Some of them were very quick to dismiss the evil eye in the name of 'science'. Some, however, admitted they have had the *ksematiasma* performed on them, but in an out-of-their-office context, namely, in a space not infused with biomedical signifieds. 'I have met a lot of doctors who believe in the evil eye. Because, you see, they are humans too. And in a few offices, I saw evil eye amulets hanging from the walls', a female Thessalonikan informant revealed. Although torn between their professional and private image, medical specialists do not cease to be 'humans'. And in this case, 'humanity' is defined by whether they believe and practise *mati* or not. When I asked a *ksematiastra* whether she regarded herself as a doctor, she replied: 'To tell you the truth ... OK, I am not a doctor, I am not a scientist, but, well, you act as a doctor at the end.' The healers usually separate their practice from 'science'. What they are performing is not something scientific, since, as they have made clear, they do not want to invade the realm of the physicians.

Still, they do hold the responsibility to improve people's health; they must act like doctors.

Besides, as Lewis' (1993) research in the West Sepik Province of Papua New Guinea has revealed, biomedical treatment does not necessarily result in efficacy. Biomedical experts kept giving the Papua New Guineans pills to swallow, in order to cure them from leprosy. Yet, the New Guineans refused this healing treatment and lied about taking the medicine, a situation which was perceived by the biomedical representatives as uncooperativeness and apathy (Lewis 1993: 202). But locals were not apathetic. The pills given to them for healing purposes lacked meaning. They were just chemicals; swallowing them would be equivalent to the ingestion of a biologically and culturally estranged substance. Locals did end up exploiting the biomedical healing system, by 'borrowing' and subsequently using penicillin powder for their sores. Biomedical authority and its scientific denotations did not count for them; they just used it when they needed it.

The evil eye ritual and spiritual healing works similarly. Although biomedicine in Greece is linked to scientificity and thus to the legitimation of illness and health discourses, *ksematiasma* offers an alternative path to healing. The invocation of spiritual forces in order to remove ill-symptoms offers effective cure. So does a visit to a physician's office. Though a different therapeutic angle, they both lead to convalescence and contribute to a person's good health as separate and/or as alternative healing resources. Despite its effectiveness in curing, however, evil eye healing is occasionally approached with a certain degree of scepticism, even by individuals who are directly involved in the healing process. For instance, Eleni, a Cretan woman in her forties, has a friend from Athens who calls her all the time, even if it is two o'clock in the morning, and asks her to do a *ksematiasma* for her. Eleni thinks her friend's attitude exceeds reasonableness. She believes that her friend self-imposes her affliction most of the time. Therefore, Eleni does not always perform the ritual, she just tells her Athenian friend that she has done so, and her friend becomes well.

Evil eye self-imposition, or *afthypovoli* (a word which derives from the Greek 'self' [*eaftos*] and 'imposition' [*ypovoli*]), is a term Rethymniots and Thessalonikans utilize when they think that the evil eye affliction and therapy are not 'real', but mentally constructed by the evil eye sufferers. Subsequently, *ksematiasma* is not 'really' efficacious but it just appears to be so: it is a placebo. Sprayed with negative connotations, the placebo phenomenon carries the preconceptions of fake healing, mental constructions, incompetent healers and a non-existent illness. The allegations against the evil eye healing appear to share commonalities with the placebo phenomenon. Two examples, one from Crete and one from northern Greece, where two very successful healers admit they have performed placebo rituals with success, describe the ambiguity with which the evil eye healing is sometimes covered. Both healers are of the opinion that, since no real healing was practised, their patients were in a self-deceptive ill state, which turned into a healthy one via a mental procedure of self-imposition.

Anna frequently meets a particular woman during common social visits. This woman always tells her she has the evil eye, and she always asks her to remove it. Anna cannot stand this situation anymore. So, last time her social contact asked her to perform a *ksematiasma*, Anna first put her cigarette down so that it would not seem that she was not actually doing anything, she pretended to say a silent prayer and the evil-eyed woman immediately felt well. Anna is certain that it is not her healing that leads the woman's body into a healthy state; it is her *afthypovoli* which does so. Kaiti, an older healer in northern Greece, was also eager to narrate a problem she had with one of her evil eye patients.

> She made me crazy, sweetheart. She was coming to my house asking me to do a *ksematiasma* everyday. And now, whenever I see her coming to church on Sundays, I avoid her. I couldn't stand her! Sometimes she had it [the evil eye], other times she didn't. I was telling her, 'I did it for you yesterday, you didn't have anything'. 'No, do it for me again!' she was insisting. So one day I told her: 'I won't do it for you, you don't have anything.' She replied: 'Of course I do, I do, I can tell.' 'How can you tell?' I asked. 'Because my husband gives me the evil eye.' 'Then', I told her, 'divorce him'. 'And how can I divorce him, he does his job, and he tells me "what a good 'thing' you have!". And then I told her to get out of my house and never come to my doorstep again. 'What can I do about your husband evil-eyeing you? Shall I be with you on the bed during the action?!'[7]

'Placebos are inert. That means they do nothing. Still, changes happen' (Moerman 2002: 14). In the Cretan case, the unperformed ritual was inert. Namely, it was not actually performed by Anna, although in the eyes of the *matiasmeni* (evil eyed) it appeared as if it was. This was enough to change the patient's sensibilities, injecting her with a play-acted yet efficacious therapeutic. In the second context, this interaction did not work. Kaiti denied what from the beginning she knew would be a stagnant therapy, even though her status as an efficacious healer would have stayed unaffected. She felt cheated. What for her patient was a constant *mati*, for her was a continuous *afthypovoli*, in which she refused to take part, since she thought the other woman had begun to confuse coincidence with cause (see Moerman 2002: 14). In both Kaiti's and Anna's cases, the evil eye suffering individuals took advantage of the healers' expertise, pushing them over the limits. Each *ksematiastra* then operated according to her personal feelings, and either went along with the patient's request or rejected it irretrievably.

> I believe that what he sees during the *ksematiasma* influences him a lot, and that is why he is immediately healed. Now, you will say that his mind thinks that 'she healed me because she did the *ksematiasma* on me', so this is a form of *afthypovoli*, he sees all these things, they go inside the brain and they create the idea that he is well, but I think that *mati* influences the life of a person, it is not only *afthypovoli* as people say.

As it is indicated in Dimitra's, another elderly *ksematiastra*'s words, what principally matters in the evil eye course of healing is the meaning response, 'the psychological and physiological effects of meaning in the treatment of illness' (Moerman 2002: 14). Even by entering the physician's office and staying there for a while, a patient is very likely to feel her ill-health symptoms reducing (2002: 12). The red colour of a pill or a picture of Snoopy on a bandage holds a better chance to heal than their blank equivalents (2002: 16). As Moerman (1979: 60) argued, 'The construction of healing symbols is healing.' That is the case with *ksematiasma*. It may be considered more of a symbolic rather than any other type of healing, which charges it with the unfortunate connotation that there are other forms of healing that are not symbolic (Csordas and Kleinman 1996: 3), rendering it non-scientific and possibly inefficacious. *Ksematiastres* (evil eye healers) heal because they provide a culturally legitimated treatment of illness (see Kleinman 1980: 362). *Ksematiasma* is a somatic as much as it is a mental course of therapeutic action, and, as Scheper-Hughes (1994: 235) has asserted: 'If mind and body are truly one, then all diseases are and must be psychosomatic – all are "somatized" as well as "mentalized". But medical anthropology has never lived up to the strength of its convictions and has never been prepared to support so radical and consequential a thesis.'

In addition to its complicated relationship with scientific-based discourses, *ksematiasma* has been strongly associated by my interlocutors with mysticism and magic. Many of the Thessalonikans and Rethymniots I interacted with during fieldwork attributed mystical and magical qualities to the ritual, mainly because the prayer used during *ksematiasma* cannot be revealed to anyone, except in the process of its transmission to another potential healer. This ritual rule of non-revelation has enfolded the ritual healing with a veil of mysticism, equating it, for them, to a New Age, magical technique; besides, according to those individuals, mysticism is synonymous with magic, and the ones who believe in the magical character of *ksematiasma* treat the explanation that the words utilized in the ritual are Christian prayers and nothing else with scepticism.

In Rethymno, the use of *gities* (spells) has been popular over the years. Some of my interlocutors referred to an elderly man, now deceased, who was a healer, and a medium. As a Cretan man explained, the healer had gained his therapeutic, mediumship and channelling abilities after killing two snakes while they were making love. He never took money; he only used his skills to help his neighbours and other Rethymniots. As I was told, *gities* are commonly used in Rethymno as a means to heal, to make someone suffer or to charm ants. I was also informed about the existence of certain magical spells one can perform to help with non-biological illnesses and social situations. I learned, for instance, what a man can do to charm his wife into making love with him; or, what action someone needs to take, if he wants to steal pigs or other animals from a house, in order to prevent the guard-dog from barking, and how a woman can make her partner loyal to her forever. All these acts can be situated inside a culturally defined field of magical performances. But, in fact, they are not so different from either the evil eye or from church practices. Of course, no religious prayers are used and Orthodoxy is not invoked in the spells I have just described. But as Malinowski (1954 [1925]: 82) wrote: 'The foundations of magical belief and practice are due to a number of experiences actually lived through, in which man receives the revelation of his power to attain the desired end.' It is all about how experience is lived, and how social actors decide to go about it. The definition of whether their performed practices are magical, religious, spiritual, or not, has to do with what sorts of linguistic and material tools are in use, and what meaning is given to them and under which circumstances. Besides, as Douglas (1996 [1970]: 9) has convincingly alleged, 'ecclesiastic and magical behaviour are both expressions of ritualism, which is concerned with the right manipulation of symbols in the right order'.

Panos, a thirty-year-old Thessalonikan, has noted that there are quite a few similarities between the ritual healing against the evil eye and baptism, since both can be regarded as religious rituals to help send the evil spirits away from a person. He has also pointed out to me that the use of other ingredients, such as oil, water and salt, and the creation of a ritual performance add to his conviction that the ritual performance against the evil eye is magical. At the same time, however, he has also admitted that *ksematiasma* does not differ much from other Church rituals. Panos has not been the only one to make such a comparative remark. Several Rethymniots and Thessalonikans with whom I spoke tried to defend the evil eye practice and the idea of energy exchange among people by referring to the common characteristics shared between the ritual healing against the evil eye and other ecclesiastical rituals.

As Stewart (1991: 207) successfully demonstrates, the Orthodox Church sacraments, especially baptism, and the ritual against the evil eye share crucial commonalities; both baptism and *ksematiasma* can be credited as paradigms of an exorcistic ritual practice. Church rituals and evil eye rituals both equal spiritual exorcism. *Ksematiasma* is a powerful performance, which chases the evil eye away. When someone goes to a priest in order to be blessed with the prayer against v*askania*, the process is more or less the same as the one the evil eye healer follows. The priest reads a prayer, while covering the evil-eyed person with his stole. When the prayer is finished, he blesses the sufferer with oil and/ or holy water. It seems that the only actual difference between the doctrinally Orthodox and the unofficial *ksematiasma* lies in who performs the ritual and where: the priest and the church carry a religiously legitimated 'sacredness', which the evil eye healer and her house supposedly lack. For the sufferer, however, what matters is to get rid of the evil eye. In his/her eyes, the priest and the lay person hold the same amount of spiritual power. And as long as their performances consist of religiously symbolic acts, they are not magical.

> *Mageia* is something different from *mati* … I believe *mageia* is more general … saying that, I do not believe in magic either. Actually, I am more negative toward magic than toward the evil eye … because the evil eye is something simpler and more specific, whereas with magic you can supposedly do 'miracles'. Of course, someone could develop this supernatural power he uses in the evil eye and do more things with it.

Such a view, expressed by Antonis, a Rethymniot man, is shared by many of my interlocutors. Magic is thought to be a more distant, more incomprehensible act of performing certain rituals, which is more difficult to understand, and is located in a particular socio-cultural context. It is believed that supernatural powers are invoked to assist with the outcome of magical performances; yet, these powers cannot be situated in a specified sphere. They are often regarded as demonic or generally evil forces. The evil eye practice, on the other hand, is not automatically dismissed. Unless they are extremely devoted Christians, Rethymniots and Thessalonikans hesitate to adopt the official Church discourse which dismisses *ksematiasma* as magical. But even if the evil eye does have something to do with magic, it is a very mild form of magic, people in my fieldsites have made clear and many equate it to current global trends of New Age spiritual orientation.

> I am spiritual, I dig all these New Age stuff. I believe a lot in energy, and alternative things, spiritual things I do, like reiki and the like, are therapies that involve energy. But, look, this energy belief that exists in the evil eye is also accepted by our religion. According to our Orthodoxy, I bless you with a prayer, or I baptize you, and all the bad energy, all the evil spirits go away. When a religion accepts that, and the fact that negative energy can be transmitted, you cannot really argue with it.

So said Euterpi, a Thessalonikan in her late twenties, who is a New Age practitioner, by her own definition, but also a Christian believer and she frequently has *ksematiasma* performed for her when she feels unwell. Euterpi defends the evil eye and the idea of energy exchange among people, by pointing out the equivalence between *ksematiasma* and church rituals, for, as she explains, they are both about removing evil after it has been transmitted through channels of negative energy. Euterpi seems certain that Orthodoxy bases its practices on a grid of energy. She knows, of course, that this theory would never be accepted by the official Christian ideology or her local priest. She is also aware that her adoption of the idea that energy is circulated around is associated with New Age spirituality. Euterpi practises yoga and reiki, does meditation and follows the basic feng shui rules in her house. Like Euterpi, there are many of my interlocutors who, having experienced New Age therapies, *ksematiasma* and religious rituals, ultimately wish to follow a very open-minded spiritual path, where they present a new spiritual and therapeutic synthesis by utilizing the concept of energy in their discourse and practice frequently and consistently. It is in these pluralistic therapeutic paths, where Orthodoxy and New Age spirituality meet and amalgamate. And it is in these novel and/or 'alternative' forms of healing, where religion and spirituality can heal in combination without entering a conflicting interaction, where the evil eye ritual healing, infused by New Age spirituality, escapes its stereotypical socio-cultural boundaries and depicts clearly a fluid shift in contemporary Greek vernacular religious practice.

5

Creative syntheses through material culture: The evil eye in the spiritual marketplace

Materiality is centrally situated in the evil eye practice. Objects that are closely related to the evil eye in terms of representation and meaning are popular in Rethymno and Thessaloniki. In the past, these objects had predominantly been blue eye-shaped plastic or glass beads, in various sizes, worn on clothes or decorating houses, which were supposed to protect people from the power of *mati*. Nowadays, the range of evil eye things has expanded, and a renewed interest triggered by fashion and New Age spirituality, in the course of the last fifteen years at least, has lifted *matakia* (evil eye-related objects) higher up on the material ladder of popularity. This material amplification does not only involve changes in the quality, quantity, form and imaginative variety of evil eye things. It also – and perhaps most importantly – has to do with a change in the evil eye practice itself. Namely, the evil eye material objects I discovered in the field, which are more spiritually pluralized than they used to be, represent a Greek turn to a more open spiritual field, where Orthodoxy and New Age spirituality are amalgamated in practice and in material creativity.

From decorative items to jewellery, from key chains to *kompologia* (worry beads), from mobile amulets to religious icons, evil eye things are everywhere to be found in both my fieldsites. In the Old Town of Rethymno, principally due to its touristic character, evil eye objects are sold in almost every shop with souvenirs, home decoration, accessories and jewellery (see Figure 15). They can also be discovered in bookshops, shops with local Cretan products, in establishments that specialize in New Age, feng shui and other objects that promote spirituality and health, at kiosks and supermarkets. In Thessaloniki, evil eye things are predominantly seen in shops selling jewellery, home decoration and accessories, in New Age shops and in feng shui specialist businesses. The Thessalonikan evil eye things tend to be more expensive and of higher quality

Figure 15 Evil eye objects outside a Rethymniot shop.

than their Rethymniot equivalents. Yet, the pace of the objects' flow and exchange of value remain equally intense in both sites.

Economic exchange creates value. Value is embodied in commodities that are exchanged. Focusing on the things that are exchanged, rather than simply on the forms or functions of exchange, makes it possible to argue that what creates the link between exchange and values is politics, construed broadly. This argument justifies the concept that commodities, like persons, have social lives.

(Appadurai 1986: 3)

Appadurai's point of theoretical departure that things have social lives, and his call to focus on their flow and valuable exchanges, has provoked criticism. His emphasis on the commodities, rather than the strategies in which the latter are embedded, has been received as an over-emphasis on materially, as opposed to culturally, embedded processes. 'It is in the strategies of selfhood and identity that "things" take on their life. Things do not have social lives. Rather, social lives have things' (Friedman 1991: 161). Of course, social lives have things. Paying attention to how things are circulating, used and living does not annihilate the agency of people who are in charge of handling them. Besides, as Simmel has argued, value is never an inherent property of objects but is a judgement made about them by the social subjects (Appadurai 1986: 3–4). Evil eye things have lives, while they are exchanged among people. During this process of social trading, they acquire and hold value. 'Politics is what links value and exchange in the social life of commodities' (Appadurai 1986: 57). Valuable evil eye objects are exchanged in the cultural context of everyday micro-politics. What has ultimately appeared on the ethnographic surface is a strong bond shared between a newly established fashion based on the evil eye objects and a novel material inclination to approach New Age spirituality.

The initial choice of the evil eye material objects that are displayed in the Rethymniot and Thessalonikan shop windows belongs to their owners. The way in which these objects flow in the marketplace and the multiple meanings they acquire as commodities are determined by the consumers. The shop owners in Rethymno and Thessaloniki have made the strong and important point that what matters most are the flow and the social lives of *matakia* (evil eye objects) after they have exited the production zone and have crossed over the consumption threshold. Ultimately, as my ethnographic research has shown, the newly developed evil eye material creativity depends upon the shop owners and the consumers of Rethymno and Thessaloniki. Shop owners and consumers, at least the ones I spoke to, have been actively involved in the development of an evil eye-related material trend and have decisively contributed to the emergence of a contemporary Greek materiality where religion, spirituality and the evil eye are all intertwined. The material popularity of the evil eye, in its creatively practised synthesis between Orthodoxy and New Age, is a very recent phenomenon. As most of my Rethymniot and Thessalonikan interlocutors have indicated, this process happened gradually, out of the need to infuse more creativity into the evil eye material objects. A shift has occurred in the evil eye materialities, which can be attributed to recent globalizing influences in the everyday life of Greeks, with special reference to varying consumerist politics and the contribution of tourism.

Raymond Williams has suggested that 'the development of modern commercial advertising is highly significant in the creation of consumerism' (Gabriel and Lang 1995: 16). Advertising has contributed greatly to the fashionable popularity of the material evil eye objects. Popular magazines are full of evil eye jewellery advertisements. Online advertising of *matakia* is prominent. An informal form of advertising, through representation on television, also takes place. During the broadcasts, serious and less formal, popular television presenters, on both national and private channels, are seen wearing *matakia* that they sometimes combine with jewellery with spiritual symbols – such as the yin and yang, the tree of life, a Buddha and so on. By visually representing them publicly, they add popular value to the evil eye things and, at a more general level, it appears that the Greek media play a significant role in broadcasting globalizing influences, including New Age trends, and in the creation and expansion of the evil eye trend. Influenced by these new spiritual material tendencies, Rethymniots and Thessalonikans, in the words of a shop owner in Thessaloniki,

> keep requesting to buy those evil eye things they see on television and in magazine ads: evil eye pendants, amulets and other similar things, such as feng shui objects, energy crystals, Chinese things, like yin and yang, other spiritual things, like the tree of life and elephants for good luck and prosperity, and the like. So, we order them and bring them.

Tourism has contributed to the process generously as well, bringing globalizing influences and requests into the Greek marketplace. Evil eye objects are very popular with tourists as such; yet, according to the shop owners in Rethymno and Thessaloniki, tourists get more demanding every year. As a New Age shop owner explained: 'They buy the evil eye things, but they also ask constantly for healing objects, like crystals, New Age things, feng shui things, and objects that have some kind of spiritual power. They even ask for Orthodox icons.' As a consequence, shop owners need to invent new ways to attract their attention and offer them what they ask for, and end up ordering for their shops, along with the classic evil eye beads and *matakia*, evil eye materialities that incorporate additional spiritual meanings, as well as New Age objects, feng shui material protective things and religious icons.

The material evil eye objects that I predominantly encountered during my ethnographic research in Rethymno and Thessaloniki can be divided into two categories. On the one hand, there are the religious *matakia*: the evil eye objects that incorporate Orthodox symbols. On the other hand, there are the New Age *matakia*: the objects that are related to both the evil eye and New Age spirituality. These objects have become very popular among Rethymniots and Thessalonikans, serving as primary indicators of a new development in the context of contemporary Greek religiosity. These objects have multiple and powerful roles and meanings within vernacular religious practice, being handled creatively in the spaces of shops, houses and bodies, frequently combining Orthodox, New Age and evil eye symbolisms, all at once.

Orthodoxy and *matakia*

During a visit to Anatoli's home in Thessaloniki, I discovered two small religious icons, which were made of blue glass, with religious figures in the middle (see Figure 16). When I asked Anatoli about these objects, she told me that for her

Figure 16 Religious icons as *matakia*.

they represent religious icons, combined with extra protection against the evil eye, because of the blue glass, as well as protecting the family against all kinds of negative spiritual energies. Anatoli told me that she first kept them in the living room, opposite the family *eikonostasi* (icon altar). But then, they did not appear appropriate to her sitting opposite the oil lamp and the Christian icons, materially representing something more than religion; hence, she moved them to her daughter's room, in order to protect her spiritually. For Anatoli, these two glass icons held a certain spiritual power and were utilized as amulets that served for a spiritual protection beyond Orthodox undertones, indicating the diverse meanings one can attribute to the evil eye things that also hold some religious connotations, and how Orthodox icons can serve as evil eye amulets while encompassing both a religious and New Age spiritual meaning.

The possession of religious icons defines one as an Orthodox Christian and is considered common among Greeks, since it is historically connected with their ethnic identity (Kenna 1985: 364). As Kokosalakis (1995: 443) has put it: 'Religious practice in Orthodoxy is unthinkable without icons. Icons over the centuries became essential carriers of the Orthodox tradition in the sense that they communicate and express the patristic ideology at a popular level.' There are two physical spaces where Orthodox icons are venerated in Greece, and where a sacred communication is established between the holy entities depicted in the icon and the devotee (Kenna 1985: 349). The first space is the interior of churches. The second is the *eikonostasi* of one's household (see Figure 17). And perhaps the church space is considered more 'appropriate', since it is more closely connected to an officially established form of veneration; yet, icons maintain their sacramental character (1985: 347) in both church and household environments. What essentially matters is the establishment of a reciprocal relationship between the devotee and the icon because, 'if the onlooker does not look at the icon and respond as a devotee, with veneration, the icon cannot act as a sacrament. Correct behaviour toward an icon not only taps its power and keeps it flowing but even seems to call forth that power initially' (1985: 359).

Possession of icons is an integral part of Greek everyday life. Icons can be seen in the houses of most Rethymniots and Thessalonikans. A person does not have to be a religious devotee to own an icon; even some of my interlocutors who characterize themselves as atheists have admitted having a few hanging from their house walls. For the faithful, icons are 'real personal bridges between the human and the divine' (Kokosalakis 1995: 443). But even when one is not religiously devoted, s/he can recognize the spiritual and mystical character of an icon, the fact that it can potentially be a vehicle of the sacred (1995: 440). When

Figure 17 Religious icons in a Thessalonikan household.

an icon is materially enriched with an evil eye symbol, however, ambiguity arises as to whether the icon maintains its sacred character. The existence of religious *matakia*, namely those material objects that combine religious figures with evil eye beads and form one single item, is a recent phenomenon. As will be further explored below, and according to my interlocutors' opinions and my ethnographic observations, it has emerged out of the need to reinvent the evil eye objects and find a way to make them more popular to Greeks and foreign tourists, as well as refresh the relationship between Orthodoxy and the evil eye, by pushing it in the direction of a more open vernacular religiosity.

In most of the Rethymniot and Thessalonikan shops I visited Christian icons and eye glass objects were evidently hung together in shop windows, on shelves, stands and walls. Whenever I entered a shop and looked for evil eye material things, I would usually find them next to crosses, or next to icons that depicted various Saints, Jesus and the Virgin Mary. I first discovered this material co-existence of religion and spirituality as I was walking down a main road in the Old Town of Rethymno back in 2005. Having already begun to cultivate the habit of paying attention to all shop windows, I found myself in front of a shop window looking at various evil eye objects, which combined blue-eye beads with crosses and icons, alongside Orthodox religious icons. A few weeks later, a friend and I went into an accessories store in the Old Town. A whole shelf full of evil eye amulets, religious icons and eye glass beads occupied two of the store's walls. I immediately called my friend to join me and see for herself, as I felt the need for an ethnographic witness's presence. When she came, she did not look so impressed. I proceeded to explain in detail why I found this particular corner of the shop fascinating. When I finished, she turned to me and plainly said: 'I guess the suppliers of the evil eyes and the icons are the same.'

In Thessaloniki, the material combination in evil eye things was equally noticeable. Most of the jewellery seen in shop windows was usually a combination of eye beads and small crosses and was arranged next to silver-framed icons. This spatial co-inhabitation left no doubt that *matakia* and religious icons are perceived as belonging to the same material category. As a young Thessalonikan woman, whose mother owned a shop in the centre of the city, has described the cohabitation:

> My mother hang all these objects in her shop, she has a whole wall full of evil eyes there, icons, evil eye amulets, beads ... they were put together. Actually, they could not be *more* together. But think about it, nowadays you can find icons with evil eyes on the top of them. Or crosses with *matakia*. Now that she has closed the shop for good, she has hung them in the house. We have so many in the house now. They are located next to the sacred icons, next to the *eikonostasi*.

In her detailed work on material Christianity in North America, McDannell (1995) has demonstrated the significance of Christian retailing, namely the selling of Christian goods for personal or household use, in contemporary American religious life. As McDannell (1995: 247) has observed, there was one particular movement of the early 1970s, the so-called 'Jesus movement', which triggered the growing popularity of religious objects, especially religious books and the Bible, in the everyday life of North Americans. For the members of the 'Jesus movement', who were evangelical Christians and combined elements of Protestantism and the 1960s spirit, Christianity was not just a matter of belief but should be approached as a lifestyle. They 'sought to experience the reality of Jesus outside of an institutionalized church structure ... The Jesus movement involved more than transforming hippies into Christians. As Protestants had done in the mid-nineteenth century, they looked to books to articulate their religious sensibility' (1995: 247).

Companies did not remain empty-handed. Taking advantage of this Christian revival, they filled up the marketplace with bumper stickers, badges, clothing patches, fashionable T-shirts, leather bible covers, expensive watches, crosses, pendants and other high-quality pieces of jewellery. Christian merchandizing became both fashionable and of high quality (1995: 249–64). 'Jesus movement artists and producers intended to establish a viable Christian alternative to the secular marketplace ... Christian consumerism, born in the previous century, had been "born again" in the Jesus movement of the 1970s' (1995: 256). However, by the late 1970s the popularity of the fashionable and high-quality Christian-oriented objects began to fade, and the next decade and a half found the American consuming public becoming more conservative. 'Just as some of the hippies grew up to be yuppies, so Christians became more politically and socially conservative. They also continued to shop at Christian bookstores' (1995: 256). In present-day America, or at least in the America of the 1990s, when McDannell's book was published, one can still find a variety of Christian merchandizing, which ranges from high-quality jewellery, standard pictures of Jesus and Gospels and Christian Heavy Metal music (1995: 259). It seems as if some of the old Christian retailing glory of the 1970s has re-emerged.

The rising popularity of religious commodities in North American society is similar to what has happened with the religious *matakia* in contemporary Greece, at least how I have ethnographically observed their popularity in the last fifteen years. American Christian retailing aimed to attract interest in Christianity, by reinventing religious objects so that they become popularly accessible. Like their American colleagues, Greek retailers have chosen to establish a material intimacy between religious icons and the popular belief in the evil eye, by placing icons and *matakia* next to each other on their shop shelves, and by promoting the religious *matakia* – evil eye amulets where eye beads and religious icons are materially amalgamated. On the other hand, the promotion of Christianity through materiality is the most important goal in the

American retailing, and the use of fashion, advertising and popular culture is mostly a means to that goal (McDannell 1995: 261). Yet, the Greek case is more ambiguous than the American one. Sometimes religious *matakia* are treated by lay people as icons with a specific Christian spiritual power; other times they are treated as amulets, which can protect against the evil eye and other forms of spiritual attacks; and yet other times they are accused of misleading the devotees into buying a fake Christian object – an object that is only pretending to be Christian in a material way. At the end, despite the diverse handling of the evil eye religious materialities, and just like Christian retailing in North America, Greek retailing is 'a striking example of how lay men and women successfully integrate religious concerns, popular culture, and profit making' (1995: 269).

> I do not believe in *matakia*, I would not use them. Watching them combined with an icon of the *Panagia*, for example, is appalling. Because the Church, belief, and saints is one thing, and the evil eye and energy is another ... I sometimes connect the evil eye with the negative aspects of the Church, you know, like with satanic things. I just think that what we call Church and what we call evil eye are two different matters. We must not combine them in the form of objects. It is a different thing to go to a priest and ask him to read the *vaskania* prayer for you. But I would never buy an object where the evil eye and religious icons are combined. Religion is something sacred to me; I do not want to combine it with something negative. *Matakia* might be something good as well, but for me they do have negative qualities, which are in no way compatible with *Panagia*.

Nikolas, a Cretan man in his fifties, expressed the above view while looking at and commenting upon an object that combined an evil eye bead with an icon of the Virgin Mary (*Panagia*) (see Figure 18). As becomes apparent from his narrative, he rejects any connection between the two. In his words, 'the evil eye is too mystical to stand next to an Orthodox icon'. Nikolas follows an official religious rhetoric, which categorizes the evil eye as a predominantly satanic force that occupies the opposite side of Christian belief. Orthodox Christianity and its Church do not recognize the role of *mati* amulets as protective things against the evil eye. Most devoted religious individuals, who strictly follow the Christian rules in leading their lives, reject the efficacy of *matakia* without discussion. When they see religious figures next to an evil eye symbol, they become angry. Such a spiritual synthesis, as they have explained, is against their religious values, and ultimately against Christianity itself. Yet, despite the fact that the Church does not officially approve of the religious *matakia*, such objects are seen right next to religious icons and rosaries in the retail businesses owned

Creative Syntheses through Material Culture 123

Figure 18 A *Panagia* (Virgin Mary) combined with an evil eye.

by the Church of Greece and/or the Bishoprics of Thessaloniki and Rethymno. Priests I talked to have acknowledged the objects' potential spiritual qualities. People in their everyday lives treat them as prophylactic amulets. Ultimately, the religious images these evil eye things carry attribute sacredness to *matakia* and legitimize them.

> I used to own *matakia*. I had a horseshoe some time ago, but now I use the cross ... I had the horseshoe hanging outside, above our front door, so that our house does not get the evil eye, because it is one of the nicest houses around ... and people also used to put red things, maybe ribbons ... they say, put a red object on you or in the house so that you do not get the evil eye ... But we removed the horseshoe at the end, because we were talking to our priest and he told us: 'These are satanic things; do not put them anywhere near your house, you have to hang the cross right away and maybe put a small red thread, which symbolizes the blood of Christ.'

Agapi, a seventy-year-old woman in northern Greece who is also a devoted Orthodox and trusts her local priest immensely, changed her material means of protection against the evil eye and her household, since the one she had chosen did not correlate with the principles of Orthodoxy, according to her trusted priest. At the same time, it might seem somewhat unforeseen that a priest would reject an evil eye amulet and suggest an equally unconventional – as far as the church practices are concerned – method of protection instead, that of the red ribbon. In this case, the unconventional material object was legitimized symbolically as an amulet by the priest, who, through representing the Church's religious authority, exercised his religious power by rejecting one object as 'satanic' and approving and attributing religious meaning to another, verifying it as an effective material means of spiritual prophylaxis.

'While religious authorities can easily say that an object has no power, I want to argue that Christians have not always listened to church authorities' (McDannell 1995: 26). Although this statement which refers to American society may contradict Agapi's attitude, it is true that people in Rethymno and Thessaloniki, both religious and non-religious individuals, frequently express disagreements with the Orthodox Greek Church. In fact, the latter has been repeatedly accused of being responsible for promoting consumerism and taking advantage of the believers. The extended material manipulation of religious belief in Tinos, in particular, and the unequivocally exploitative attitude of various monasteries, where people are in a way forced to buy icons, *komposhinia* (rosaries) and even *matakia* – all of which are supposed to have been sacralized, but in reality have probably not been, as some priests, monks and individuals who volunteer to aid at churches and monasteries have admitted to me – do not escape the attention of my interlocutors. 'I have been told that there are *matakia* in Tinos, here in Crete, and in monasteries around Greece. That is so bad. As far as I am concerned, they should not sell these things. I think this is happening due to marketing reasons', is how Sifis, a Rethymniot elderly man, has expressed his repulsion towards the situation.

Religiously oriented material objects are also embedded in Greek cultural spaces where they show a not so 'innocent' disposition of social circulation. The island of Tinos constitutes such a context. Every year on the 15th of August, the day of the Dormition of *Panagia* (Virgin Mary), thousands of Greeks and non-Greeks visit the island. The central church of Tinos, where one of the most miraculous icons of *Panagia* is to be found, is flooded by Orthodox and other Christian adherents. *Dekapentaugoustos*, the 15th of August that is, is extensively celebrated, as it is considered one of the most important days in Orthodox Christianity. My interlocutors who have visited the island on that day have referred to the multiplicity of amulets, evil eye objects and other relevant material objects one can buy in the market setup just outside the church of *Panagia*. 'If you walk along this street that leads all the way up to the *Panagia*'s church, you shall see all these peddlers selling evil eye amulets next to *Panagia*'s icons', a Rethymniot man told me. Most of the Greeks who have visited Tinos have been critical of this material co-habitation, especially because the sellers seem to them to be taking advantage of the sacredness of the day in the name of consumption and profit. Besides, for the devoted Christian I have talked to, items sold in such a way can never be sacralized and thus cannot be utilized as religious objects.

The bookshops that officially belong to the Church of Greece, which I discovered in my fieldsites, portray how Christianity has become commercialized in its quest for popularity. These belong to the Bishoprics of Rethymno and Thessaloniki, with direct links to the Orthodox Church of Greece, and are usually conveniently located close to Rethymno's and Thessaloniki's main churches. When one enters these bookshops, apart from the large variety of religious books that dominate the space, one can also find religious rosaries and amulets. For example, what caught my ethnographic gaze before going in-store of the bookshop of the Church of Greece in Thessaloniki was the existence of silver pomegranates – which are considered to be lay amulets and sold for good luck and against the evil eye – covered with decorative crystals, next to Christian icons in the shop window. Inside the shop, a big framed photo of the Archbishop dominated one corner, and, underneath the picture, a stand with rosaries and other small amulets, as well as icons, claimed a spatial presence. The most surprising items I discovered, however, were evil eye amulets that combined a cross with an evil eye; taking into consideration the fact that these shops represented the Orthodox Christian Church and its ideologies, meaning that the symbol of the evil eye would be rejected as non-ecclesiastic, the existence of such objects within the bookshops seemed religiously displaced yet strategically placed.

These bookshops have brought Christianity and the church closer to peoples' everyday life. Rethymniots and Thessalonikans have the chance to go for religious shopping to buy religious books, rosaries, icons, legitimized Christian amulets that are supposed to be sacralized at a church liturgy; at the same time, however, they sell, unofficially, lay-oriented objects that carry a vernacular religious meaning, such as the pomegranates mentioned above and even evil eye amulets that carry both the image of a cross, a Jesus or the Virgin and a blue eye bead (see Figure 19). These last objects are legitimized as Orthodox amulets, since they are found and potentially bought at official religious spaces, approved by the official Church authorities. They represent a novel material door that

Figure 19 An evil eye amulet, sold at an ecclesiastic shop.

has opened in the context of practising vernacular religion through materiality, which is indicative of a shift within the Church circles in their pursuit of a more popular presence in Greeks' everyday spiritual life.

When people buy icons, religious *matakia*, bottles of holy water, rosaries and other such objects from the street vendors of Tinos, in other Greek monasteries and churches and in the official Orthodox Church bookshops, they might not always believe in their sacred qualities. As many of Rethymniots and Thessalonikans have noted, even the crosses, *komposhoinia*, bottles of holy water and icons that are sold in monasteries, churches and official bookshops managed by Orthodox religious authorities in their cities respectively are most likely not sacralized. Yet, as McDannell (1995: 41) explains: 'The religious souvenir participates in the power of the original experience. Our modern commercial economy makes it easier to fabricate and purchase religious souvenirs, but the material ephemera of Christian history attest to the enduring need to re-experience religious memories through objects.' Religious visitors at Tinos, for example, treat those objects as religious souvenirs. Foreign tourists in Rethymno and Thessaloniki mostly treat religious *matakia* as Greek souvenirs, since these objects combine two primary symbols of Greek culture: that of the denominational religion in Greece and that of a popular Greek belief. Greeks can treat these objects as religious souvenirs, dismiss them for not being 'proper religious icons' and for possessing the evil eye symbol. More often than not, however, religious *matakia* are bought as prophylactic amulets, as icons that may not have been sacralized by a priest but still possess sacred qualities and offer protection against evil spiritual powers and the evil eye.

A male interlocutor of mine in Rethymno, who is the owner of a shop full of religious icons, evil eye amulets and religious *matakia*, made a noteworthy statement (see Figure 20). I was standing opposite a stand full of religious evil eye objects, observing a couple of them where the evil eye and Orthodoxy were clearly merging: a big, round, blue evil eye was hanging from religious icons of Jesus and *Panagia*. The owner came to stand next to me and we started discussing the meaning of those objects. A few seconds later he turned to me and said: 'Even if they [the evil eye and Orthodoxy] had not shared any kind of relationship up to now, well, now they do', pointing to the material co-inhabitation of religious icons and the evil eye in the space of his shop.

By putting an evil eye and a religious symbol materially together, a meaningful emergence, in physical, spatial and in ideological terms, arises. As my interlocutor eloquently asserted, the relationship they had carried before does not really matter any longer. What counts is their present co-existence, and the way in

Figure 20 Material co-inhabitation of religious icons and the evil eye.

which this interaction is interpreted, negotiated and practised by people. Two kinds of valuable evil eye-related signifieds exist: the material/commoditized on the one hand and the spiritual on the other (cf. Davenport 1986: 108). 'Icons tie the material world with the spiritual, material objects to abstract ideas. In one sense, of course, every religious object makes such a connection. But what is significant about icons for many of the devout is not the abstract meaning icons supposedly convey; rather, it is the experience of the spiritual world that they make possible' (Dubisch 1995: 72). As happens with icons, materiality and spirituality merge in the religious *matakia*. Being empowered by Christian symbolism and by the evil eye belief, these objects help people experience the spiritual world through a material pathway, and a new version of vernacular religion, through materiality, emerges.

Evil eye amulets and religious icons reside in the same physical space and interact inside their shared cultural space. Evil eye and Orthodox Christian ideology frequently co-inhabit material objects, which can then be interpreted as evil eye amulets, religious protective amulets or both. The market has the power to influence the consuming public and make the evil eye religious items popular. The churches, the monasteries and the shops that sell evil eye objects alongside religious items might have been thinking strategically: by putting the religious and the evil eye material realms together, they may hope that the Christian-related objects, with their symbolically carried sacredness, can – symbolically at least – transfer some of their religious sanctity to the *matakia*. But even if such a strategy is employed, people in Rethymno and Thessaloniki are generally aware of the cultural game, and they have the power to handle the objects: to choose what kind of amulets they should buy and what kind of meaning, religious, spiritual, commoditized, or a combination of all, they should endow the objects – and their vernacular religious value – with.

Material prophylaxes: Creating meaningful objects

Rethymniots and Thessalonikans mainly treat *matakia* as objects of prophylaxis against the power of *mati*. These objects vary. They are not necessarily things that incorporate the eye as a powerful symbol, although the eye objects dominate and are supposedly considered more spiritually and protectively powerful. They are not necessarily material. Bodily acts are also performed as a representation of a spiritualized prophylaxis. Any thing and any act that is implanted with the spiritual power to protect against a potential evil eye attack becomes a *mataki* amulet. Humans, animals, households, cars, shops, yards are all in need of protection. The amulets offer a prophylactic route to cultural security and personal and spiritual comfort.

Matakia, namely the evil eye material objects, can act as *fylahta*: as amulets which possess (spiritual) prophylactic power and protect people from the evil eye and other forms of negative energy. Religious icons, crosses and other objects with strong Orthodox symbolism can also be *fylahta* (amulets) and protect people from evil powers, especially the devil. At the same time, icons can also play a prophylactic role against the evil eye, while *matakia* can protect against the devil and other evil spiritual powers. Devoted Orthodox Rethymniots and Thessalonikans are usually the ones who prefer the use of religious *fylahta*, which, as they believe, can guard them against all forms of evil. Less observant

Orthodox believers and/or even atheists primarily prefer the use of *matakia* and New Age goods that they treat as protecting amulets. Consequently, there is a variety of dynamics in how people approach the evil eye material objects. Evil eye believers and non-believers, devoted Christians and atheists, or religious individuals who partly accept the evil eye in their lives all carry different opinions as to how to handle the objects, as to what is considered a commoditized object and/or an amulet, and how much religious symbolism, efficacy and spiritual power an item contains. What actually matters, and what makes those matters meaningful, is the spiritual power that *matakia*, as *fylahta*, are infused with, and how this power is interpreted by people.

> I think *matakia* help people. It is like you have a *fylahto* and you feel it protects you, or something that was given by a beloved friend to protect you; *matakia* function inside this logic. I do not have a *mataki*. I have amulets from time to time. If I am doing something that stresses me, I buy some objects. These objects I consider protective charms.

The distinction Nantia, a young woman in Thessaloniki, makes between *matakia* and amulets is worthy of note. She is someone who does not believe in the power of the evil eye. And it is for that reason, as she has explained to me, that she does not carry any form of protection against the evil eye. She does recognize that, unlike herself, some people can treat *matakia* as amulets. Yet, she is not certain whether these are effective or not. As she has specified, she frequently owns items, bought by her, or given to her by people she loves, some of which can be evil eye or New Age items, which she translates as amulets since she feels they possess a protective power against any kind of bad energy. These charms are her spiritual blanket: a material way to make her feel better in relation to what spiritually lies above. At the same time, however, Nantia claims that she would not adopt the same stance towards *matakia*, as their role is more circumscribed and she would feel trapped in a belief she does not really want to allow into her life and be dependent on. I have met quite a few people in both my ethnographic sites that choose to attribute the same kind of logic to the amulets. They believe that adopting them in their lives would mean accepting the evil eye as a practice. But, since they do not want to make the evil eye practice part of their lives, they prefer to buy other items and infuse them with alternative spiritual signifieds of efficacious prophylaxis. By transforming them into amulets, my informants are reassured that the objects will bring good fortune into their lives and protect them from negative energies, bad interpersonal influences and evil spiritual forces.

Aleksandra's aunt in Thessaloniki gave her two gold rings as protective charms against the evil eye: one with a blue bead, the other with two dolphins. Alexandra has not taken them off her finger since. From what she told me, her aunt sacralized the rings by reading prayers over them, and by wearing them during a church liturgy a few times. For Aleksandra, the two rings have sacred qualities and are covered with mysticism. They bear similarities to a religious fetish. As Aleksandra told me, they have protected her numerous times from people's evil eyes and negative energies. Her aunt sacralized them secretly, without seeking the help of a priest; therefore, Aleksandra thinks that the rings possess a spiritual power which is more mystical than religious, since it derives from her aunt's praying and not from an official Orthodox blessing. This lay sacralization performed by her aunt has been kept a secret, out of fear that these rings would lose their mystical protective power should the aunt's vernacular material sacralization be revealed; and because of their sacralized power, Aleksandra treats them with care and secrecy, for she believes they could be potentially dangerous should she not be careful in the handling of them. 'Those rings are my fetish', Aleksandra has remarked, insisting upon their spiritual, mystical, sacred and secret qualities.

Pietz (1985, 1987, 1988) is one of the most prominent theorists who has placed the notion of the fetish in the centre of their analysis. Fetishes, according to Pietz (1985: 14; 1988: 106), are material objects that are perceived by people as endowed with a mysterious power and which possess determinate values. The fetish, 'as an idea and as a problem, and as a novel object not proper to any prior discrete society, originated in the cross-cultural spaces of the coast of West Africa during the sixteenth and seventeenth centuries' (1985: 5). The term 'fetish' was first used in the fifteenth century by Portuguese traders on the West African coast. During the seventeenth century, it became a popular term among the rest of the European countries, indicating an object with a spiritual power of its own (1987: 24). The notion of the fetish, therefore, was constructed by European Christians and was used as a pejorative characterization against Africans, based on the assumption that African gods and spirits were not transcendental but immanent. The term 'fetish' is not used in this book in a derogatory sense, but rather as a notion that captures the power invested in objects. Like Aleksandra, quite a few of my interlocutors have referred to the notion in order to characterize certain material objects they have in their possession, which, as they believe, possess spiritual energies and which people in Rethymno and Thessaloniki utilize as amulets. Together with its usefulness in comprehending emic conceptualizations of material objects and their relation to the spiritual, the notion of the fetish can be useful in terms of etic analysis; it can help negotiate the relationship between immanence and transcendence, and between the material and the spiritual, by placing the multiple ambiguities of *matakia* under a clearer focus.

In general terms, Christians in Western countries perceive their religion as transcendental and criticize non-Western and non-Christian societies for the immanent orientation of their spiritual cosmos. However, at least as far as my research has allowed me to observe, the everyday cosmos of Greeks is transcendental and immanent, spiritual and material. Although sometimes Greek Orthodox believers struggle to keep their objects completely symbolic and not immanently occupied with spirits, their everyday spiritual practices show otherwise. This ambiguous stance of Rethymniots and Thessalonikans is particularly relevant in the ways in which they handle and perceive religious *fylahta*, icons and *matakia*.

I met Anastasia, a middle-aged devoted Christian, in Rethymno. She insisted upon the insignificance of the evil eye things. The only kind of amulets that really exist and are legitimized, she stated, are those objects that are infused with some kind of religious connotations: objects that are blessed during a church inauguration, or with Holy Oil which comes directly from the Patriarchate of Constantinople, material parts of the cloth of the Chancel Table and the like. She showed me her *fylahto*, which incorporates a small piece of the Holy Cross, as well as holy bread crumbs. Anastasia admitted that she used to own a *mataki*. Yet, after having asked the Bishop of Rethymno what she could do in order not to get the evil eye, and after he had forbidden her to use *matakia* that are sold in the market, she followed his suggestion. She created her *fylahto* by asking her local priest to provide her with wooden Holy Cross pieces. She then added a couple of holy breadcrumbs, wrapped the Holy Cross pieces and the holy bread in a cloth, and she has always carried her Christian legitimate *fylahto* with her ever since. Anastasia's *fylahto* is close to being a religious fetish. Its existence should not be revealed to other people, others should not touch it and should not even see it, as Anastasia asserted, or else its sacred power will be lost. Since Christianity is considered by Anastasia and by my other Orthodox observant informants as the ultimate protective force against the devil, they place most confidence in Orthodox Christian religious objects, their religious *fylahta* that is, where religious *matakia* are included, and their efficacious prophylaxis.

When I say I believe, I do not believe that an object can perform miracles. It is not the object that performs the miracle; it is the spirit that does it, it is God himself that does it. The *Panagia* icon we were talking about, which people say is sacred because it has sacred relics inside it ... why should the icon itself be sacred? It is the *Panagia* who, as a mother of God, is sacred and her spirit who protects us. If I pray to my own *Panagia* icon, she is the one who will perform the miracle for me, not the wood. That's why I'm telling you, it's not the material object I believe in.

In the above ethnographic account, Eleni, a middle-aged woman in Thessaloniki, asserts that it is the spirit of the *Panagia* that makes the icon powerful enough to perform miracles, and not just the wooden frame and the material icon as such. She denies the efficacy of the matter, while making a distinction between the efficacious importance of the material and the spiritual. She recognizes the role of the material only when it is endowed with meaning, and with particular qualities of belief. It is what the material object represents that is important, not the object as such. Pietz famously made a distinction between a fetish and idol. According to his analysis, a fetish consists of 'irreducible materiality' and is not an iconic representation of something else, whereas an idol is an iconic image of an immaterial and transcendent reality. As he writes: 'The truth of the fetish resides in its status as a material embodiment: its truth is not that of the idol, for the idols' truth lies in its relation of iconic resemblance to some immaterial model or entity' (Pietz 1985: 7). Drawing on Pietz's schema, icons are for Eleni more idols than fetishes. Yet, she also believes that it is through the material that a communication with the spiritual can be achieved.

Eleni also follows the Orthodox doctrinal view. The Orthodox doctrine makes a clear distinction between the material and spiritual qualities of an icon. According to the Seventh Ecumenical Council, icons should not be conceived as idols, and their veneration – and not worship – should be performed towards the holy figures represented and not to the icons' material existence (Kokosalakis 1995: 438). In the words of Bishop Kallistos Ware (1997 [1963]: 32): 'When an Orthodox kisses an icon or prostrates himself before it, he is not guilty of idolatry. The icon is not an idol but a symbol; the veneration shown to images is directed, not towards stone, wood and paint, but towards the person depicted.'

Yet, Orthodox believers pray to the holy figures depicted in the icons as if they were real live subjects (Kokosalakis 1995: 443). Indeed, plenty of my informants said to me that they talk to the holy figures depicted in their icons as if they were members of their family. They talk to them as immanent beings of the natural world. The material presence of the icons is important to them. They want to feel the icons. By touching them, people in Rethymno and Thessaloniki feel the icons' spiritual power. They also believe that some of the icons' sacredness is transmitted through tactile communication with their owners. Deviating from the doctrinal Orthodox beliefs on idolatry, my informants implicitly attribute animacy to them, while recognizing their spiritual power and transcendental presence as well as the importance of their materiality. Rethymniots and Thessalonikans treat religious icons as both idols and fetishes. Religious and spiritually syncretic *matakia* are treated in the same way. In fact, these objects are considered powerful and are believed to be multiply efficacious for they depict religious figures, the evil eye and/or New Age symbols. By wearing them on their bodies, holding them or simply gazing at their material presence, my informants admit they feel their material as well as their spiritual presence of these objects, which can protect them against all forms of spiritual threat.

As has been analysed so far, there are three kinds of evil eye objects, of *matakia*, that is: the 'classic' protective evil eye charms, usually made of blue glass or plastic, which depict an eye; the religious *matakia*, most of which combine an eye symbol with a Christian symbol, but some people may also utilize religious objects (such as crosses or other types of religious *fylahta*) as evil eye prophylactic items; and there are the *matakia* that amalgamate New Age ideologies with an evil eye symbol, and, sometimes, with a cross or an icon too. With the exception of the deeply devoted Christians, who reject *matakia* from the start, the majority of the individuals I met recognize the power of all three forms of *matakia*, as long as these are sacralized in some way. Sacralization through blessing from a priest is a normal practice for religious icons and religious *fylahta*, even if they are used for protection against the evil eye – as in Anastasia's case. But since the Church does not officially recognize the evil eye symbol, *matakia* need to follow other pathways to become sacralized. In addition to the priestly power, there is the lay power that can turn a material thing that lacks any other signifieds into an object of spiritual power, into a charm of spiritual prophylaxis.

For the adherents of the Pentecostal Charismatic Church that Meyer (1998) has studied in Ghana all commodities are fetishes which threaten the personal identity and integrity of their owners. The only road to defetishization is through prayer (Meyer 1998: 751, 752). Meyer refers to an incident where a local priest had sexual dreams after buying a pair of underpants in the local market.

When he threw the object away, the dreams stopped. After his experience, he asked all his church members to say a prayer over every purchased commodity they owned, before entering their homes. They were to ask God to sanctify the things they had bought, and by doing so they would prevent any destructive powers already incorporated in the object from damaging the owner's life (1998: 752).

Whereas Ghanaian Pentecostalists want to eradicate any spiritual powers from materialities, defetishize them through prayer and turn them into mere commodities, in the case of *matakia* a reverse procedure seems to be taking place. Rethymniots and Thessalonikans use Christian prayers to turn the evil eye objects into charms, aiming to infuse the commodities with spiritual prophylactic power; they turn the evil eye materialities into fetishes. Furthermore, neither Pietz's distinction between a fetish and an idol nor Orthodoxy's doctrinal views seem to be relevant for my ethnographic findings. During their everyday practice, my interlocutors treat all three forms of *matakia* as being endowed with both material and spiritual qualities. The images depicted on *matakia* (whether these are eye shapes, crosses or Orthodox figures), their symbolisms and connotations, and their potential spiritual power are crucial for my interlocutors. At the same time, however, their presence as material objects is considered equally important. Rethymniots and Thessalonikans want to touch, see, feel the materiality of their charms on their body; they need to sense a *fylahto*'s spiritual power in a tactile way. *Matakia* can be characterized as both idols and fetishes; for the majority of my interlocutors, *matakia*'s image depictions and their materiality are both thought to be spiritually powerful.

Ultimately, it is about how people in Rethymno and Thessaloniki create meaningful objects. *Matakia* lose and earn meaning constantly, depending on how they are handled by individuals. Besides, 'their meanings are inscribed in their forms, their uses, their trajectories' (Appadurai 1986: 5). Sometimes people accept *matakia* that have already been loaded with evil eye meaning. At other times they discard the initial meaning and create their own instead. Goods structure perception and facilitate social interaction (Howes 1996: 2). It is the perception of things and the modes in which they are related to the evil eye practice, in addition to how people operate inside this mobilized materiality, that leads the *matakia* charms to meaningful trajectories. People and objects are 'so complexly intertwined that they cannot be disentangled' (Hoskins 1998: 2). This close relationship, together with the emotional reactions to objects, and their sensory handling, renders the material meanings ascribed by individuals multiple and divergent.

New Age Spirituality and *matakia* in the spiritual supermarket

Rethymno is a tourist town. Thousands of foreign visitors overflow this popular Cretan town, especially during the summer and autumn months. Those tourists bring foreign and popular socio-cultural tendencies from all over the world. New Age spirituality constitutes an example of such global trends. Most of the Rethymniot shops that sell healing crystals, oil, incense, feng shui and evil eye objects were initially established, according to their owners, mainly for the benefit of the foreign tourists. Gradually, the shops began to attract Greek tourists and locals, many of whom are now well acquainted with and initiated in New Age spirituality. When it comes to Thessaloniki, New Age shops, yoga centres and alternative healing spaces have gained increasing popularity in the last decade or more. In these spaces, some of the most commonly found material objects are amulets that combine a religious symbol with a blue eye bead and a New Age symbol (see Figure 21). These objects are hardly considered 'spiritually appropriate' by the Church, priests and devoted Orthodox adherents. Yet, they have become an alternative version of a simple evil eye bead, and these are very popular with both New Age practitioners and loose religious Orthodox believers, many of whom find such amulets spiritually effective, and buy them for themselves or to offer them as presents to their loved ones as material protections against all sources of negative energy and the evil eye.

A female Rethymniot in her mid-forties, who owns a New Age shop in the Old Town of Rethymno, has been quite explicit in her attempt to establish a connection between what hides behind the evil eye and the world we live in. What initially attracted me to enter her shop were, as usual, the various evil eye objects hanging from a wooden stand: from the 'classic' bracelets and key rings to the more impressive silver hands of Fatima and other symbols which were combined with eye beads. Moving inside, the place was full of healing rocks and spiritual crystals, Chinese and Indian artefacts, feng shui objects, incense and a variety of other New Age objects. The owner clarified that she holds a diploma in feng shui and went on to explain to me that every human being has an aura, which can be either positive or negative, and which aura s/he transmits to others. The energy of someone's aura affects people, it influences them, and as a result they feel the symptoms of the evil eye on their bodies. The absorbing visit to her shop came to an end, after she showed me which crystals can be used as a protection against the evil eye, as well as against stronger forms of energy attack.

Creative Syntheses through Material Culture 137

Figure 21 A New Age spiritual symbol meets the evil eye at a spiritual healing centre.

She told me that many tourists visit her shops, but 'I also have local clients, who come here. Some of them are religious, Orthodox, you know. And they don't come just to buy a present for their friends' birthdays, which they also do. They also come just for a coffee, and we just sit down, and we talk about feng shui, energy, the evil eye, spirituality … about all these spiritual things'.

In his comparative study about New Age shops in Israel and in New Zealand, Zaidman (2007) observed that New Age is enjoying a gradual development in both countries. More and more New Age shops were opening, in both major and small towns. A wide range of New Age goods were available in the marketplace, and people were attracted to buy them. The most popular objects, found in both Israel and New Zealand, were incense, crystals and oils. In each one of the two countries, however, one could additionally find goods that are associated with its national religion (Zaidman 2007: 259–60). New Age shops, as it seems, adapted their best-selling stock in such a way that they comfortably accommodated the already familiar religious field, while adapting to the globalized needs of people to shop for New Age goods. New Age Greek shops work equivalently. In the Rethymniot and Thessalonikan cases, Christian, New Age and evil eye objects are not only brought spatially and socially together, but they very often become one item. The stock of goods under sale is adapted to cover for the current needs of the spiritual marketplace, which, especially during the last decade, depends significantly on the circulation of New Age spiritual objects. At the same time, an attempt is made to familiarize the mostly 'foreign' connotations and uses of these objects, but introducing them into a safe symbolic space where the evil eye and religious items already reside.

While I was in Thessaloniki, I discovered a shop that sold exclusively different types of stones and crystals, which were meant to be used for spiritual healing purposes, as well as a large variety of *matakia*. The owner, a polite middle-aged man, was very willing to discuss both my evil eye research and his 'energetic stones', as he called them. He even took a book out of a desk drawer, which dealt with the shared intimacy between the stones and a person's star sign; then, he offered his advice on which stones would be good for a Piscean's (my star sign) prosperity and health. The conversation turned to the evil eye. He pointed to an object with an eye glass bead, a small silver Christ and a silver garlic all combined on it. I asked Kostas what he thought about the synthesis of an evil eye, a religious figure and a good luck symbol. His reply was that he did not mind the mix, as long as there were religious symbols evidently placed on the objects. He immediately declared that if these protective things carried symbols from China, for instance, he would never accept them. But since they carried sacred symbols instead, these material objects could definitely function as amulets.

Kostas recognizes the evil eye as an 'alternative form of spirituality', as he put it, but he thinks that it is not so different from the official religious practices of Orthodoxy, from other 'practical ways, such as garlic' to ward off evil powers, the devil and negative energies or from healing stones. He therefore is not against the idea of an evil eye material amalgamation in terms of spirituality, as long as such material synthesis does not escape the Greek cultural boundaries; in that way, one's identity cannot face intra-cultural hazards. His rhetoric against foreign spiritual influences, however, is incompatible with his actions. His shop is predominantly occupied by the presence of healing stones that carry energy and spiritual power, and he is aware of the New Age connections these objects carry. These goods are not 'officially' consistent with Orthodoxy, and up until recently they have not been part of any kind of Greek spiritual practice. They represent and belong to a recently developed New Age cultural wave that has not been inherently Greek, but which, nevertheless, has become an integral part of the changing Greek spiritual landscape at the level of vernacular religiosity.

In North America, the New Age movement is explicitly condemned by many Christians. For them, New Age is a '"pagan" religion combining the egocentric follies of secular humanism and the evil machinations of the devil' (McDannell 1995: 264). As a consequence, crystals, herbal medicines, tarot cards and the rest of the New Age material culture 'present a serious religious rival to the biblical orientation of conservative Christians' (1995: 264). Conservative Greek Orthodox Christians also condemn New Age material culture. However, in general terms, people in my fieldsites, who range from religious disciples to atheists, appear to be sympathetic towards the material combination of New Age and evil eye ideologies. Many of the Cretans and northern Greeks I have interviewed buy these *matakia* so that they bring positive energy to their house, which they have decorated according to the rules of feng shui. Many times, they place *matakia* and New Age objects next to religious icons. They regard these *matakia* as amulets that can protect them from the evil eye, from the devil and from all types of negative energy.

In present-day Greece, the popularity of evil eye and New Age material objects continues to grow, and, at least most of the people I met in my fieldsites, appear to be eclectic and shop in the spiritual market (Sharma 1993: 17). The rising consumerist market of New Age and evil eye goods can be considered to be a 'religious consumerist supermarket, which thrives in the competition and the offer of various spiritual goods' (York 2001: 367). The idea of the 'spiritual supermarket', especially in relation to the New Age, has often been used in a negative and even derogatory manner; yet, as Bowman (1999: 182; c.f. Redden 2016: 232) asserts, it is an 'accurate, value-free characterization of the contemporary situation, in which many people are experiencing greater religious consumer choice than ever before due to globalized spiritual commodification'. It furthermore indicates the significance of New Age spirituality in the public sphere (Aupers and Houtman 2006). Cretans and northern Greeks are presented with an ample choice of New Age and evil eye goods, being given the freedom to look and shop around the spiritual supermarket of contemporary Greek religiosity, according to their individual spiritual needs. The presence of New Age materialities in Greece signifies a material intimacy among religion, spirituality and the evil eye in a spiritual supermarket that constantly renews its stock of material goods and leads vernacular religiosity towards novel spiritual directions.

The materiality of the evil eye is indicative of a change in contemporary Greece. Religious icons, evil eye beads and New Age symbols co-habit material objects and spaces. And this is not a co-habitation that lacks interaction. When a Jesus icon and an eye-shaped glass bead amalgamate into one single item, the signifieds and the symbolisms they carry merge as well. Before these spiritually synthesized objects made a distinct appearance in the Greek market and gained such popularity, Orthodox, evil eye and New Age symbolisms were hard to find in combination and co-habitation. People occasionally wore a golden crucifix and an evil eye bead together; yet, these were two different objects, which could easily and immediately be separated. Of course, the choice of putting a religious and an evil eye symbol together is particularly important. It is a practice that continues to date which is of great significance as far as the renewed affinity between Orthodoxy, spirituality and the evil eye is concerned.

The interaction between evil eye, Christian and New Age spiritual symbolisms has only emerged in very recent years. This phenomenon constitutes a material representation of a spiritual mobility in contemporary Greece, and of a movement towards new spiritual itineraries that are not exclusively Orthodox. My research has discovered *matakia*, *matakia* with religious icons and other Orthodox depictions, *matakia* which are New Age oriented. This newly revived material presence in vernacular religious practice designates the complex way in which people believe, practise and imaginatively negotiate the evil eye; moreover, it vividly portrays the strong position the evil eye inhabits between Orthodoxy and New Age spirituality.

6

The pluralistic landscape of Greek religiosity: Religion and spirituality at a Global Age

In one of the most central and busiest streets of Thessaloniki, the sign 'Feng Shui World' caught my ethnographic attention, once again (see Figure 22). I had passed in front of this shop a couple of times already and it was either crowded, which meant that I would not really have the chance to gain a lot of information from the owners, or closed. One day I found it empty, at last, and I stepped inside. Instead of the Chinese couple of owners I had glimpsed before, a Greek young woman was there to offer her assistance. I was disappointed; I would have preferred the Chinese owners to be present, so that I could extract more useful ethnographic data – or so I thought. The shop assistant, when I explained about my research and asked whether she would be kind enough to answer some of my questions, replied that, although the Chinese owner of the shop was not around, she would be happy to discuss the evil eye subject with me. She proved to be Cretan, a detail which surprised and pleased me at the same time; it was a link between my fieldsites that could not pass unnoticed. Perceiving this coincidence as a sign that I was on the right ethnographic path, we talked about feng shui, the evil eye and spiritual energy. Maria told me that the idea of the evil eye had always existed in her family, but she never fully believed in it. Since she started working in the feng shui shop and was constantly dealing with the idea of energy and the ways in which it is manifested spiritually, her relationship with the evil eye had become persistently stronger.

Meanwhile, my attention was immediately caught by the wall behind the desk where Maria was sitting: it was fully covered by a carpet with Chinese ideograms, and a *mataki* was hung on it (see Figure 23). This was an image that represented symbolically not just Maria's own shift in her relationship with feng shui and the evil eye, but also how the evil eye has shifted to include New Age spirituality in the core of its practice. I asked Maria about the reason why the owners chose to bring an evil eye in their feng shui shop and make the two co-inhabit the

Figure 22 'Feng Shui World'.

same space materially and spiritually. Maria replied that this mostly has to do with energy, since, as the Chinese owner and his wife have explained to her, the Chinese people believe in the existence of energy. *Mati*, she continued, according to her, to the Chinese owners and most of their Greek clients, is exactly that: an exchange of energy among people. Therefore, the evil eye is introduced alongside feng shui, as both are practices that involve energy; it has also been an attempt on behalf of the Chinese owner to indicate the degree of cultural sameness between the Chinese culture and Thessalonikan culture. Drawing his clients' gaze on the carpet with the Chinese ideogram and the evil eye, and placing feng shui and evil eye objects in such a way that they amalgamate spatially, symbolically and spiritually, the owner has aimed for a strategy to incorporate his own cultural conceptualization of energy through feng shui into the concept of energy of a Greek popular belief, creating a performative representation of cultural and spiritual hybridity.

Konstantina, a female Cretan interlocutor in her mid-thirties, has described persuasively this hybrid relationship between the evil eye and New Age spiritual

Figure 23 Eastern spirituality meets the evil eye.

practices: 'Feng shui and the like are the same as *mati*. Well, feng shui has now become fashionable, but, actually, it is like the evil eye in a different form.' Alexia, a female student in Thessaloniki, has expressed a similar opinion. We were eating in a Chinese restaurant one afternoon in Thessaloniki, with a couple of other young people, when the discussion turned, as usual, to the topic of my research. Alexia then stated that she does not believe in the evil eye, most likely because it has never happened to her. Yet, she thinks that both the evil eye and feng shui are fashionable in contemporary Greece. If she were to provide an explanation, she told me, she would say it is all about negative energy that is transmitted between people. 'Since we are in a Chinese restaurant, let me tell you that I accept feng shui. Actually, the evil eye is something like feng shui, isn't it? It is all about energy.'

Feng shui is one of the most popular practices I encountered in the field, and it claims a highly fashionable position within the Greek vernacular practice of New Age spirituality. Being part of oriental medicine and philosophy, it is 'based on the premise that along with all the physical aspects of our world that we can see, hear, touch, smell and taste, there is a movement of a subtle flow of electromagnetic energy' (Brown 1996: 1). Like the evil eye, it is based on the existence of energy within and outside the realm of the sensory. *Mati* and feng shui have both been conceived by people in Rethymno and Thessaloniki as following parallel spiritual paths: they are both founded on fields of energy. This link is primarily established by younger Rethymniots and Thessalonikans, aged between twenty and forty years old, students and young professionals. In addition to their treatment of both the feng shui and the evil eye as fashionable spiritual practices, they regard the presence of feng shui in Greece as a sign that the country is part of a globalizing world and of a changing religious landscape that pushes the evil eye into global trends, accommodating non-Orthodox spiritual pathways. This link, furthermore, demonstrates for them one's ability to escape social, personal, spiritual and religious narrow-mindedness by embracing, or simply claiming awareness about, a spiritual practice that originates outside the context of Greek religiosity – it hence symbolically transforms a person into a citizen of the world. Taking a commonly held Greek belief, such as the evil eye, and uniting it with an internationally known spiritual ideology, such as the feng shui, the evil eye is spiritually appropriated in such a way that is pushed onto a globalized spiritual market, creating a new breed of pluralistic religiosity.

New religious pluralism, globalization and spiritual transcendence

As Mapril and Blanes (2013: 4) assert: 'In countries such as Spain, Portugal, Italy and Greece religious pluralism was always present, but simultaneously obscured by hegemonic and repressive regimes with specific strategies concerning religious adherence and manifestation.' A few excellent ethnographies have been published in recent years, which demonstrate the changing religious landscapes of southern European countries where Christianity used to play the role of the hegemonic and dominant state religion. These works show that in the last decades Christianity and New Age spirituality appear to experience a co-existence rather than rupture in vernacular religious practice (see, among others, Palmisano 2010; Fedele 2012; Cornejo-Valle 2013; Roussou 2013; Clot-Garrell and Griera 2019). When it comes to Greece, more specifically, I do not wish to argue that the country had a homogeneous religious past, where Christianity was dominant, and pluralism was not part of the spiritual picture. Yet, my research has revealed that the contemporary Greek spiritual field has reached a new age of pluralism, where the dominant religion, namely Orthodox Christianity, still possesses a central role, but its boundaries have become more fluid to allow interaction with globalized spiritual influences such as the New Age at the level of vernacular religiosity.

The spiritual landscape of contemporary Greece, at least the one I managed to observe during my fieldwork and my subsequent visits to Greece, has been through a process of 'easternization'. Greeks recognize 'the importance of Eastern religious themes in what is usually called "New Age spirituality" and their general spread into the wider culture' (Bruce 2002: 118). This is a Western socio-cultural phenomenon that Bruce characterizes as 'the Easternization of the West'. This process of 'easternization', which has claimed a part in Rethymniots' and Thessalonikans' vernacular religious life, does not denote a shift to the secular. Orthodoxy is still present in Rethymniot and Thessalonikan everyday practices. 'Easternization' signifies that global trends have invaded the Greek religious landscape. Consequently, the way people interpret and manifest their spiritual actions has become more pluralistic.

Peter Berger (2007: 19) has provided a convincing argument where he links the new emergence of religious pluralism with the effects of globalization. This 'new religious pluralism', as he calls it, has implications on two levels. The first level is institutional: the clergy loses its socially given authority, and lay people become active agents in a religious market that is constantly seeking new religious clientele (2007: 21). The second level is cognitive: individuals can choose their religion, which is not a taken-for-granted part of their consciousness any longer, but is freely chosen and subjectivized (2007: 23). The pluralism I ethnographically discovered in Greece can be interpreted as a phenomenon that belongs to a process of globalization, having derived from the articulation of global socio-cultural and spiritual influences. Ever since 2005, when my fieldwork started, and I gained the opportunity to closely observe how Greeks practise their spiritual quests for more than a decade now, and how they express their selves through it, the quest for new globalized spiritual confrontations has seemed present. Rethymniots and Thessalonikans have begun to develop novel spiritual paths and test their religious aspirations, in relation to or independently of Orthodoxy, in terms of discourse, practice and belief. As a result, the contemporary Greek spiritual identity is no longer rigidly attached to Orthodox Christianity.

Despite the fact that Orthodox Christianity and globalization share a long historical and social trajectory (see Roudometof 2014), the Orthodox Greek Church has resisted globalization, which can allegedly lead to secularization. The idea of secularization, which has resuscitated the perception that 'God is dead', a phrase that Nietzsche had famously employed theoretically in order to describe the decline of people's belief in God (see Bruce 2002: 60–74), has been strongly criticized by social scientists. As Berger, one of the most well-known social scientists who strongly support the theory of desecularization,[1] puts it, 'The assumption that we live in a secularized world is false. The world today, with some exceptions, is as furiously religious as it ever was, and in some places more so than ever' (Berger 1999: 2; cf. Bhargava 1998: 1). And perhaps religious institutions might have lost their power in many societies, Berger (1998) continues. However, people in their everyday lives continue to be influenced by old and new religious beliefs and practices. Luckmann (1990: 127) agrees that religion is well established in the modern world. He sees human experience as a continuous flow of 'little', 'intermediate' and 'great' transcendences, which are organized and controlled differently in different societies. 'Modern social constructions of religious significance shifted away from the "great" other-worldly transcendences to the "intermediate" and also to the minimal transcendences of modem solipsism, whose main themes tend to bestow a sacred status upon the individual' (1990: 127).

Greece is experiencing a socio-cultural and spiritual transcendence. This transcendence is not constituted by the movement from Orthodox Christianity towards a secularized state. The strictly confined boundaries that doctrinal Orthodoxy and its adherents had been building up have lost their sturdiness in contemporary Greece. Actually, the boundaries have almost collapsed, leaving the ground free for religious creativity and new spiritual confrontations. Despite its gradual disengagement from religion, the Greek state is still deeply intertwined with Orthodox Christianity and the politics involved in the relationship between them. As has been shown earlier in the book, Orthodoxy and spirituality go hand in hand, and many factors have contributed greatly to an Orthodox turn towards more mystical and popular spiritual paths. Orthodoxy, hence, is not all about liturgical dogmas and canonical ritualisms, but can be spiritually creative and open to mysticism. The inflow of New Age spirituality in the Greek religious landscape has been subtle. At the same time, Greeks in my fieldsites do not take Orthodoxy's supremacy for granted; they still appear to be capable of making free spiritual choices, without being extremely influenced by the Church's official discourse and resistance towards globalization and secularization.

Resisting religion, embracing spirituality

In 2015, United Nations decided to declare 21st June as the International Day of Yoga. After receiving the news, the Holy Synod of Greece, namely the official body of Orthodox Christianity, communicated officially its condemn of the practice of yoga, due to the fact that belongs to another spiritual tradition, incompatible to Orthodoxy. Similar official Orthodox reactions continued in the next years. In 2017, for example, an Orthodox Bishop of a city close to Thessaloniki made a declaration that yoga does not correlate with Orthodox faith since it is based on spiritual traditions and beliefs that belong to non-Christian religious principles.[2] This declaration went viral among Orthodox circles and strict Orthodox believers, who applauded such an opinion against 'all this New Age spiritual nonsense', as a Thessalonikan Orthodox devotee commented to me, while we were discussing the Bishop's words. In 2018 and 2019 many more Bishops as well as local priests voiced an official opinion about yoga and other similar spiritual practices, using characterizations such as 'dangerous trends' and that 'these are satanic things'. Lectures have been organized against yoga and other non-Orthodox practices. Religious blogs, which bare nationalistic undertones emphasizing on the concept of 'Helleno-Orthodoxy', are becoming popular among strictly dogmatic Orthodox circles, clergy and adherents.[3] It appears that the additional visibility yoga gained after 2015 had begun to threaten the religious authority of the Orthodox Church and the clergy, both officially and at the level of vernacular practice.

Yoga has come up in the course of many discussions I had with people in both my fieldsites. There appears to be a kinship between yoga and the evil eye, which mainly has to do with the way energy is communicatively circulated in both. As Strauss (2005) remarks, yoga can accept multiple definitions. It mainly has to do with the development of one's wellbeing, health and spirituality. It can be an attitude, a philosophy, a set of practices or a way of being in the world (Strauss 2005: 2). Yoga originated in India. However, nowadays it has become an integral part of contemporary ideologies and practices all over the world. In the words of the anthropologist: 'Yoga can be understood as a practical method for acquiring spiritual capital' (2005: 9). The practice of yoga is very popular among most of my Rethymniot and Thessalonikan interlocutors, who link yoga practice to the evil eye, by expressing the opinion that they both have to do with energy and with a communication with something spiritual. Younger women and men of a middle-class background, between their mid-twenties and forties, have seemed especially keen to regularly attend yoga classes. Their religious identity ranges from those who have rejected Orthodox Christianity to those who attend Church liturgies from time to time; and from those who believe in the evil eye and have had *ksematiasma* performed on them to those who completely deny *mati*'s existence, or who are completely indifferent towards everything and approach yoga, and the evil eye too, out of simple curiosity.

'The yoga centre was in the basement. Every time I went down the stairs, I could see this huge icon of Christ hanging from the wall in the entrance. You know, basically to prevent people from thinking that yoga is something *parathriskeftiko* (New Age).' This is how Melina, a woman in her mid-twenties, spatially described the place where she practises yoga in Thessaloniki. The owner of the yoga centre is her friend. Placing an icon that is obviously linked to and represents Orthodoxy in such an obvious place has been strategically and meaningfully used, in order to bring two religious cosmologies together into a peaceful co-existence and possible spiritual synthesis. Yoga is not simply an Indian spiritual practice that has nothing common with Orthodoxy. Quite the opposite: they are both concerned with a quest for the spiritual. Melina's friend adapted yoga in such a way that it would fit into the Greek context.

> I think it mainly has to do with our thought. But I have heard from a friend of mine, who teaches yoga, that our body functions as a positive and negative pole. That is, you are able, through bodily contact, to move the energy around in a circular way. And the pole that is superior influences both people who participate in the circle.

This is how Danai, a woman in Thessaloniki, describes her experience with yoga, as she has practised it with the help of a friend. She provides an explanatory model with regard to the origins of the evil eye. In yoga, the human body holds both positive and negative energy. It is the interaction with another person, and his/her own energy, that determines whether the energy exchange between them shall be positive or negative. If negative energy prevails, the evil eye may occur. Some of my interlocutors in Rethymno and Thessaloniki, who are Christian devotees, have placed yoga under the umbrella of New Age and have characterized it as non-Christian and non-religious. Others, who attend church liturgies quite often and define themselves as good Christians, but who are also ideologically open to accept the existence of non-Orthodox spiritual practices, are more flexible. Although they do not usually practise yoga themselves, and if they do it is only for exercise purposes, they respect people who take up yoga as a physical as well as a spiritual practice. I have met yoga practitioners who are relatively or quite religious; however, what the Church thinks does not really appear to matter much to them. They do not see anything wrong in practising yoga on Sunday afternoons, after having attended a liturgy. They do not see anything wrong in synthesizing spiritualities.

Reiki is another popular practice that bears a particular resemblance to *ksematiasma*. As people in Thessaloniki and Rethymno have observed, both are types of healing based on the channelling of energy. Afroditi, for example, a Rethymniot woman in her fifties, is an Orthodox believer. She always wears a golden chain with a cross and a *mataki* on her neck. She thinks that the evil eye healing is based on Orthodoxy, and it is this communication with the sacred during *ksematiasma* that helps her heal people. At the same time, Afroditi is in favour of eastern spiritual philosophy. She is keen on yoga, and she believes that energy circulation constitutes one major function of the world. But what regards as more important in her spiritual pathways is that she is a reiki healer. Eastern spirituality is part of her everyday way of living. So is Orthodoxy. The embrace of yoga, reiki, orthodox prayers and *ksematiasma* 'collapses time and space within embodied practice, conjoining disparate pasts from different places within a particular present' (Klassen 2005: 378). Through their embodied practices, Afroditi and the rest of my interlocutors who have adopted both Orthodoxy and New Age spirituality in their lives create a spiritually pluralized present that collapses the boundaries between Orthodox Christianity and eastern spirituality, and, most importantly, they amalgamate those seemingly very different cosmologies into one.

Athina is a Thessalonikan shop owner in her sixties. I discovered her feng shui shop as I was walking around my Thessalonikan neighbourhood. The window was full of small Chinese objects, labelled according to their potential usage. They promised positive developments in the love domain, spiritual growth, good luck and good health. One glass ball caught my eye. The label next to it declared: 'Protection against the evil eye.' Intrigued, I entered the shop. She asked me how she could help, and I explained how interesting I found the glass ball in her shop window, since this was the topic of my research. She was very willing to assist. She took the ball out of the window so that I could have a closer look and stated that this was the feng shui object for protection against the evil eye (see Figure 24). Then, she pointed towards the glass eyes, *matakia* that were hanging from a wall. When asked if these Greek-style *matakia* were also

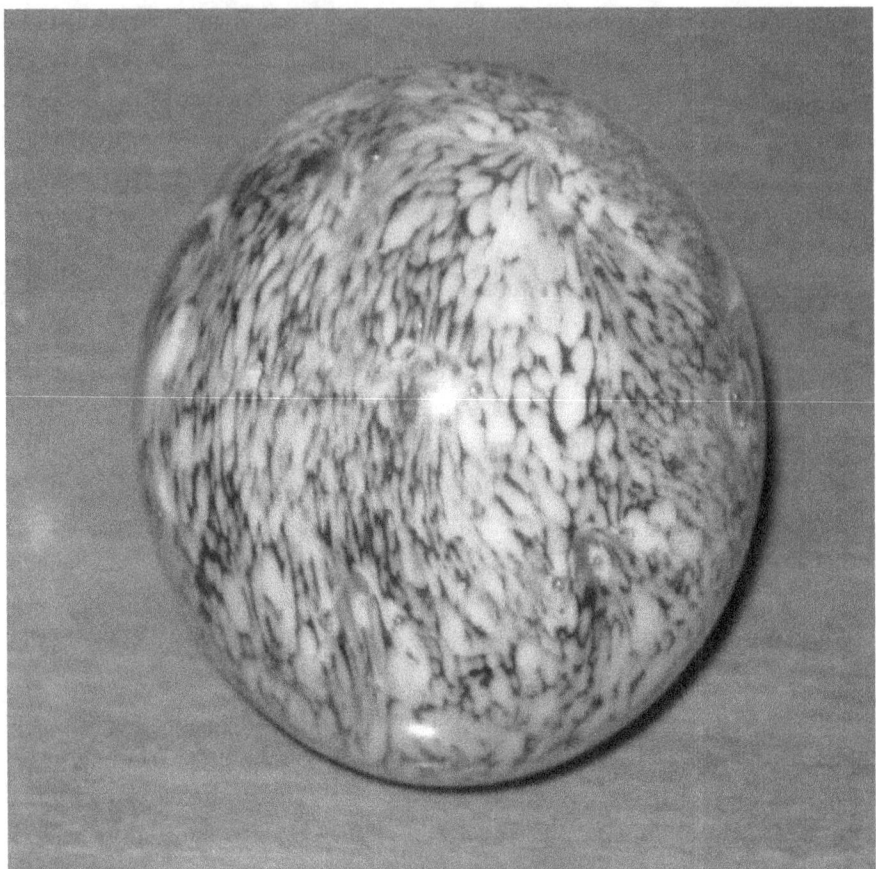

Figure 24 Feng shui protective object against the evil eye.

considered part of the feng shui practice, she replied by showing me an object which was composed of two small silver figures next to a *mataki*, a feng shui item that, as Athina explained, is usually bought because it offers prosperity in romantic relationships. Apart from its aid with marriages and relationships, this object skilfully depicted marriage between two cultures: feng shui and the evil eye had found each other.

Before I left, I noticed a couple of objects displaying an intimacy already encountered in the field: combined religious icons and evil eye things were standing opposite me once again. When I enquired about these, Athina replied that 'the Church believes in *vaskania*'. Then, she proceeded to explain that, when she first opened the feng shui shop, she was uncertain whether it would be accepted by Orthodox Christianity. Being religious herself, she asked her confessor[4]: 'Father, what shall I do? People ask for feng shui objects.' The priest came to visit the shop, so as to look at the objects and offer his opinion on their spiritual suitability. Since, as she clarified, he did not see anything that would insult Orthodoxy, and since people wanted these objects, he gave his permission. Athina was relieved and carried on with the final arrangements for opening her feng shui establishment.

Perhaps it was only this specific priest who did not see any conflict arising between Orthodoxy and feng shui practice. Still, this ethnographic incident is indicative of the fact that feng shui is not necessarily perceived by priests as spiritually threatening at a level of vernacular religious practice. Athina is a religious woman; therefore, her explanation that she wanted to open the shop to help people find what they want seems to have touched the priest's humanitarian feelings. If lay people want feng shui objects, they should have them. Maybe the priest did not realize the spiritual signifieds that feng shui objects can carry. Perhaps, he did not determine that feng shui objects depict a path to spirituality which could be in conflict with doctrinal Orthodoxy. The significance, however, does not lie in the reasons why the priest let Athina open her shop. The importance of what happened rests on the fact that a priest walked into Athina's establishment, saw the feng shui things, saw *matakia*, saw the material combination of the two and did not feel any spiritual danger. Whether he was the exception to the orthodox rule, or not, this was one more incident I encountered during my fieldwork which demonstrates that Orthodoxy and the Church have lowered their strictly doctrinal walls. It is a sign that Orthodox Christianity and New Age spirituality are not, or no longer, at cultural war. On the contrary, they can ideologically and performatively co-exist, interact and mix.

As many of my interlocutors have observed, when one goes to the priest and asks him to read a prayer against the evil eye, the process is the same as the one followed by the lay evil eye healer, the yoga teacher or the reiki alternative healer. Namely, they all use sacred symbolism, varying from religious icons and the cross to yin and yang and other alternative spiritual symbols; it is this combination of sacred symbols, in addition to utilizing a discourse about exchanging and distributing sacred energy, which leads to successful healing. In general, my research in Crete and northern Greece showed how people in Greece combined the more widespread and religiously accepted belief in the evil eye with alternative healing practices such as yoga and reiki, the use of New Age spiritual objects and the concept of energy and feng shui ideologies, among others (see Figure 25). Without being fully aware of it yet, they had already been using a globalized spiritual influence, that of the New Age discourse and

Figure 24 A conscious spiritual amalgamation of New Age and Orthodoxy.

ideology, in their practices of vernacular religiosity. The evil eye has offered them a 'religiously correct' opening of ritual performativity and, simultaneously, a vehicle to believe beyond the official ecclesiastical ideology, while creating a spiritual entanglement between Christian and world religious practices.

Believing and belonging

When talking about the evil eye, Rethymniots and Thessalonikans have continually talked about belief (*pisti*): belief in the evil eye, belief in God, belief in religion, belief in spiritual forces, belief in energy exchange, belief in the supernatural. My interlocutors have presented their various forms of believing, while describing how their beliefs, and according to what and who they believe, affect their stance towards the evil eye. At the same time, in the course of talking about their belief, Rethymniots and Thessalonikans have willingly or less explicitly situated themselves in the cosmos. They have shown how the evil eye inhabits a physical, or embodied, space, a 'location where human experience takes on material form' (Low and Lawrence-

Zuñiga 2003: 2). And how it also populates a spiritual space: an area situated beyond the scientifically 'natural' world.

One word I kept encountering during fieldwork was the verb *pistevo* (*I believe/ to believe*). Its meaning is ambivalently open. *Pistevo* states religious belief. People *pistevoun* (believe) in God, Jesus, *Panagia* and the saints. Furthermore, the Creed is known in Greek as give the Greek 'The Symbol of *Pisti*' or as '*Pistevo*' (the first word of the Creed, equating to the Latin credo) according to the less official terminology. At the same time the notion transcends its religious connotations and signifies a more generalized form of believing. One believes in an idea, a friend or a politician. And, of course, an individual can claim *pisti* in *mati*. As Sotiria in Thessaloniki has put it: 'We have *pisti* in God, because he created the world and protects us. But we can say "*pistevo* in Mitsotakis[5]", or *pistevo* that this is black', or "*pistevo* in your abilities to do something or that you can give me the evil eye". And if I believe in it strongly, it shall become true.' As Sotiria argues, *pisti* also implies trust that can be placed in people and institutions. When asked about their opinion concerning the evil eye, people in Rethymno and Thessaloniki immediately state their belief or their disbelief with regard to it. '*Pistevo* in *mati*' or 'I do not *pistevo* in it at all' are two of the most common phrases people have used in order to describe their trust and distrust, their religious affiliation and approval or disapproval towards the evil eye.

The notion of belief has raised concerns and criticism among anthropologists. Needham (1972) is perhaps one of its stronger critics. His *Belief, Language and Experience* (1972) begins with the narration of a dream, where Needham was trying to discuss the statement 'I believe in God' with one of his Penan informants in Indonesia (Needham 1972: 1–2).

> The Penan had no formal creed, and so far as I knew they had no other conventional means for expressing belief in their God. Nevertheless, I had been accustomed to say, to myself at any rate, that they believed in a supreme God. Yet it suddenly appeared that I had no linguistic evidence at all to this effect. Not only this, but I realized that I could not confidently describe their attitude to God, whether this was belief or anything else, by any of the psychological verbs usually found apt in such situations.
>
> (1972)

Needham questions the applicability of belief as a cross-cultural analytical category. He asserts that notions of belief tend to be culture-specific and not universal, and he points to the Western roots of 'belief', which he considers an exclusively Western category that may not be applied outside the 'West'. 'Like the promise, belief is an artificial contrivance for the convenience and advantage of society, and to the furtherance of these interests men have indeed "feigned" a new act of the mind' (1972: 150). Needham asserts that belief statements are mere social performances, strategies for the advantage of society with no further meaning and no necessary truth value engaged to them. Ultimately, he concludes that the notion of belief has no analytical value and it should be abandoned.

Needham is not the only anthropologist who has drawn attention to the problems of the notion of belief and has called for its abandonment. Pouillon has been critical of the term, noting that 'a believer believes in God, he feels no need to say that he believes in God's reality; he believes in it implicitly; precisely because in his eyes there can be no doubt about it: the existence of God is not believed in, but perceived' (Pouillon 1982: 2). Therefore, 'one could say that it is the unbeliever who believes that the believer believes in the existence of God' (1982). Ruel (2002 [1982]) follows a similar critical approach and places emphasis on the relativist character of 'belief', by examining it within the context of Christianity. He points out that in the New Testament, 'the verb *pistevo* is often used in the sense of to be converted, to become a Christian, and the word *pistis* as the belief held collectively by the early Christians as a common conviction, uniting them as community' (Ruel 2002 [1982]: 102). Belief, hence, has become a marker of Christian identity; Christians are believers. As Ruel (2002 [1982]: 110) argues, 'Clearly, it is not possible, not even desirable, to limit the word "belief" to its specifically Christian use. Yet at the same time we should make clear that it has a Christian use and that this use must affect its connotations in contexts other than Christian.'

A very interesting publication of the journal *Social Analysis*, with the title 'Against Belief?' as its main theme, is dedicated to the subject. The volume editors argue 'for the virtues of writing "against" – rather than "with" – the term [belief] in ethnographic texts', stating that they had been dissatisfied with 'the term "belief" as a general analytical tool in studying phenomena usually classed as religious', and that they find 'belief' inadequate (Lindquist and Coleman 2008: 1). I agree with Needham (1972), Ruel (2002 [1982]), Pouillon (1982) and Lindquist and Coleman (2008) that an anthropologist should not impose ethnographic authority on the people s/he studies by forcing the notion of belief into the analysis. Namely, an anthropologist should not attempt to translate a Western notion into a non-Western one and should not use an etic notion as an emic one. I also agree that 'belief' is a predominantly Western term, which has played a specific role in the Christian context, and cannot and should not be applied universally. Yet, ignoring the ethnographic and theoretical significance of belief in my research would be a mistake. Greece belongs to the West. 'Belief' exists as part of the Rethymniot and Thessalonikan everyday vocabulary. Although it possesses religious connotations, its use in the contemporary Greek context is broader. Through talking about their beliefs, my interlocutors have expressed their convictions; they have talked about their thoughts, their doubts and their experiences. Although it is difficult to define specifically, since its meanings and uses vary significantly and change cross-culturally, the concept of belief can offer important insights about socio-cultural phenomena and has definitely been beneficiary as far as the evil eye practice is concerned.

According to Pouillon (1982: 7), the Hadjerai people of the African country of Chad believe in the existence of invisible spirits, the *margay*, like they believe in their own existence. The anthropologist continues: 'or rather, they do not believe in it: this existence is simply a fact of experience' (1982). To draw an analytic parallel, those who believe in the evil eye believe in it as they believe in their own being. People who clearly affirm that they believe in *mati* consider it as part of their everyday social life, practice and experience. *Mati* is very much existent and actively present in their lives; and it is their belief in it which makes the evil eye real for them. 'I do not go to church liturgies, unless I feel the need to do so for my personal serenity. I feel God's presence stronger inside the church. I do not fast, I do not confess, I am not Christian in the typical sense. I am Christian in belief, not in religion.' Marilena, a young Thessalonikan woman, explains where her relationship with religion in general and Orthodox Christianity in particular stands. She seems to think that following the official doctrinal rules is what religion is all about. Since she is not a strict follower of Orthodoxy's demanding activities, she cannot claim to be part of a religion. She also presents the idea that one is religious when one practises religion, through attending regular church services, through confessing, through fasting. But when it comes to her, Marilena believes in Orthodoxy, but rarely practises it. Therefore, as she says, Christianity is part of her in the form of belief, but not of actual religious participation and practice. But she does practise religion: she occasionally goes to church; she has been to priests to have herself blessed; she is a firm believer in the evil eye and has had *ksematiasma* performed on her. She practises her belief.

Dubisch has effectively argued that 'insofar as Greek Orthodox Christianity is very much about *practice*, about *doing* rather than simply about *believing*, ritual activities, whether *within* or *outside* the boundaries of the church, actually constitute religion for many Greeks' (Dubisch 1995: 60, my emphasis). The evil eye constitutes a practice which involves ritual activity, and which is ostensibly situated both within and outside the boundaries of the Church and Orthodoxy.

One could argue that, by moving the evil eye closer to practice and experience, I might imply that practice and experience are more tangible than belief. The evil eye is strongly connected with issues of believing. Simultaneously, evil eye belief does not only consist of abstract ideas and intellectual representations. It is a belief that comes to be acted in practice. Evil eye belief is practised through the action and activation of sensory experiences, bodily sensations, emotional responses and perceptual correspondences. At the same time, it is part of a wider religious belief system and the Greek religious identity which, as Marilena has expressed with her words above, can be more complex and less defined for many Greeks; it can be a matter of believing without belonging, or belonging but without actively practising their belief.

The notion of 'believing without belonging' became popular in 1994, when the sociologist of religion Grace Davie developed it analytically and thoroughly in her now well-known and classic book entitled *Religion in Britain since 1945: Believing without Belonging*. In her book, Davie established the idea that, despite the fact that we live in a world where religion has – supposedly – ceased to play a central role in the public as well as the private domain, people continue to believe without attending church liturgies or participating in any other form of religious activities; namely, they are gradually letting go of the churches and 'believe without belonging' (Davie 1994). Drawing principally on European Values Survey data, her argument is based on the fact that the majority of people in Britain 'see no need to participate with even minimal regularity in their religious institutions' (1994: 2); however, they do not cease to believe in God. Consequently, the British should be characterized as 'unchurched' rather than 'secular' (1994: 12–13). Despite Davie's important contribution to crucial debates on secularization and the politics of religion in the contemporary world, her argument has raised a variety of criticisms to date, almost twenty years after it was first published.

A basic line of criticism lies in the fact that 'believing without belonging' seems to be Christian-centric and hence its analytical usefulness can only be applied to the study of Christian believers. As Hunt (2003: 164) puts it, 'Believing without belonging implies that the belief has some Christian content, but many people have little actual knowledge of the Christian faith. It is belief, yes, but not belief in an orthodox Christian God, rather a belief in "something."' In addition, as Day (2010) remarks, a vagueness characterizes the term 'belief', while its meaning is not defined thoroughly; consequently, 'by omitting certain words she [Davie] is creating an ellipse, conveying the meaning of "belief" as "belief in God" or "belief in Christianity"' (2010: 11). Day argues that Davie's thesis is 'implausible', given that ultimately 'assertions of belief are expressions of belonging' (2010: 19). On a similar basis of criticism against Davie's notions, Voas and Crockett (2005: 25) go as far as to suggest that '"believing without belonging" was an interesting idea, but it is time for the slogan to enter honourable retirement'.

Davie herself has identified certain shortcomings and limitations that can be observed in her work on belief and belonging. In particular, she has admitted that 'believing without belonging' has seemed more descriptive than explanatory, relying partly on statistical measurement and as a result it is vague rather than socio-culturally specific. As a result of her self-critical reflection, she has ended up formulating the term 'vicarious religion' instead. In her own words (Davie 2007: 22):

> Ongoing reflection about the current situation, however, has led me to reconsider this relationship [of believing and belonging], utilizing, among other tools of analysis, the concept of 'vicarious religion'. More than anything else, it represents an increasing dissatisfaction with a way of thinking that almost by definition pulls apart the ideas of believing and belonging; it concentrates instead on the subtle and complex relationships that continue to exist between these two variables.

Davie (2007: 22-3) goes on to explain that 'vicarious religion' 'has been coined in order to convey the notion of religion performed by an active minority but on behalf of a much larger number, who (implicitly at least) not only understand, but, quite clearly, approve of what the minority is doing'.[1] She concludes that 'vicarious religion' is more accurate as a concept than the idea of 'believing without belonging', since it does not simply go beyond the dichotomy but furthermore 'points to the complex cultural and political histories that are likely to shape vicariousness in any given society' (2007: 26). In spite of Davie's own recognition that belief and belonging are no longer sufficient enough as analytical concepts in order to debate over current issues of religious practice in present-day Europe, I have decided to make use of them in this chapter. Contrary to Voas and Crockett (2005: 13), who express the opinion that 'despite the interest in the idea of BWB [believing without belonging], we maintain that it is now more misleading than helpful as a way of describing the contemporary situation', I argue that the terms remain efficacious as tools of the anthropological study of religion in the modern world. Of course, I do not neglect the serious criticisms Davie's conceptualization of 'believing without belonging' entails.

Taking thus into consideration the potential weaknesses of the term(s), I find 'believing' and 'belonging' a much more useful tool – than 'vicarious religion', for instance – as far as my own analysis is concerned. The people with whom I have held conversations during my fieldwork have actually expressed themselves in terms of belief and belonging; they have constantly and consistently been using phrases such as 'I believe' or 'I don't believe' (in religion, the Catholic Church, the priests, in God and sacred imaginary in general), relating their beliefs to their sense of cosmological belonging in the world, identifying themselves as 'religious' or as 'spiritual', and making sense of their self by articulating their religious and/or spiritual aspirations. Consequently, I have chosen to respect the emic side of the analytical and ethnographic process, namely my interlocutors' use of the terms 'believing' and 'belonging' and incorporate it in the etic part of my analysis, by re-interpreting Davie's conceptualization, and exploring what the notions of 'believing' and 'belonging' can unveil about contemporary Greek religiosity.

As has been noted by Hunt (2003: 164), 'Sacred space can be found in traditionally religious places, even for people who are generally dismissive of organized religion.' Hunt (2003) observes that, despite the popular view expressed by her interlocutors that the Church is 'an institution full of hypocrites', many of them 'still speak of the importance of attending church services at Christmastime.' In my research I have equally met many people who dismiss the Church, albeit not denying the efficacy of religious belief. In the Greek case the opposite stands as well. People who define themselves as strong Christian believers do not hesitate to try New Age practices and, more generally, become entangled with new and alternative to Orthodoxy spiritual trajectories. Such spiritual openness from both sides creates an interactive field of Greek religiosity, where Christianity and new forms of spirituality fuse rather than collide.

Davie's conceptualization can therefore still offer a helpful analytical basis as a means to understand contemporary religious (and not necessarily Christian-oriented) experience. For the Greeks, it is not just a matter of 'believing without belonging', but an issue of belonging *and* believing; the two concepts, in my ethnographic case, appear to be interactive rather than antithetical. Belief, as shown above, constitutes part of people's everyday vocabulary; they utilize the term in order to describe their diverse spiritual trajectories and to reflect upon their religious belonging. Their attitude towards (their) believing and belonging is multiple and adaptable. Rethymniots and Thessalonikans can believe in Christ, Virgin Mary or the Archangels, but at the same time refuse any form of attachment to Christianity. They can belong to the Orthodox Church, while believing in the religious efficacy of alternative forms of spirituality. They can belong to a religious institution without necessarily believing in it, or they can define themselves as spiritual, and attend church liturgies from time to time. They can believe and belong simultaneously, or they can challenge their beliefs and belonging according to individual necessities and socio-cultural influences. At the end, practising New Age spirituality does not mean automatically that one has cut his/her bonds with his/her religious institution; and identifying oneself as a Christian does not imply a rigid stance towards new forms of spirituality. Instead, an interactive relationship between New Age spirituality and Christianity seems to have been formed in the current context of vernacular Greek religiosity.

Individualizing religion: Spi/ritual proximity and revolution

In her excellent article based on the narratives of three North American Anglicans, Klassen (2005) explains how liberal Protestants blend Christian and Asian religious rituals together, resulting in the creation of their own amalgamated spirituality. Through this process, which Klassen calls 'ritual proximity', they develop a strategy where a pluralistic ritualism is applied and practised, and new lineages of religious inheritance within webs of Christian ritual are constructed (2005: 377). The anthropologist also points out the irony of such a ritual adaptation (2005: 378). American Protestants had socio-culturally and religiously colonized their Asian counterparts. Now, however, they have in turn been spiritually colonized themselves. As a result of this historic underlining, some of their fellow Christians accuse them of heresy, while others perceive their syncretism as exoticism.

Greece has not been involved in any serious and organized crusade to impose Orthodox Christianity on eastern cultures. The irony of reversed spiritual colonization that Klassen has observed, therefore, bears no substance. Yet, as in the liberal Protestants' case, accusations have been cast towards those Rethymniots and Thessalonikans who have adopted, and adapted to, a pluralistic religious ritualism. Since, however, the majority of my interlocutors seem to have become engaged in such a spiritual synthesis in a variety of socio-cultural degrees, voices against a creative use of ritual proximity and mixture are heard but are not fundamentally influential. The evil eye practice is considered to belong to Orthodox Christianity and at the same time it escapes this ownership. It is a Christian act as much as it is a non-ecclesiastic practice. And when New Age spiritual ideologies enter the evil eye practice, a ritual, performative and rhetorical proximity is generated.

Klassen has observed sun salutations in a church sanctuary, the use of biblical verses for meditation needs and the channelling of healing energy through an anointing service (Klassen 2005: 378). In comparison with Klassen, I have not witnessed yoga sun salutations inside the space of a church, but, like her, I have observed and been aware of practices such as meditation with religious verses, sending energy in the context of reiki exchange during a baptism and/ or a wedding Christian ritual, primarily to wear off the evil eye from the newly baptized and the newly wed, or keeping a New Age crystal in one's pocket during Sunday mass, in order to prevent the potentially envious gazes of co-church goers transmit negative energy and the evil eye. Furthermore, the same people who go to church for the Sunday liturgy get attacked by the evil eye, perform *ksematiasma* for others, do yoga and reiki. They refer to *mati* as yet another everyday practice that contributes to the maintenance of their positive energy level, to the extermination of negative aura which might surround them, to their good spiritual and physical health. Or they just rhetorically engage a fashionably contemporary language, articulating the vocabulary of New Age spiritual practices and placing the evil eye in a pluralistic field of energetic spi/ ritualisms.

North American Protestants construct ritual adaptations of a standardized religious practice. They distance themselves from their religious colonial 'heritage' and they go on to 'pursue a mingling of rituals, religions, spirits and energies in their twenty-first-century versions of a healing mission' (Klassen 2005: 380). Greek Orthodox Christians follow a similar cultural renovation – less explicitly, perhaps, yet equally vigorously. Rethymniots and Thessalonikans act creatively. They choose whether or not to follow Orthodoxy. Simultaneously, they look around for new resources that can keep them spiritually alert. The evil eye is an excellent path for that cause, since it offers a 'religiously correct' opening beyond the official Church ideology; and I am using the signifier 'correct', in the sense that the evil eye practice utilizes Orthodox rhetorics and performances, and, despite the fact that the Church rejects the *ksematiasma* that is performed by lay healers, the practice is widely connected with the legitimized aspect of spiritual activities. At the same time, the evil eye, as handled in contemporary Greece, stands on a ground that articulates a ritual proximity with worldly religious practices, spiritual quests and energies.

There is a general assumption that religion in Europe is facing erosion, since Christianity is losing its position as the dominant cultural tradition (Knoblauch 2003: 270) – an assumption, which brings the issue of secularization again into the picture, raising the question whether religion is disappearing from Europe, or is

European religion simply changing (Stark, Hamberg and Miller 2005: 3). Greece has not turned into a secular state and has not been disenchanted. Religion still plays a central part in Greek everyday life. Yet, the need to communicate with the sacred is moving away from collective spiritual impositions and is becoming a matter of individual choice.

> According to the individualization theory, individual religiosity has emancipated itself from the custody of the large religious institutions; religious preferences are increasingly subject to the individual's autonomous choices. Churches no longer define comprehensive belief parameters; individuals instead decide on their own worldviews and spiritual orientations.
> (Pollack 2008: 171)

Rethymniots and Thessalonikans have begun to individualize their religiosity. They acknowledge their status of inhabiting a space which becomes spiritually vibrant under the influence of contrasting fields of energy. Orthodox practices, New Age practices and the evil eye: they all incorporate energetic discourses and offer different routes to spiritual unsettlement. They are practised together or in different combinations, and while encountering each other, they recreate and transform the religious landscape of contemporary Greece. The Weberian notion of charisma, which 'is outside the realm of everyday routine and profane sphere' (Weber 1964: 358), has changed meaning. By engaging their senses and ritually performing, by attending church liturgies and doing sun salutations at home, by combining reiki and *ksematiasma* healing treatments, by adopting feng shui *matakia*, by explaining evil eye affliction in energetic terms, my interlocutors have shown that spiritual charisma is not incorporated by a spiritual elite only. It is not restrictedly obtained by priests or other religious specialists. A spiritual charisma is up for grabs for individuals during their everyday journey to spiritual growth.

It has been widely asserted that the age of religion has come to an end, and the world has entered a New Age of spirituality, which is devoid of doctrinal and organized religious ideologies (Shimazono 1999: 125; cf. Heelas and Woodhead 2005: 6–7; Heelas 2006: 224; Marler and Hadaway 2002; Hill et al. 2000; Knoblauch 2008). This subjective-life spirituality, or the mind–body–spirit spirituality, as Heelas (2006: 224) explains, is a spirituality that rests on experience; it is experienced as sustaining life. One does not have to follow a dogma or a Church strictly. People are free to pursue whichever individually created spiritual path inspires and helps them more in the context of their everyday lives. The turn to subjective religiosity has been criticized, and those who choose to individualize their religious identity have been accused of practising religion in a selfish way. Perhaps the best answer to the criticism against the argument concerning the individualization of contemporary religiosity can be expressed through the words of Marion Bowman (1999: 182):

> The charge that self-religion is essentially selfish religion is an oversimplification which tends to overlook the fact that much religious activity is essentially about looking after the spiritual well-being of the individual self or soul (…). There has always been an extent to which personal religiosity has been a very individual collage of beliefs and practices drawn from both official and vernacular traditions, influenced largely by personal experience and perceptions of efficacy. Individuals within what might be thought of as fairly monolithic religious traditions have woven very idiosyncratic fabrics of belief. Scholars have tended, for the most part, to ignore this.

The practice of vernacular individualized religiosity is creatively revolutionary, rather than selfish. In their now classic book that analyses in depth the question of whether the world is going through a 'spiritual revolution', Heelas and Woodhead (2005) claim that 'traditional forms of religion, particularly Christianity, are giving way to holistic spirituality, sometimes still called New Age' (Heelas and Woodhead 2005: x). Heelas and Woodhead, with a team of other researchers, decided to test the claim by conducting empirical research in the market town and regional centre of Kendal, in the north West of England (2005: 8). Their research brought up a distinction between people who held strong religious beliefs and who belonged to a church congregation, and those who had turned to subjective-life spiritualities and who belonged to alternative health care and spirituality groups. Furthermore, what the researchers discovered was the fact that Church attendance had considerably dropped in the Kendal area since the 1960s. In contrast, the spiritual groups' creation and attendance had experienced a significant elevation. Heelas and Woodhead conclude that there is no point in asking whether the Kendal residents are experiencing a spiritual revolution. The spiritual revolution has already taken place.

The European religious landscape has changed (Martikainen 2007; Pollack 2008). New forms of spirituality have made their way in and have been received with a renewed religious interest. Greece seems to be taking part in this spiritual revolution. Orthodox Christianity has lost its dominance, and nowadays goes hand in hand with subjective-life spiritualities. People have realized that they can free themselves from the confinement which has been imposed on them by the Church. They have the choice to follow Orthodoxy or to reject it altogether.

They can be Christian adherents and simultaneously experiment with other spiritual practices. Rethymniots and Thessalonikans have gained the freedom to creatively act in the religious landscape of contemporary Greece in multiple ways, and individualize their religiosity to the degree they desire. Through their everyday evil eye and other spiritual practices, they have found a way to bring Orthodox and New Age spirituality together into a new age of spiritual creativity.

7

Conclusion

Quite a few months had already passed since I had returned to London from the first period of my ethnographic field research on the evil eye. I was spending most of my time in the shared office, working on the writing up of my doctoral thesis among colleagues in our anthropology departmental building. When friends and colleagues discovered that I could perform the ritual against the evil eye upon my return from the field, many of them asked me to perform the ritual healing against the evil eye on them. I refused to do so; I felt that the shared space of our anthropology department and office was not an 'appropriate' place where I could concentrate thoroughly and do a *ksematiasma*, while treating my newly gained ability to perform a healing ritual with the respect it – anthropologically, ethnographically and socio-culturally – deserved. In addition to the lack of 'ritual suitability', I was afraid. My healing had always been successful: the times I had performed the healing during fieldwork I was usually able to relieve the evil-eyed person's body from the ill-symptoms by embodying them myself; yet, getting rid of the ill-symptoms transference was very difficult for me, if not impossible. Almost every time I had performed a healing, I would then have to ask my mother, my aunt or other healers to ritually perform a *ksematiasma* for me in turn, so as to take the symptoms of an evil eye that I embodied as part of the therapeutic exchange away from me.

One of my close friends, a Japanese woman, had been under bodily distress for quite a long time. She was of the opinion that someone was giving her the evil eye, that she was the recipient of a constantly transmitted negative energy. We were always talking about how I should at some point perform the ritual for her. However, I had already mentioned the difficulty I had in getting rid of the symptoms. She never insisted on having her evil eye removed by me and I never suggested it. Until one evening she entered the room where I was sitting. Instantaneously, I felt something negative, I started yawning and I was unable to stop. I decided that the time had arrived; I should perform a *ksematiasma* for her. And so I did. After I finished, she told me that she was feeling worse. I was taken aback. She decided to return to her house and lie down and rest, and left me yawning and gradually developing additional bodily symptoms of illness. Fifteen minutes passed, my yawning had stopped, but I was feeling very strange. My whole body was numb. It was as if someone else was regulating my moves, as if I had lent my body to someone else who could entirely manipulate me. Colleagues were talking to me, and I could barely create words in my mouth. My senses were fogged under a perceptual blackout. Panic started rising inside. I called my mother, explained that I had just performed a *ksematiasma*, after which I had developed severe bodily symptoms – the strongest side effects I had ever experienced in the post ritual phase of *ksematiasma*. When she called back, I was feeling slightly better. My mother informed me that three women, including her, had performed the *ksematiasma* for me; and she forbade me to perform the evil eye healing ever again. Then she told me that I was suffering from a really strong evil eye, but there was something strange about it. Instead of the usual eye-like oil shape in the surface of the water, a strange island-like figure was formed. It looked familiar, so she had opened the encyclopaedia and looked at the world map. The island oily shape was Japan. Astonished, I admitted that I had tried to remove the evil eye from a Japanese friend. I stayed on the phone while being given a strict lecture about the effects of messing with spiritual forces and mixing religions. After more *ksematiasmata* from my kin in the course of the next few days, my fully perceiving self was back in charge.

It took a while before I saw my friend again. It appeared as if this incident had created a period of awkwardness between us. After I got over my fear of losing my bodily perception again, and she perhaps stopped feeling guilty of causing this loss to me, we finally met. The negative power that was being sent to her body was very strong, she assumed. She could fight it back, but my body was not as strong; therefore, it reacted badly to the invasion. We concluded that, by tentatively mixing different spiritual traditions, we had provoked the spiritual. Actually *I* had, by attempting to battle a foreign – to me, my culture and the [Greek] evil eye – spiritual attacker with the use of an Orthodox Christian weapon. And my body was battered back.

This incident has indicated that believing, perceiving and practising the evil eye are not a cultural game. Not that my friend and I treated it as one. Yet, ours was a forced performance. My friend did not ask for the healing, and I was not absolutely certain whether I wanted to offer it. The terms of the evil eye context were not properly negotiated and cleared between us. Admittedly, my performance was unsuccessful. The failure was not due to a rejection of our commonly agreed spiritual synthesis. It seemed to be a rejection of the out-of-the-Greek-context spiritual synthesis, in particular. When it came to a meeting of Greek and Japanese culture and ideology outside Greece, the two could not work together, interact and amalgamate. Yet, as I have shown throughout the book, eastern spiritual and Greek spiritual ideas and practices can be amalgamated by Greeks and sometimes by non-Greeks in Greece. This is what happened in the end. The spiritual synthesis, which was initially developed between my Japanese friend and I, had to be domesticated and controlled wholly within the Greek socio-cultural terms. Once the performance was returned to Greece to be handled, through the medium of an experienced healer, through my mother and my relatives that is, in this particular case, it was back on the cultural road of performative success: both my Japanese friend and myself had felt better.

This incident offers an excellent representation of the creative agency that is characteristic of the evil eye practice and the spiritual syntheses that are happening in contemporary Greece. My friend comes from a country where spirituality is well developed. Reiki originates in Japan, and the exchange of energy is an important constituent of Japanese culture. Eastern spirituality and the evil eye, therefore, met in our *ksematiasma* performance. Three individuals were involved in this incident of spiritual synthesis, all of whom dynamically contributed to the ritual action: my friend (as an evil eye sufferer and a representative of eastern spirituality), myself (as an indigenous anthropologist and an evil eye healer) and my mother (as an Orthodox adherent, and a typical Greek *ksematiastra*). And perhaps the spiritual synthesis commenced with the engagement of my friend and I in the ritual. Yet, it was my mother, the symbolic representative of the lay people in Rethymno and Thessaloniki I studied, who, exactly like them, and despite her seeming disagreement, demonstrated considerable agency and mixed religion, spirituality and the evil eye into one performance of a creative spiritual synthesis.

With the evil eye as its central theme, the main objective of this book has been to demonstrate the dynamic ways in which lay people in Crete and northern Greece practise their religion and spirituality in the context of their vernacular negotiations of religiosity. Although they have not let go of the Church, the majority of the individuals I spoke to have questioned the position which Orthodox Christianity holds in contemporary Greece and have begun to follow non-Orthodox spiritual itineraries. Their need to pursue other spiritual directions in parallel to practising Orthodoxy is inspired by global trends and their desire to discover new ways of communication with the sacred.

Most of the Rethymniots and Thessalonikans I talked to belong to two categories. There are those who define themselves as Orthodox Christians, but who also remain friendly and ideologically open to other paths of establishing a communication with the spiritual and sometimes combine Christian and New Age spiritual practices. And there are those who have gradually disengaged themselves from Orthodoxy without totally cutting the link to it, and who usually seek to express themselves through New Age paths of spirituality. But even those who keep their defences against following new paths of spirituality well raised have recognized that something in the Greek religious landscape is changing today.

Rethymno and Thessaloniki: Comparative notes on ethnographic findings

As it has become apparent from my dual-sited ethnography, Rethymno and Thessaloniki share more socio-cultural similarities than differences, at least as far as my topic of research is concerned. This is possibly the reason why no sharp distinctions or arguments between the two have appeared in the main part of this book. The most important comparative element that was brought up during research and its subsequent analysis was that Greeks in two very different loci of the country have begun to combine Orthodoxy and New Age spirituality, and approach the evil eye and their spiritual quests in dynamic, creative ways. Some potential convergences and divergences shared between Rethymno and Thessaloniki are summarized below.

Urban and rural

Rethymno and Thessaloniki are both considered to be urban spaces and I ethnographically chose them because of their urban character, for I wanted to move away from the stereotype of the evil eye as an exclusively rural practice. Indeed, the majority of evil eye studies, in Greece as well as in the rest of the world, have been conducted in small villages. I decided to follow a different ethnographic path. What I came to realize, however, is that the urban and the rural are not characterized by spatial rigidity. The communication between them is constant and can influence and can be formed by people's everyday practices. As showed earlier in the book, it is quite common for Rethymniots and Thessalonikans to visit and/or phone friends and relatives who live in rural areas and ask them to perform rituals against the evil eye. *Ksematiasma* at a distance also occurs within urban settings. It is symptomatic of the busy urban life my interlocutors lead. At the same time, it establishes a communication between urban and rural environments, and collapses the alleged distinction between them.

Relatedness

Ksematiasma – whether performed at a distance or face to face – is indicative of the way in which the evil eye appears to travel through social webs of relatedness in both Rethymno and Thessaloniki. The evil eye ritual healing is predominantly practised among relatives, friends and neighbours, that is, among kin and symbolic kin members. In order for the healing to be successful, the evil eye afflicted person and the healer need to share a certain level of intimacy and social relatedness. At the same time, relatedness can result in evil eye affliction. *Matiasma* occurs within the boundaries of the neighbourhood. People gaze at and/or gossip about their neighbours and they give them the evil eye. People give the evil eye to their kin or gossip about members of their extended family and, consequently, bewitch them. It is not random that *matiasma* caused by close relatives is considered most powerful of all and very difficult to extinguish.

Evil eye affliction caused through webs of relatedness is not always bad, however, and the novel idea of *kalo mati* verifies such an idea. People in Rethymno and Thessaloniki are hesitant to accept and/or explicitly declare that a close relative, friend or social acquaintance feeds negative feelings of jealousy towards them. Instead, they explain evil eye affliction that is caused within webs of relatedness as *kalo mati*: as a *matiasma* which derives from the exchange of excessive positive feelings. In that way, they safeguard their social relationships. At the same time, those few who have admitted they can give the evil eye to friends and relatives speak about their *kalo mati*, and, as a result, the danger of stigmatizing their identity as evil eye givers lessens. Consequently, Rethymniot and Thessalonikan social relatedness carries a dual significance in the evil eye process: it can provide a socio-cultural and ritual shelter against the evil eye, but it can also endanger people's embodied selves by causing evil eye affliction, albeit not, or not always, in an 'evil' way.

Gender

According to a popular stereotype, when it comes to the evil eye practice women prevail. Evil eye affliction is supposedly caused mainly by women who, at the same time, purportedly dominate in the field of *ksematiasma*. In Rethymno and

Thessaloniki, the evil eye is given by both men and women. At the same time, the ritual healing expertise is not confined within the boundaries of female social activity. Men also take an active social and ritual role in the evil eye process. Crete is considered a particularly patriarchal society, and the majority of spiritual activities, including the evil eye healing, are supposed to be female tasks. In Rethymno, however, I met many men who were popular healers and performed the *ksematiasma* on a regular basis for their fellow male and female Rethymniots.

In Thessaloniki, the number of female healers was greater than that of their male counterparts. A large number of Thessalonikan young women were successful evil eye healers. Another gendered stereotype was thus transcended in my northern Greek fieldwork: a *ksematiastra* need not be an old woman in a village, who uses the evil eye ritual healing as a means to strengthen her restricted – compared to men – power in the society she lives in. A *ksematiastra* can be a young woman with a busy urban lifestyle, who performs *ksematiasma*, along with reiki, yoga and feng shui, as a spiritual means to improve the health of her social circle. The most common stereotypical image, held by Greeks and painted by folklorists and anthropologists of Greece, holds the evil eye expert to be an old woman in a 'traditional', rural setting. This view remained apparent during the course of my research. Yet, it has been joined by the image of Cretan male healers, by the image of young Thessalonikan women who are New Age practitioners and by the image of older Rethymniot and Thessalonikan women who perform *ksematiasma* while incorporating ideas of energy in the discourses during their vernacular religious practice.

Perception

Sensory perception plays a vital role in the process of *matiasma* and *ksematiasma*. Daily sensory communication affects Rethymniots and Thessalonikans and frequently results in evil eye affliction. At the same time, sensory interaction is central to the ritual healing of *ksematiasma*. Triggering the senses of the evil-eyed person is needed for an efficacious healing to be achieved. Most scholarly analyses of the evil eye have treated vision as the queen of the five senses. I wanted to move away from such a westernized model of analysis, which emphasizes the supremacy of the visual. In any case, the pluri-sensorial attitudes of Cretans and northern Greeks left me with no choice but to explore their paradigm and develop an analysis where all five senses are treated as equals.

The five-sense schema of experiencing the world is heavily determined by scientific explanatory models concerning perception. Positivist science presupposes that what is real in our cosmos is confined within the boundaries of five-sense natural perception. Everything else that escapes those boundaries is a matter of belief, not perception. A number of Rethymniots and Thessalonikans, both young and old, men and women, who were very science-conscious, followed a similar epistemological discourse and challenged the idea that the evil eye exists. They argued that the evil eye is not tangible and cannot be perceived with the five senses; thus, it belongs to a supernatural sphere of existence, which is not rational since it cannot be scientifically verified.

The majority of my interlocutors in both Rethymno and Thessaloniki have not rejected the evil eye in the name of science. It is true that they have followed the scientific explanatory model and have shown in practice how perception through the five senses is involved in the evil eye. Rethymniots and Thessalonikans thoroughly described the various ways in which they experience the evil eye on and through their somatic perception and physical body. At the same time, however, their practice indicates that the evil eye is entangled with a form of perception that transcends the five-sense scientifically constructed schema. According to my interlocutors, *mati* is somatically perceived. It is felt. It is experienced. It is sensed. So is the supernatural. For Rethymniots and Thessalonikans, at least the ones who accept and practise the evil eye, the evil eye belongs in the sphere of the extra-sensory, and often they connect it with extra-sensory, supernatural and spiritual experiences which they regard to be closer to New Age spirituality than their Orthodox religious belonging. The evil eye and the spiritual energy are embodied, believed and perceived, within and beyond the five senses. The rigid dichotomizations between scientific and supernatural, belief and perception, natural and supernatural appear to have collapsed.

Materiality

Another commonality between my two fieldsites was the popularity which the material form of the evil eye enjoyed in both Rethymno and Thessaloniki. As analysed earlier, evil eye material objects could be found in Rethymniot and Thessalonikan shops, houses, cars and on people's bodies. People in Rethymno and Thessaloniki utilized them mostly as charms, namely as prophylactic objects against the evil eye, against any kind of evil, against any form of negative energy. Perhaps the most crucial *matakia* I discovered were the ones that amalgamated evil eye, Christian and New Age symbols. These spiritually pluralistic evil eye objects were very popular and fashionable throughout my fieldwork. They depicted a newly developed spiritual pluralism in contemporary Greece.

The insistent popularity of *matakia* in my fieldsites was triggered and maintained by shop owners and consumers in Rethymno and Thessaloniki. They were the social agents who introduced, promoted, consumed, circulated and handled the syncretic *matakia* in creative and dynamic ways.

The wide circulation and consumption of the spiritually syncretic evil eye objects can be considered a response to global trends and the global marketplace. The establishment of New Age and feng shui shops in Rethymno and Thessaloniki have been largely prompted by the popularity New Age objects enjoy among tourists. Furthermore, Chinese goods, especially clothing and other cheap products, have invaded the Greek marketplace for almost a decade now and have become popular with Greeks. Alongside the Chinese shops, feng shui and other eastern-oriented shops have made an appearance. Greek media promote global trends, New Age spirituality and the evil eye. All these factors and the contact with other cultures have contributed to the material popularity which New Age spirituality enjoys in Rethymno and Thessaloniki. The evil eye is still connected with Orthodoxy. Religious *matakia* that combine Orthodox icons and evil eye symbols are significantly popular in Rethymno and Thessaloniki. Yet, the evil eye has also regained popularity under a fresh socio-cultural light; the Orthodox and evil symbols of *matakia* are joined by New Age material symbols. Religion and spirituality are materially brought together. A syncretic materiality, which corresponds to the spiritual landscape of contemporary Greece, has been created.

Religion and spirituality at the crossroads

The evil eye and Orthodoxy are closely connected. The Orthodox Church accepts *vaskania* and considers the evil eye to be the work of the devil. The Church and clergy do not accept the ritual healing against the evil eye as it is performed by lay healers. However, the distinction between laity and clergy, between a *ksematiastra* and a priest, between lay and doctrinal interpretations of the prevailing religion collapses in vernacular religious practice. Lay evil eye healers are Orthodox believers and almost always recite Orthodox Christian prayers and use Orthodox symbolisms in the evil eye ritual healing, interpreting the Orthodox doctrine in their own ways. Furthermore, during their everyday lives, priests accept the spiritual authority of lay healers, and sometimes they even ask these lay healers to perform the *ksematiasma* for them. Consequently, whether they are laity or clergy, people in Rethymno and Thessaloniki have nowadays obtained the choice to manifest their religious practices in multiple ways. They interpret and handle Orthodoxy according to their personal everyday spiritual needs, amalgamating it with other forms of spirituality, whenever they feel it is necessary.

Following the religious leadership of Archbishop Christodoulos in the Church of Greece (1998–2008), Orthodoxy became more approachable for a wider range of believers. Christodoulos' strategy of dropping some of the Church's rigidity increased church-going among Greeks of the younger generation. Yet, it also transformed Orthodoxy into a porous religion, and this push of Orthodoxy to become popular amongst young people could be interpreted and practised openly and in a variety of ways, even by the clergy. In the years of Christodoulos, the road towards the emergence of a spiritually open religiosity became slowly yet steadily cultivated. However, the socioeconomic crisis that hit Greece, especially from 2010 onwards, resulted in the rise of right-wing political parties, whose discourse linked nationalistic arguments with a twisted and extreme emphasis on 'Helleno-Orthodoxy'. These parties gained followers and provoked large waves of religious fanaticism. Despite this fact, contemporary Greek religiosity has continued to show signs of fluidity in vernacular practice. The popularity of New Age spirituality has in fact grown in the period of crisis, with many Greeks resorting to alternative forms of spirituality, instead of the Orthodox Church and its priests, to find spiritual support.

New Age has claimed a vivid position in the contemporary Greek religious landscape. New Age practices are adopted by Rethymniots and Thessalonikans in parallel to attending church liturgies and giving, receiving, ritually performing and becoming healed from the evil eye. Contemporary global trends with regard to spiritual quests and practices have not left Greeks unaffected and apathetic. The extensive use of 'energy', a concept that is directly linked to New Age ideologies, as part of people's everyday discourse in Rethymno and Thessaloniki is indicative of the influence new forms of spirituality have exercised on the everyday life of Greeks. Secularization, 'the idea that society moves from some sacred condition to successively secular conditions in which the sacred evermore recedes' (Hammond 1985: 1), does not appear to prevail in contemporary Greece. Greeks remain spiritually active in both Orthodox and New Age terms. Yet, as my evil eye research has shown, the religious landscape of contemporary Greece is becoming more individualized, and the boundaries of Greek vernacular religion have become extended, allowing for the presence and co-inhabitation of New Age spirituality in the until recently almost exclusive Orthodox *topos* of spi/ritual domination. It is not simply about Orthodoxy, or even about superstition, any longer. The evil eye is also about energy, about pursuing New Age spirituality, even by Orthodoxy's firm followers, in a context which transcends Orthodox Christianity and, instead, creates a syncretic and pluralistic Greek spiritual landscape that has brought religion and spirituality at a crossroads.

Crossroads are spiritually powerful spaces. According to a popular Greek belief, they are possessed by spirits, and people need to make the sign of the cross with their fingers if they want to avert spiritual assault (cf. Stewart 1991: 103). The particular crossroads I encountered in the evil eye are a cultural space where religion and spirituality encounter each other. It has also proven to be an ethnographic space. The contemporary Greek religious landscape is at the crossroads. It is experiencing a turn to individual spirituality, and the beginning of a spiritual revolution. The evil eye practice stands at the centre of this cultural crossroad. Orthodoxy comes down to meet the evil eye from one street; atheism approaches from another route; New Age spiritual practices arrive from a third path. At the heart of the crossroad these currents all confront each other, creatively interact and enter a procedural action of socio-cultural symbiosis. Then, they continue their travel spiritually refreshed. Their amalgamation has given rise to a vernacular form of spiritual creativity in contemporary Greece. The evil eye practice has emerged in this study as the cultural link, which has brought Orthodoxy and New Age spirituality together. Greece is currently undergoing a process of spiritual synthesis, as the evidence accumulated above shows. Whether (Orthodox) religion is to prevail (New Age and eastern), spirituality to take over, or a spiritual syncretism to become even more strengthened, remains to be experienced.

Rethymniots and Thessalonikans have entered a process of redefining the traditional concept of the evil eye, enriching it with a new kind of Western mysticism that is popular in the rest of Europe and America. For some of my interlocutors, who are more aware of the existence of the New Age movement and alternative therapeutic pathways, the act of introducing contemporary, spiritual, global trends to the evil eye practice has been more of a conscious effort to 'modernize' a 'traditional' practice, while maintaining its Greek cultural heritage. For most of the Cretans and northern Greeks I spoke to, however, this act of amalgamating religious and spiritual discourses and ritual performances through the practice of the evil eye has happened spontaneously, through the process of living their religion in a vernacular context. The blending of the classically as religiously interpreted concept of the evil eye with contemporary New Age spiritual interpretations has, hence, been less of an intentional effort of one to act as a citizen of the contemporary world when it comes to religio-spiritual practice and more of an unstructured creation of a pluralistic field of religion, spirituality and healing, imaginatively assembled while one handles, performs, expresses and lives his/her (practices of) vernacular religion creatively in a changing world.

Notes

Chapter 1

1. I found it crucial to protect the Rethymniots and Thessalonikans whom I spoke to by disguising their identity. Consequently, all the names of my interlocutors that are used in the book are pseudonyms.
2. *Palo santo*, literally 'sacred wood' in Spanish, is a tree that primarily grows in South America and is considered to have mystical qualities, often being utilized by shamans and other spiritual healers in South America during their healing rituals. Burning a *palo santo* stick is supposed to have strong spiritual healing qualities, and its fragrant smoke that leaves behind promotes physical, spiritual and mental health and fills a room with positive energy, removing all forms of evil spiritual forces. In Greece, its use has become popularized by New Age spiritual healers and practitioners very recently, and I only encountered it early in 2019 for the first time.
3. 'Orthodoxy' and 'Orthodox Christianity' are employed alternatively throughout this text and are equal to Greek Orthodoxy. Moreover, the word 'Orthodox' with a capital 'O' refers to Orthodox Christianity and the Church, whereas 'orthodox' with a small 'o' refers to the conforming to traditional or established standards in religion, namely to strict doctrinal conservatism.
4. The statistical and demographic information concerning Rethymno and Thessaloniki comes from the National Statistical Service of Greece (www.statistics.gr) and the Prefectures of Rethymno and Thessaloniki respectively.
5. The term *ftharmos*, which derives from the ancient Greek *ofthalmos*, and the term *mati*, which is used in modern Greek, are synonyms and they both mean 'eye'.
6. As Hirschon (2008: 192) explains, 'The Greek word for obligation, *ypochreosi*, reveals the tension generated by this notion, for the word itself incorporates the idea of "debt", *chreos*. Thus, in Greek, the notion of obligation is one of "indebtedness". To be obliged, therefore, entails being *in debt*, or rather, literally, "under debt."'

Chapter 2

1. Some of the most popular widely known Greeks, who have expressed neo-Orthodox ideas, are Christos Yannaras, a professor of Philosophy and Theology;

Kostas Zouraris, another university professor; writer Kostis Moskof; popular composer and singer Dionysis Savvopoulos; Father Georgios Metallinos, a priest who has appeared on Greek television programmes numerous of times; Metropolitan Hierotheos Vlachos; as well as famous Greeks, who have linked their music with Greek history, such as Mikis Theodorakis and Giannis Markopoulos (Makrides 1998: 141–3).

2   For more information with regard to the Patriarchate of Constantinople, Orthodoxy and its organization, see the official website of the Patriarchate of Constantinople, www.ec-patr.org.

3   As Prodromou (2004a: 64) puts it: 'Radiating out like a set of pokes from this centre is a far-flung network of churches designated as either autocephalous or autonomous in order to identify their degrees of independence from their respective historic Patriarchates, or "mother churches."'

4   A few more Greek islands also have their own Archiepiscopates established and do not belong to the Church of Greece, but to the Ecumenical Patriarchate. For more details on Crete and the islands, see the official site of the Archiepiscopate of Crete www.iak.gr.

5   Archbishop Christodoulos passed away in 2008 after a battle with cancer. Since I am completing this book after his death, perhaps I should refer to him as the late Archbishop. However, I have decided not to; for a large part of my research, he was the Archbishop of the Church of Greece, and his presence evidently influenced my informants and my ethnographic data as a consequence. I shall thus be referring to Christodoulos as the 'Archbishop' in this book, with a danger of anachronism; yet, any other choice would be misleading as far as my ethnographic research is concerned.

6   Although PASOK lost its power in the national elections of 2004, during the first period of my fieldwork the influences of the modernizing tendencies of PASOK were still vividly present. Many individuals Rethymno and Thessaloniki continuously expressed to me their hope that PASOK would soon be back in power and help Greece move forward in the international political arena.

7   I will not go here into the historical, political and socio-cultural details of the effect of the economic and refugee crisis in contemporary Greece, as there are many excellent works dedicated on the subject (Cabot 2014; Dalakoglou and Agelopoulos 2017; Doxiadis and Placas 2018; Kirtsoglou and Tsimouris 2018).

Chapter 3

1   Kleinman (1980: 72) has famously argued for a distinction between disease, the 'malfunctioning of biological and/or psychological processes', and illness, the

'psychosocial experience and meaning of perceived disease'. Although he later came to rethink the issue and consequently changed his mind about his initial statement, his dichotomized medical schema of the biological and the medically accurate versus the symbolic and the medically malfunctioning is still popular. By referring to the evil eye symptomatology as 'illness', I definitely do not follow an illness vs disease binarism. Instead, I use the term 'illness' in order to indicate both the biological and the socio-cultural aspects of the symptoms of illness my informants experience.

2   Appearing at the end of the 1980s, and reaching its full development during the 1990s, the 'anthropology of the senses' grew out of the theoretical turn and interest towards bodily modes of knowing, and it has since managed, not only to broaden social theories of embodiment so that the senses are incorporated, but, most importantly, to discard visual reductionism and, at the same time, elevate the significance of each sense separately, whilst jointly approaching all the senses, in every cultural setting, as equal (Howes 1991a, 1991b: 3, 4, 11). Some of the most well-known representatives of the 'anthropology of the senses' are Stoller (1989), Taussig (1993), Classen (1990, 1993, 1994), Howes (1991a, 1991b, 1996, 2003), Seremetakis (1994) and Geurts (2002).

3   According to the Greek educational system, one has to take exams in order to get into university. But these exams are quite difficult, and, although public schools are supposed to prepare high school students for this process, the knowledge they offer is inadequate. Therefore, the majority of students spend a great amount of time and money in tutorial classes. To pass the exams without tutorials is considered to be a great achievement. Marina not only achieved that, but her attempt to study and enter university in her mid-thirties, while having a family and two kids, is regarded as another major achievement, bound to raise envy, gossip and provoke evil eye affliction.

4   These are the three largest and most popular milk brands in Greece.

5   Vasilopita is the name of the cake prepared by Greek Orthodox Christians on New Year's Eve. A coin is placed inside the cake, which is then cut and served immediately after the New Year arrives – but not before, since that would bring bad luck to the household. Whoever receives the slice with the coin will enjoy a year of good luck.

Chapter 4

1   The word 'reiki' means 'universal life-force energy'. It was first discovered by the Japanese priest Mikao Usui in the late nineteenth century, who developed a special type of healing by channelling healing energy (Quest 1999: 6).

2   In almost every Greek household, people, whether religiously devoted or not, dedicate a corner in the house to create a family altar, an *eikonostasi* (literally, an icon stand), which is usually filled with Christian icons and an oil lamp. This altar is supposed to protect the household from evil forces and the devil, and it is the place where members of the family go to pray and/or establish a form of communication with the sacred.

3   Although I have met both female and male healers who perform *ksematiasma*, the women are the ones who prevail in the ritual performance. I have chosen, therefore, to use the Greek term of evil eye healer that points to the female identity of the healer, namely *ksematiastra*, throughout the text, given that the grammatically masculine version of the term is not really used in the Greek evil eye discourse.

4   It has been argued that the characterization of an individual as a 'patient' suggests passivity (Sharma 1992: 28). Yet, I do not use the term with such a meaning. I find the word useful, since it suggests a person who is suffering from an illness, but who is also actively involved in her medical interpretations and therapeutics.

5   For example, one main criticism against the Orthodox Christian Church is its exclusion of women from its hierarchical ranks. For a thorough discussion of the issue, see Sotiriu (2004, 2010).

6   The holistic health movement appeared in the United States in the 1970s, having grown out of various socio-cultural influences, the need to go back nature, a turn to eastern spirituality and mysticism, the feminist movement and so on (Baer 2003: 234–5).

7   Kaiti became so angry with her patient and threw her out of her house due to the sexual hint. What the other woman was actually saying is that her husband was evil eyeing her while they were having sex, because she was good at it. This declaration, coming from a middle-aged woman towards an elderly lady (Kaiti, that is), insulted Kaiti, since she violated her ethics as a woman and as a healer.

Chapter 6

1   Berger was one of the first scholars to support the 'secularization' theory (Berger 1967). Later, however, he came to overturn his initial theoretical views and proceeded to develop his 'desecularization' theory instead (Berger 1999).

2   Source: www.vimaorthodoxias.gr

3   A very popular webpage that was mentioned to me by some devoted Christians, but also by some New Age practitioners in order to point to the sources of what they regard as spiritual backwardness, was the one called *Orio Pisteos* (Boundary of Faith). It is a Thessalonikan-based religious group, involving many local priests and faithful Orthodox devotees, with a strong nationalistic flavour, which functions

with the support of the Bishop of Thessaloniki. Part of the website is based on providing information about 'religious heresies', as they are titled, which includes, among others, yoga, reiki, homeopathy, esotericism and *Nea Epohi* (New Age). Interestingly enough, the use of *Nea Epohi* is only used by official ecclesiastic circles and websites to designate New Age, rather than by its practitioners themselves, who usually use the term in its English version. *Orio Pisteos* also organizes frequent lectures and seminars against all practices of *Nea Epohi*, yoga and all practices that its members regard as heretic. For more information, see www.oriopisteos.eu/
4   Confessor is an Orthodox priest who has the power to hear confession, and who usually possesses the role of one's spiritual mentor.
5   Kyriakos Mitsotakis is the current prime minister of Greece.

References

Alivizatos, N. (1999), 'A New Role for the Greek Church?', *Journal of Modern Greek Studies*, 17: 23–40.
Ammerman, N. (2014), 'Finding Religion in Everyday Life', *Sociology of Religion*, 75 (2): 189–207.
Appadurai, A. (1986), 'Introduction: Commodities and the Politics of Value', in A. Appadurai (ed.), *The Social Life of Things: Commodities in Cultural Perspective*, 3–63, Cambridge: Cambridge University Press.
Aune, K. (2014), 'Feminist Spirituality as Lived Religion: How UK Feminists Forge Religio-spiritual Lives', *Gender & Society*, 29 (1): 122–45.
Aupers, S. and D. Houtman (2006), 'Beyond the Spiritual Supermarket: The Social and Public Significance of New Age Spirituality', *Journal of Contemporary Religion*, 21 (2): 201–22.
Baer, A. H. (2003), 'The Work of Andrew Weil and Deepak Chopra: Two Holistic Health/New Age Gurus: A Critique of the Holistic Health/New Age Movements', *Medical Anthropology Quarterly*, 17 (2): 233–50.
Bakalaki, A. (1997), 'Students, Natives, Colleagues: Encounters in Academia and in the Field', *Cultural Anthropology*, 12 (4): 502–6.
Berger, P. (1967), *The Sacred Canopy: Elements of a Sociological Theory of Religion*, New York: Doubleday.
Berger, P. (1999), 'The Desecularization of the World: A Global Overview', in P. Berger (ed.), *The Desecularization of the World: Resurgent Religion and World Politics*, 1–18, Washington, DC: Ethics and Public Policy Center.
Berger, P. (2007), 'Pluralism, Protestantization, and the Voluntary Principle', in T. Banchoff (ed.), *Democracy and the New Religious Pluralism*, 19–29, Oxford: Oxford University Press.
Bernard, R. (2002), *Research Methods in Anthropology: Qualitative and Quantitative Methods*, Walnut Creek, California and Oxford: AltaMira.
Bhargava, R. (1998), 'Introduction', in R. Bhargava (ed.), *Secularism and Its Critics*, 1–28, Oxford: Oxford University Press.
Blum, R. and E. Blum (1965), *Health and Healing in Rural Greece. A Study of Three Communities*, Stanford, CA: Stanford University Press.
Blum, R. and E. Blum (1970), *The Dangerous Hour. The Lore of Crisis and Mystery in Rural Greece*, New York: Scribners' and Sons.
Boddy, J. (1988), 'Spirits and Selves in Northern Sudan: The Cultural Therapeutics of Possession and Trance', *American Ethnologist*, 15 (1): 4–27.

Bourdieu, P. (1984), *Distinction: A Social Critique of the Judgement of Taste*, Cambridge, MA: Harvard University Press.
Bowman, M. (1999), 'Healing in the Spiritual Marketplace: Consumers, Courses and Credentialism', *Social Compass*, 46 (2): 181–9.
Bowman, M. and Ü. Valk (eds.) (2012), *Vernacular Religion in Everyday Life: Expressions of Belief*, Sheffield and Bristol: Equinox.
Brown, S. (1996), *Principles of Feng Shui*, London: Thorsons.
Brown, F. M. (1997), *The Channeling Zone: American Spirituality in an Anxious Age*, Cambridge, MA and London: Harvard University Press.
Bruce, S. (1998), 'The Charismatic Movement and the Secularization Thesis', *Religion*, 28: 223–2.
Bruce, S. (2002), *God Is Dead: Secularization in the West*, Oxford and Malden, MA: Blackwell Publishers.
Butler, J. (1990), 'Performative Acts and Gender Constitution: An Essay in Phenomenology and Feminist Theory', in S. E. Case (ed.), *Performing Feminisms:Feminist Critical Theory and Theatre*, 270–82, Baltimore, MD and London: The Johns Hopkins University Press.
Cabot, H. (2014), *On the Doorstep of Europe: Asylum and Citizenship in Greece*, Philadelphia: University of Pennsylvania Press.
Campbell, J. (1964), *Honour, Family and Patronage*, New York and Oxford: Oxford University Press.
Chryssanthopoulou, V. (1993), 'The Construction of Ethnic Identity among the Castellorizian Greeks of Perth, Australia', D.Phil Thesis, Wolfson College, University of Oxford.
Chryssanthopoulou, V. (1999), 'To Kako Mati stous Ellines tis Australias: Taftotita, Syneheia, Neoterikotita', *Arhaiologia kai Tehnes*, 72: 22–30.
Chryssanthopoulou, V. (2008), 'The Evil Eye among the Greeks in Australia: Identity, Continuity and Modernization', in J. C. B. Petropoulos (ed.), *Greek Magic: Ancient, Medieval and Modern*, 106–18, London and New York: Routledge.
Classen, C. (1990), 'Sweet Colors, Fragrant Songs: Sensor Models of the Andes and the Amazon', *American Ethnologist*, 14 (4): 722–35.
Classen, C. (1993), *Worlds of Sense: Exploring the Senses in History and across Cultures*, London and New York: Routledge.
Classen, C. (1994), *Aroma: The Cultural History of Smell*, London and New York: Routledge.
Clot-Garrell, A. and M. Griera (2019), 'Beyond Narcissism: Towards an Analysis of the Public, Political and Collective Forms of Contemporary Spirituality', *Religions*, 10: 579.
Cornejo Valle, M. (2013), 'Individual Spirituality and Religious Membership among Soka Gakkai Buddhists in Spain', in A. Fedele and K. Knibbe (eds.), *Gender and Power in Contemporary Spirituality: Ethnographic Approaches*, 62–77, London: Routledge.

Cowan, J. (1991), 'Going Out for Coffee? Contesting the Grounds of Gendered Pleasures in Everyday Sociability', in P. Loizos and A. Papataxiarchis (eds.), *Contested Identities: Gender and Kinship in Modern Greece*, 180–202, Princeton, NJ: Princeton University Press.

Csordas, T. (1993), 'Somatic Modes of Attention', *Cultural Anthropology*, 8 (2): 135–56.

Csordas, T. (1997 [1994]), *The Sacred Self: A Cultural Phenomenology of Charismatic Healing*, Berkeley: University of California Press.

Csordas, T. and A. Kleinman (1996), 'The Therapeutic Process', in C. F. Sargent and T. M. Johnson (eds.), *Medical Anthropology: Contemporary Theory and Method*, 3–20, Westport, CT and London: Praeger.

Dalakoglou, D. and G. Agelopoulos (eds.) (2017), *Critical Times in Greece: Anthropological Engagements with the Crisis*, London and New York: Routledge.

Danforth, L. (1989), *Firewalking and Religious Healing: The Anastenaria of Greece and the American Firewalking Movement*, Princeton, NJ: Princeton University Press.

Davenport, H. W. (1986), 'Two kinds of value in the Eastern Solomon Islands', in A. Appadurai (ed.), *The Social Life of Things: Commodities in Cultural Perspective*, 95–109, Cambridge: Cambridge University Press.

Davie, G. (1994), *Religion in Britain since 1945: Believing without Belonging*, Oxford: Blackwell.

Davie, G. (2007), 'Vicarious Religion: A Methodological Challenge', in N. Ammerman (ed.), *Everyday Religion: Observing Modern Religious Lives*, 21–36, Oxford: Oxford University Press.

Day, A. (2010), 'Propositions and Performativity: Relocating Belief to the Social', *Culture and Religion*, 11 (1): 9–30.

Desjarlais, R. (1996), 'Presence', in C. Laderman and M. Roseman (eds.), *The Performance of Healing*, 143–64, New York and London: Routledge.

Dickie, M. (1995), 'The Fathers of the Church and the Evil Eye', in H. Maguire (ed.), *Byzantine Magic*, 9–34, Washington, DC: Dumbarton Oaks Research Library and Collection.

Dionisopoulos-Mass, R. (1976), 'The Evil Eye and Bewitchment in a Peasant Village', in Clarence Maloney (ed.), *The Evil Eye*, 42–62, New York: Columbia University Press.

Douglas, M. (1996 [1970]), *Natural Symbols: Exploration in Cosmology*, London and New York: Routledge.

Doxiadis, E. and A. Placas (eds.) (2018), *Living under Austerity: Greek Society in Crisis*, New York and Oxford: Berghahn.

Du Boulay, J. (1974), *Portrait of a Greek Mountain Village*, Oxford: Clarendon Press.

Du Boulay, J. (1991), 'Cosmos and Gender in Village Greece', in P. Loizos and E. Papataxiarchis (eds.), *Contested Identities: Gender and Kinship in Modern Greece*, 47–78, Princeton, New Jersey: Princeton University Press.

Dubisch, J. (1986), 'Introduction', in J. Dubisch (ed.), *Gender and Power in Rural Greece*, 3–41, Princeton, NJ: Princeton University Press.

Dubisch, J. (1995), *In a Different Place: Pilgrimage, Gender, and Politics at a Greek Island Shrine*, Princeton, NJ: Princeton University Press.
Eller, C. (1993), *Living in the Lap of the Goddess: The Feminist Spirituality Movement in America*, New York: Crossroad.
Favret-Saada, J. (1980), *Deadly Words: Witchcraft in the Bocage*, Cambridge: Cambridge University Press.
Fedele, A. (2012), *Looking for Mary Magdalene: Alternative Pilgrimage and Ritual Creativity at Catholic Shrines in France*, Oxford: Oxford University Press.
Fedele, A. and K. Knibbe (eds.) (2013), *Gender and Power in Contemporary Spirituality: Ethnographic Approaches*, London and New York: Routledge.
Friedman, J. (1991), 'Consuming Desires: Strategies of Selfhood and Appropriation', *Cultural Anthropology*, 6 (2): 154–63.
Gabriel, Y. and T. Lang (1995), *The Unmanageable Consumer: Contemporary Consumption and Its Fragmentations*, London: Sage.
Galt, A. (1982), 'The Evil Eye as a Synthetic Image and Its Meanings on the Island of Pantelleria, Italy', *American Ethnologist*, 9: 664–81.
Gefou-Madianou, D. (1993), 'Anthropologia Oikoi: Gia mia kritiki tis "gigenous anthropologias"', *Diavazo*, 323: 44–51.
Gefou-Madianou, D. (1998), 'Anastohasmos, Eterotita kai Anthropologia Oikoi: dilimmata kai antiparatheseis', in D. Gefou-Madianou (ed.), *Anthropologiki Theoria kai Ethnographia: Sighrones Taseis*, 365–435, Athens: Ellinika Grammata.
Geurts, K. L. (2002), *Culture and the Senses: Bodily Ways of Knowing in an African Community*, Berkley: University of California Press.
Gilsenan, M. (1996), *Lords of the Lebanese Marches: Violence, Power and Culture in an Arab Society*, London: I.B. Tauris.
Gupta, A. and J. Ferguson (eds.) (1997), *Anthropological Locations: Boundaries and Grounds of a Field Science*, Berkeley: University of California Press.
Hallam, E. and T. Ingold (2007), 'Creativity and Cultural Improvisation: An Introduction', in E. Hallam and T. Ingold (eds.), *Creativity and Cultural Improvisation*, 1–24, Oxford and New York: Berg.
Hammond, P. (1985), 'Introduction', in P. Hammond (ed.), *The Sacred in a Secular Age. Toward Revision in the Scientific Study of Religion*, 1–8, Berkeley: University of California Press.
Handelman, D. (1973), 'Gossip in Encounters: The Transmission of Information in a Bounded Social Setting', *Man* [New Series], 8 (2): 210–27.
Hanegraaff, W. (1996), *New Age Religion and Western Culture: Esotericism in the Mirror of Secular Thought*, Leiden: Brill.
Hardie, M. (1925), 'The Evil Eye in Some Greek Villages of the Upper Haliakmon Valley in West Macedonia', *Journal of the Royal Anthropological Institute*, 23: 160–72.
Harding, S. (1975), 'Women and Words in a Spanish Village', in R. R. Reiter (ed.), *Toward and Anthropology of Women*, 283–308, New York: Monthly Review Press.

Hart, L. K. (1992), *Time, Religion and Social Experience in Rural Greece*, Lanham, MD: Rowman and Littlefield.

Hastrup, K. (1998), 'Ithagenis Anthropologia: Mia antifasi stous orous?', in D. Gefou-Madianou (ed.), *Anthropologiki Theoria kai Ethnographia: Sighrones Taseis*, 337–64, Athens: Ellinika Grammata.

Hastrup, K. (2001), 'Othello's Dance: Cultural Creativity and Human Agency', in J. Liep (ed.), *Locating Cultural Creativity*, 31–45, London and Sterling, VA: Pluto Press.

Hayden, R. (2002), 'Antagonistic Tolerance: Competitive Sharing of Religious Sites in South Asia and the Balkans', *Current Anthropology*, 43 (2): 205–31.

Heelas, P. (1996), *The New Age Movement: The Celebration of the Self and the Sacralization of Modernity*, Oxford: Blackwell.

Heelas, P. (2006), *Spiritualities of Life: 'New Age' Romanticism and Consumptive Capitalism*, Malden, MA and Oxford: Blackwell.

Heelas, P. and L. Woodhead (2005), *The Spiritual Revolution: Why Religion Is Giving Way to Spirituality*, Oxford: Blackwell.

Herriot, M. J. (1997), 'Feminist Spirituality, Theology and Anthropology', in F. A. Salamone and W. R. Adams (eds.), *Explorations in Anthropology and Theology*, 47–66, Lanham, MD and Oxford: University Press of America.

Herzfeld, M. (1981), 'Meaning and Morality: A Semiotic Approach to Evil Eye Accusations in a Greek Village', *American Ethnologist*, 8: 560–74.

Herzfeld, M. (1986), 'Closure as Cure: Tropes in the Exploration of Bodily and Social Disorder', *Current Anthropology*, 27 (2): 107–20.

Herzfeld, M. (1991), *A Place in History: Social and Monumental Time in a Cretan Town*, Princeton, NJ: Princeton University Press.

Herzfeld, M. (2001), *Anthropology: Theoretical Practice in Culture and Society*, Oxford: Blackwell; Paris: UNESCO.

Hill, C. P. et al. (2000), 'Conceptualizing Religion and Spirituality: Points of Commonality, Points of Departure', *Journal for the Theory of Social Behaviour*, 30 (1): 51–77.

Hirschon, R. (1993 [1978]), 'Open Body/Closed Space: The Transformation of Female Sexuality', in S. Ardener (ed.), *Defining Females: The Nature of Women in Society*, 51–72, Oxford and New York: Berg.

Hirschon, R. (1998 [1989]), *Heirs of the Greek Catastrophe: The Social Life of Asia Minor Refugees in Piraeus*, Oxford: Clarendon Press.

Hirschon, R. (2008), 'Presents, Promises and Punctuality: Accountability and Obligation in Greek Social Life', in M. Mazower (ed.), *Networks of Power in Modern Greece: Essays in Honour of John Campbell*, 189–208, New York: Columbia University Press.

Hirschon, R. (2009), 'Religion and Nationality: The Tangled Greek Case', in R. Pinxten and L. Dikomitis (eds.), *When God Comes to Town: Religious Traditions in Urban Contexts*, 3–16, London and New York: Berghahn Books.

Hoskins, J. (1998), *Biographical Objects: How Things Tell the Stories of People's Lives*, New York and London: Routledge.

Howes, D. (ed.) (1991a), *The Varieties of Sensory Experience: A Sourcebook in the Anthropology of the Senses*, Toronto, Buffalo, London: University of Toronto Press.

Howes, D. (1991b), 'Introduction: "To Summon the Senses"', in D. Howes (ed.), *The Varieties of Sensory Experience: A Sourcebook in the Anthropology of the Senses*, 3–21, Toronto, Buffalo, London: University of Toronto Press.

Howes, D. (1996), 'Introduction: Commodities and Cultural Borders', in D. Howes (ed.), *Cross-Cultural Consumption: Global Markets – Local Realities*, 1–16, London and New York: Routledge.

Howes, D. (2003), *Sensual Relations: Engaging the Senses in Culture and Social theory*, Ann Arbor: University of Michigan Press.

Hristodoulou, T. (2003). *Eksorkismoi, Eksorkistes kai Vaskania*, Athens: Omologia.

Hunt, K. (2003), 'Understanding the Spirituality of People Who Do Not Go to Church', in G. Davie, P. Heelas and L. Woodhead (eds.), *Predicting Religion: Christian, Secular and Alternative Futures*, 159–69, Aldershot: Ashgate.

Ingold, T. (2000), *The Perception of the Environment: Essays in Livelihood, Dwelling and Skill*, London and New York: Routledge.

Kemp, D. and J. Lewis (eds.) (2007), *Handbook of New Age*, Leiden: Brill.

Kenna, M. (1985), 'Icons in Theory and Practice: An Orthodox Christian Example', *History of Religions*, 24 (4): 345–68.

Kenna, M. (1995), 'Saying "no" in Greece: Some Preliminary Thoughts on Hospitality, Gender and the Evil Eye', in S. Diamanakos et al. (eds.), *Les Ami sets les Autres. Melanges en l'honneur de J. Peristiany*, 133–46, Athens–Paris: EKKE– Maison des Sciences de l'Homme.

Kirtsoglou, E. (2013), 'The Dark Ages of the Golden Dawn: Anthropological Analysis and Responsibility in the Twilight Zone of the Greek Crisis', *Suomen Antropologi: Journal of the Finnish Anthropological Society*, 38 (1): 104–08.

Kirtsoglou, E. and Tsimouris, G. (2018), 'Migration, Crisis, Liberalism: The Cultural and Racial Politics of Islamophobia and "Radical Alterity" in Modern Greece', *Ethnic and Racial Studies*, 41 (10): 1874–92.

Klassen, P. (2005), 'Ritual Appropriation and Appropriate Ritual: Christian Healing and Adaptations of Asian Religions', *History and Anthropology*, 16 (3): 377–91.

Kleinman, A. (1980), *Patients and Healers in the Context Culture*, Berkeley: California University Press.

Knoblauch, H. (2003), 'Europe and Invisible Religion', *Social Compass*, 50 (3): 267–74.

Knoblauch, H. (2008), 'Spirituality and Popular Religion in Europe', *Social Compass*, 55 (2): 140–53.

Kokosalakis, N. (1995), 'Icons and Non-Verbal Religion in the Orthodox Tradition', *Social Compass*, 42 (4): 433–49.

Koss-Chioino, D. J. (2006), 'Spiritual Transformation, Ritual Healing and Altruism', *Zygon*, 41 (4): 877–92.

Laderman, C. and M. Roseman (1996), 'Introduction', in C. Laderman and M. Roseman (eds.), *The Performance of Healing*, 1–16, New York and London: Routledge.
Latour, B. ([1991] 1993), *We Have Never Been Modern*, Cambridge, MA: Harvard University Press.
Lewis, G. (1993), 'Double Standards of Treatment Evaluation', in S. Lindenbaum and M. Lock (eds.), *Knowledge, Power and Practice*, 189–218, Berkeley, Los Angeles, London: University of California Press.
Lewis, I. M. (1966), 'Spirit Possession and Deprivation Cults', *Man*, 1 (3): 307–29.
Liep, J. (2001), 'Introduction', in J. Liep (ed.), *Locating Cultural Creativity*, 1–13, London and Sterling, VA: Pluto Press.
Lindquist, G. and S. Coleman (2008), 'Introduction: Against Belief?', *Social Analysis*, 52 (1): 1–18.
Lossky, V. (2005), *The Mystical Theology of the Eastern Church*, Reprinted edition, Cambridge: James Clarke & Co.
Low, M. S. and D. Lawrence-Zuñiga (2003), 'Locating Culture', in S. M. Low and D. Lawrence-Zuñiga (eds.), *The Anthropology of Space and Place: Locating Culture*, 1–47, Malden, MA and Oxford: Blackwell Publishing.
Luckmann, T. (1990), 'Shrinking Transcendence, Expanding Religion?', *Sociological Analysis*, 51 (2): 127–38.
Luhrmann, T. M. (1989), *Persuasions of the Witch's Craft: Ritual Magic in Contemporary England*, Cambridge, MA: Harvard University Press.
Lykiardopoulos, A. (1981), 'The Evil Eye: Towards an Exhaustive Study', *Folklore*, 92 (ii): 221–30.
Makrides, V. (1998), 'Byzantium in Contemporary Greece: the Neo-Orthodox Current of Ideas', in D. Ricks and P. Magdalino (eds.), *Byzantium and the Modern Greek Identity*, 141–53, Aldershot: Ashgate.
Makrides, V. and L. Molokotos-Liederman (2004), 'Orthodoxy in Greece Today', *Social Compass*, 51 (4): 459–40.
Malinowski, B. (1954 [1925]), *Magic, Science and Religion and Other Essays*, New York: Doubleday.
Mapril, J. and R. Blanes (2013), 'Introduction: Sites and Politics of Religious Diversity in Southern Europe', in J. Mapril and R. Blanes (eds.), *Sites and Politics of Religious Diversity in Southern Europe: The Best of All Gods*, 1–15, Leiden: Brill.
Marcus, G. (1995), 'Ethnography on/of the World System: The Emergence of Multi-Sited Ethnography', *Annual Review of Anthropology*, 24: 95–117.
Marcus, G. (1998), 'Ta Meta tin Kritiki tis Ethnographias', in D. Gefou-Madianou (ed.), *Anthropologiki Theoria and Ethnographia: Sighrones Taseis*, 67–108, Athens: Ellinika Grammata.
Marler, P. L. and C. K. Hadaway (2002), '"Being Religious" or "Being Spiritual" in America: A Zero-Sum Proposition?', *Journal for the Scientific Study of Religion*, 41 (2): 289–300.

Martikainen, T. (2007), 'Changes in the Religious Landscape: European Trends at the Dawn of the Twenty-First Century', *Swedish Missiological Themes*, 95 (4): 365–85.

Massey, D. (1994), *Space, Place and Gender*, Cambridge, Oxford: Polity Press.

McDannell, C. (1995), *Material Christianity: Religion and Popular Culture in America*, New Haven, CT and London: Yale University Press.

McGuire, M. (1990), 'Religion and the Body: Rematerializing the Human Body in the Social Sciences of Religion', *Journal for the Scientific Study of Religion*, 29 (3): 283-97.

McGuire, M. (1993), 'Health and Spirituality as Contemporary Concerns'. *The Annals of the American Academy of Political and Social Science*, 527: 144–54.

McGuire, M. (2008), *Lived Religion: Faith and Practice in Everyday Life*, Oxford: Oxford University Press.

Meyer, B. (1998), 'Commodities and the Power of Prayer: Pentecostalist Attitudes Towards Consumption in Contemporary Ghana', *Development and Change*, 29: 751-76.

Mitchell, J. (1997), 'A Moment with Christ: The Importance of Feelings in the Analysis of Belief', *Journal of the Royal Anthropological Institute*, 3 (1): 79-94.

Mitchell, J. (2001), 'The Devil, Satanism, and the Evil Eye in Contemporary Malta', in P. Clough and J. P. Mitchell (eds.), *Powers of Good and Evil: Social Transformation and Popular Belief*, 77–103, New York and Oxford: Berghahn Books.

Moerman, D. (1979), 'Anthropology of Symbolic Healing', *Current Anthropology*, 20 (1): 59-80.

Moerman, D. (2002), *Meaning, Medicine and the 'Placebo Effect'*, Cambridge: Cambridge University Press.

Molokotos-Liederman, L. (2004), 'Sacred Words, Profane Music? The Free Monks as a Musical Phenomenon in Contemporary Greek Orthodoxy', *Sociology of Religion*, 65 (4): 403–16.

Morris, B. (2006), *Religion and Anthropology: A Critical Introduction*, Cambridge: Cambridge University Press.

Narayan, K. (1993), 'How Native Is a "Native" Anthropologist?', *American Anthropologist*, 95 (3): 671–86.

Needham, R. (1972), *Belief, Language and Experience*, Oxford: Basil Blackwell.

Okely, J. (1992), 'Anthropology and Autobiography: Participatory Experience and Embodied Knowledge', in J. Okely and H. Callaway (eds.), *Anthropology and Autobiography*, 1-28, London and New York: Routledge.

Pachis, P. (2004), 'Religious Tendencies in Greece at the Dawn of the Twenty-First Century – An Approach to Contemporary Greek Reality', in A. Leopold and J. Jensen (eds.), *Syncretism in Religion: A Reader*, 348-61, London: Routledge.

Palmisano, S. (2010), 'Spirituality and Catholicism: The Italian Experience', *Journal of Contemporary Religion*, 25 (2): 221–41.

Palmisano, S., and N. Pannofino (eds.) (2017), *Invention of Tradition and Syncretism in Contemporary Religions: Sacred Creativity*, London: Palgrave McMillan.

Pandolfi, M. (1990), 'Boundaries Inside the Body: Women's Sufferings in Southern Peasant Italy', *Culture, Medicine and Psychiatry*, 4 (2): 255–73.
Panourgia, N. (1995), *Fragments of Death, Fables of Identity: An Athenian Anthropography*, Madison: The University of Wisconsin Press.
Petropoulos, J. C. B. (2008a), 'Introduction: Magic in Modern Greece', in J. C. B. Petropoulos (ed.), *Greek Magic: Ancient, Medieval and Modern*, 85–6, London and New York: Routledge.
Petropoulos, J. C. B. (ed.) (2008b), *Greek Magic: Ancient, Medieval and Modern*, London and New York: Routledge.
Petrus, T. (2006), 'Engaging the World of the Supernatural: Anthropology, Phenomenology and the Limitations of Scientific Rationalism in the Study of the Supernatural', *Indo-Pacific Journal of Phenomenology*, 6 (1): 1–12.
Pietz, W. (1985), 'The Problem of the Fetish, I', *Res*, 9: 5–17.
Pietz, W. (1987), 'The Problem of the Fetish, II: The Origin of the Fetish', *Res*, 13: 23–45.
Pietz, W. (1988), 'The Problem of the Fetish, IIIa: Bosman's Guinea and the Enlightment Theory of Fetishism', *Res*, 16: 105–23.
Pina-Cabral, J. (1986), *Sons of Adam, Daughters of Eve: The Peasant Worldview of the Alto Minho*, Oxford: Clarendon Press.
Pollack, D. (2008), 'Religious Change in Europe: Theoretical Considerations and Empirical Findings', *Social Compass*, 55 (2): 168–86.
Pouillon, J. (1982), 'Remarks on the Verb "To Believe"', in M. Izard and P. Smith (eds.), *Between Belief and Transgression: Structuralist Essays in Religion, History and Myth*, 1–8, Chicago, IL and London: University of Chicago Press.
Poulin, A. P., and W. West (2005), 'Holistic Healing, Paradigm Shift, and the New Age', in R. Moodley and W. West (eds.), *Integrating Traditional Healing Practices into Counseling and Psychotherapy*, 257–68, Thousand Oaks, London, New Delhi: Sage.
Primiano, L. (2012), 'Afterword. Manifestations of the Religious Vernacular: Ambiguity, Power and Creativity', in M. Bowman and Ü. Valk (eds.), *Vernacular Religion in Everyday Life: Expressions of Belief*, 382–94, Sheffield and Bristol, CT: Equinox.
Primiano, L. N. (1995), 'Vernacular Religion and the Search for Method in Religious Folklife', *Western Folklore*, 54 (1): 37–56.
Prodromou, E. (2004a), 'The Ambivalent Orthodox', *Journal of Democracy*, 15 (2): 62–75.
Prodromou, E. (2004b), 'Negotiating Pluralism and Specifying Modernity in Greece: Reading Church–State Relations in the Christodoulos Period', *Social Compass*, 51 (4): 471–85.
Quest, P. (1999), *An Introduction to Reiki: A Step-by-Step Guide to Reiki Practice*, London: Piatkus.
Redden, G. (2016), 'Revisiting the Spiritual Supermarket: Does the Commodification of Spirituality Necessarily Devalue It?', *Culture and Religion*, 17 (2): 231–49.
Reed-Danahay, D. (1997), 'Introduction', in D. Reed-Danahay (ed.), *Auto/Ethnography: Rewriting the Self and the Social*, 1–17, Oxford and New York: Berg.

Roudometof, V. (2005), 'Orthodoxy as Public Religion in Post-1989 Greece', in V. Roudometof, A. Agadjanian and J. Pankhurst (eds.), *Eastern Orthodoxy in a Global Age: Tradition Faces the Twenty-First Century*, 84–108, Walnut Creek: Altamira Press.

Roudometof, V. (2014), *Globalization and Orthodox Christianity: The Transformations of a Religious Tradition*, New York: Routledge.

Rountree, K. (2010), *Crafting Contemporary Pagan Identities in a Catholic Society*, Surrey: Ashgate.

Roussou, E. (2011), 'Orthodoxy at the Crossroads: Popular Religion and Greek Identity in the Practice of the Evil Eye', *Journal of Mediterranean Studies*, 20 (1): 85–105.

Roussou, E. (2013), 'The New Age of Greek Orthodoxy: Pluralizing Religiosity in Everyday Practice', in J. Mapril and R. Blanes (eds.), *Sites and Politics of Religious Diversity in Southern Europe: The Best of All Gods*, 73–92, Leiden: Brill.

Roussou, E. (2017), 'The Syncretic Religioscape of contemporary Greece and Portugal: A Comparative Approach on Creativity through Spiritual Synthesis', in S. Palmisano and N. Pannofino (eds.), *Invention of Tradition and Syncretism in Contemporary Religions: Sacred Creativity*, 155–17, London: Palgrave McMillan.

Roussou, E. (2018), 'Spiritual Movements in Times of Crisis: An Anthropological Account of Alternative Spirituality in Portugal and Greece', in G. Chryssides (ed.), *Minority religions in Europe and the Middle East: Mapping and Monitoring*, 52–64, London and New York: Routledge.

Ruel, M. (2002 [1982]), 'Christians as Believers', in M. Lambek (ed.), *A Reader in the Anthropology of Religion*, 99–113, Malden, MA: Blackwell Publishing.

Schechner, R. (1987), 'Victor Turner's Last Adventure', in V. Turner (ed.), *The Anthropology of Performance*, 7–20, New York: PAJ Publications.

Scheper-Hughes, N. (1994), 'Embodied Knowledge: Thinking with the Body in Critical Medical Anthropology', in R. Borofsky (ed.), *Assessing Cultural Anthropology*, 229–42, New York and London: McGraw-Hill.

Seremetakis, C. N. (ed.) (1994), *The Senses Still: Perception and Memory as Material Culture in Modernity*, Boulder, CO: Westview Press.

Sharma, U. (1992), *Complementary Medicine Today: Practitioners and Patients*, London and New York: Tavistock/Routledge.

Sharma, U. (1993), 'Contextualizing Alternative Medicine: The Exotic, the Marginal and the Perfectly Mundane', *Anthropology Today*, 9 (4): 15–18.

Shimazono, S. (1999), '"New Age Movement" or "New Spirituality Movements and Culture"?', *Social Compass*, 46 (2): 121–34.

Smith, M. (1977), *Jesus the Magician. Charlatan or Son of God?*, New York: Harper and Row.

Sointu, E. and L. Woodhead (2008), 'Spirituality, Gender, and Expressive Selfhood', *Journal for the Scientific Study of Religion*, 47 (2): 259–76.

Sotiriu, E. (2004), 'Contested Masculine Spaces in Greek Orthodoxy', *Social Compass*, 51 (4): 499–510.

Sotiriu, E. (2010), 'The Traditional Modern: Rethinking the Position of Contemporary Greek Women in Orthodoxy', in V. Roudometof and V. Makrides (eds.), *Orthodox Christianity in 21st Century Greece*, 131–53, Aldershot: Ashgate.

Stark, R., E. Hamberg and A. S. Miller. (2005), 'Exploring Spirituality and Unchurched Religions in America, Sweden, and Japan', *Journal of Contemporary Religion*, 20 (1): 2–23.

Stewart, C. (1989), 'Hegemony or Rationality? The Position of the Supernatural in Modern Greece', *Journal of Modern Greek Studies*, 7: 77–104.

Stewart, C. (1991), *Demons and the Devil: Moral Imagination in Modern Greek Culture*, Princeton, NJ: Princeton University Press.

Stewart, C. (2004), 'Relocating Syncretism in Social Science Discourse', in A. Leopold and J. Jensen (eds.), *Syncretism in Religion: A Reader*, 264–85, London: Routledge.

Stirrat, R. L. (1992), *Power and Religiosity in a Post-Colonial Setting: Sinhala Catholics in Contemporary Sri Lanka*, Cambridge: Cambridge University Press.

Stöckligt, B. M. H. et al. (2015), 'Healing Relationships: A Qualitative Study of Healers and Their Clients in Germany', *Evidence-Based Complementary and Alternative Medicine*, 2015: 1–8.

Stoller, P. (1989), *The Taste of Ethnographic Things: The Senses in Anthropology*, Philadelphia: University of Pennsylvania Press.

Strauss, S. (2005), *Positioning Yoga: Balancing Acts Across Cultures*, Oxford: Berg.

Sutcliffe, S. (2003), *Children of the New Age: A History of Spiritual Practices*, London: Routledge.

Sutcliffe, S. and M. Bowman (2000), *Beyond 'New Age': Exploring Alternative Spirituality*, Edinburgh: Edinburgh University Press.

Sutcliffe, J. S. and I. S. Gilhus (2013), 'Introduction: "All Mixed Up" – Thinking About Religion in Relation to New Age Spiritualities', in S. J. Sutcliffe and I. S. Gilhus (eds.), *New Age Spirituality: Rethinking Religion*, 1–16, Durham: Acumen.

Taussig, M. (1993), *Mimesis and Alterity: A Particular History of the Senses*, New York: Routledge.

Turner, V. (1987), *The Anthropology of Performance*, New York: PAJ Publications.

Turner, E. (1993), 'The Reality of Spirits: A Tabooed or Permitted Field of Study?', *Anthropology of Consciousness*, 4 (1): 9–12.

Van Vleet, K. (2003), 'Partial Theories: On Gossip, Envy and Anthropology in the Andes', *Ethnography*, 4 (4): 491–519.

Veikou, H. (1998), *To Kako Mati: I kinoniki kataskevi tis Optikis Epikoinonias*, Athens: Ellinika Grammata.

Voas, D. and A. Crockett (2005), 'Religion in Britain: Neither Believing nor Belonging', *Sociology*, 39 (1): 11–28.

von Stuckrad, K. (2005), *Western Esotericism: A Brief History of Secret Knowledge*, Durham: Acumen.

Vozikas, G. (2009), 'Rural Immigrants and Official Religion in an Urban Religious Festival in Greece', in R. Pinxten and L. Dikomitis (eds.), *When God Comes to Town:*

Religious Traditions in Urban Contexts, 65–78, New York and Oxford: Berghahn Books.

Ware, B. K. (1995), *The Orthodox Way*, Revised edition, Crestwood, New York: St Vladimir's Seminar Press.

Ware, T. ([1963] 1997), *The Orthodox Church*, New edition, Harmondsworth: Penguin Books.

Weber, M. (1964), *The Theory of Social and Economic Organization*, London: Collier Macmillan Publishers.

Wood, M. (2007), *Possession, Power and the 'New Age': Ambiguities of Authority in Neoliberal Societies*, Aldershot: Ashgate.

York, M. (2001), 'New Age Commoditisation and Appropriation of Spirituality', *Journal of Contemporary Religion*, 16 (3): 361–72.

Zaidman, N. (2007), 'New Age Products in Local and Global Contexts: A Comparison between Israel and New Zealand', *Culture and Religion*, 8 (3): 255–70.

Websites

https://www.patriarchate.org/administrative-structure-of-the-ecumenical-patriarchate (last accessed 20 December 2019).

http://www.iak.gr/gr/ekklisia-kritis/index.html (last accessed 20 December 2019).

https://www.statistics.gr/el/statistics/-/publication/SAM03/- (last accessed 10 February 2020).

https://www.vimaorthodoxias.gr/tags/tag/%CE%B3%CE%B9%CE%BF%CE%B3%CE%BA%CE%B1/(last accessed 1 March 2020).

https://www.oriopisteos.eu/search/label/%CE%9D%CE%95%CE%91%20%CE%95%CE%A0%CE%9F%CE%A7%CE%97# (last accessed 21 May 2020).

Index

agency 12–13, 27, 73–4, 115, 167
Ammerman, Nancy 50
anthropology at home 18–24
Appadurai, Arjun 114–15, 135
atheism 9, 39, 118, 130
aura 47, 136, 160
authority. *See* Orthodox Christian authority

bad luck. *See* gkantemia
belief
    and experience 78–9, 155–6
    and/without belonging 5, 156–9
    notion of 152–9
Berger, Peter 145–6, 179n.1
biomedicine 104–7
blessing 53, 94–6, 111, 131–4
Bourdieu, Pierre 81
Bowman, Marion 5, 7, 139, 162
Bruce, Steve 4–5, 145–6
Butler, Judith 55

care 104–5
channelling 51–2, 93, 102–5, 149, 160
charisma 8, 102, 161
charms. *See* material culture amulets
Chinese cultural influences 116, 138, 141–3, 149, 172
Christianity. *See* Orthodox Christian, Orthodoxy
Chryssanthopoulou, Vassiliki 10
church
    attendance 26, 36–41, 148–9, 155–6, 162
    liturgies 36, 38–41, 47, 126, 155
    rituals, *see* Orthodox Christian sacraments
    shrines 36–7, 41–2
Classen, Constance 56, 60, 62
clergy. *See* priest
cosmology 75, 80, 148–9, 158
creativity

definition of 13, 27, 50
incidences of spiritual 4–5, 83, 90–1, 97–8, 103, 166–7
material, *see under* material culture
crisis 5, 44, 50, 173
cross, sign of 37, 85–8, 91
Csordas, Thomas 88, 91–2, 101–2

Danforth, Loring 10, 72, 91
Davie, Grace 5, 156–8
Desjarlais, Robert 89–90
devil 70–5, 93, 96, 129, 139, 179n.2a
devotion 40, 70, 93, 118, 122–4, 129–32, 179n.3b
divine 4, 45, 91, 102, 118. *See also* sacred
doctor. *See* biomedicine
dreaming 2, 77, 134–5, 153
Dubisch, Jill 10, 41, 99, 128, 155
Du Boulay, Juliet 10, 80

eikonostasi 37, 40, 85, 118–120, 179 n. 2a
emotion 3, 54–6, 78–9, 89–90, 104–5
empiricism 79
energy 46–7, 51–3, 71–5, 92–6, 112, 142–4
envy 2, 10, 56, 63, 70, 169
ethnography
    auto-, *see* anthropology at home
    multi-sited 16–17
evil eye
    affliction 51, 54–60, 169
    and baptism 110–11
    as *ftharmos* 17
    the good (*kalo mati*) 56, 68–9, 169
    materialities, *see* material culture
    and relatedness 14, 169
    research in Greece 9–12
    self-imposed 66, 107–9
    as social control 10–12
    and social status 10–11, 72, 80–1, 84
    as *vaskania* 69–71, 75, 94–5, 111, 122, 150

and women 39–40, 95–9, 169–70, 179 n. 5
exorcism 10, 79, 93–6
extra-sensory perception. *See* senses and perception

feeling. *See* emotion
feng shui 47, 141–4, 149–51
firewalking 10, 71
fluidity 14, 16, 50, 99–100, 145
folklore 9–12, 35–6, 170
fylahta. See material culture amulets

gender and power 72, 93–100
gkantemia 64–6
globalization 81, 144–5, 172–3
glossofagia 56, 59, 62–4, 66
gossip. *See glossofagia*

Hastrup, Kirsten 13, 18, 27
Heelas, Paul 47–8
healer
    lay 93–7
    and patient 87–92, 100–5, 108–9, 179n.4
    as scientist 106–7
healing
    alternative 39, 79, 107, 112
    efficacy of 90–2, 97, 106–9
    and emotions 104–5
    holistic 104–5, 179n.6
    long-distance 92–3
    radical empathy in 105
    and the senses 88–90, 101, 170–1, *see also* senses
Herzfeld, Michael 10–11, 14–15, 62, 78, 87
Hirschon, Renée 35–40
Howes, David 55, 62, 135

icon stand. *See eikonostasi*
illness
    bodily symptoms of 54–5, 64, 85, 101–9
    and embodiment 100–1
    as opposed to disease 177n.1
    as suffering 101
    transference of 100–1, 104
imagination 13, 27, 92
individualization 4, 7, 159–63, 173

jealousy. *See* envy

Kenna, Margaret 10, 118
Klassen, Pamela 149, 159–60
Kleinman, Arthur 109, 177n.1
Knoblauch, Hubert 8, 160
Koss-Chioino, Joan 105
ksematiasma. See ritual against the evil eye

Luhrmann, Tanya 47, 76

magic 10, 75–6, 79–80, 109–12
material culture
    amulets 118, 122–32, 136–9, 171–2
    and consumerism 41, 115–16, 121, 124, 139
    creative synthesis of 115, 122, 138–40, 148
    fetish 131–5
    icons 36–7, 41, 117–22, 125–9
    New Age 136–140
    as prophylaxis against the evil eye 124, 127, 129–35
    religious 117–29
    souvenirs 127
    value 114–16
matiasma. See evil eye affliction
McDannell, Colleen 120–4, 127, 139
McGuire, Meredith 3, 50, 79, 105
meditation 8, 47, 50, 103, 160
Meyer, Birgit 134–5
mind-body-spirit 47, 49, 101–2, 105
miracle 75, 111, 133
misfortune. *See gkantemia*
Mitchell, Jon 73, 78
Moerman, Daniel 108–9
monastery 95, 124–5, 127
Morris, Brian 75
mysticism
    and New Age spirituality 79–81, 109–10
    in Orthodox Christian circles 8, 44–6

native anthropology. *See* anthropology at home
Needham, Rodney 153–4
New Age
    criticism against 7, 33
    definition of 3, 7–9, 47–8, 105

of Greek religiosity 29–31, 44–50
Greek term of 49
objects, *see under* material culture
and Orthodox Christianity 4–9, 49, 56, 112–15, 140
new religious pluralism. *See under* pluralism

occultists 48–9
Okely, Judith 20
Orthodox Christian
　authority 38, 44, 84, 93–100, 105–6, 124
　bookshops 70, 113, 125–7
　Church of Greece 17, 31–4, 39, 43, 125, 173
　faith 38–9, 118–19, 179n.3b
　Patriarchate of Constantinople 17, 31–3, 43, 132
　sacraments 32, 87, 96, 111, 118
Orthodoxy
　and Greek identity 4, 32, 44
　Helleno- 30–1, 147, 173
　and the Kollyvades movement 45–6
　neo- 32, 46
　in official education 31–2, 70–1
　role of Archbishop Christodoulos in 33, 173

pagan 76, 139
palo santo 1–2, 47
Panagia 87, 122–5, 133
performance. *See under* ritual
Pietz, William 131, 133, 135
placebo 107–8
pluralism
　new age of 31, 145
　new religious 145
　spiritual 49
possession (spirit) 71–5, 94
Pouillon, Jean 154–5
prayer
　of evil eye ritual healing 83–8, 90–1, 97–8, 102, 111–12
　Hesychast method of 45–6
　for sacralization of objects 131, 134–5
　secrecy of evil eye 97, 109–10
　against *vaskania* 94–5, 111, 122
priest 29–30, 42–3, 93–100, 124, 145–7, 150–1, 172–3
Primiano, Leonard 5

reiki 47, 83, 149
religion
　lived 3, 5, 50
　material, *see* material culture
　patchwork 50
　and spirituality 3, 6–9, 53, 112, 172–4
　as synonymous to Orthodoxy 7
　vicarious 157
ritual
　against the evil eye 84–8, 92–3, 97–100
　performance of 87–93
　proximity 159–60
Roudometof, Victor 32, 146

sacred 91–3, 97, 102–5, 151, 158
sacraments. *See under* Orthodox Christian
Schechner, Richard 87–8
Scheper-Hughes, Nancy 109
science 79, 106–7, 170–1
secularization 35–41, 146–7, 160–1, 173
senses
　anthropology of 178n.2
　of gaze 3, 56–62
　of hearing 56–7
　and perception 75–9, 170–1
　the pluralistic experience of 59, 62, 88–90, 170–1
　of smell 56, 59
　and visualism 60–2, 78
Seremetakis, K. Nandia 59
shaman 75, 176n.2
Sharma, Ursula 139
Shimazono, Susumu 8
space
　as crossroads 172–4
　of the neighbourhood 56–60
　sacred 158
　urban and rural 13–14, 60, 92, 168–9
spells 80, 110
spiritual
　easternization 145
　marketplace 115–16, 121, 138
　revolution 162, 174
　supermarket 139–40
　transcendence 132–4, 146
spirituality. *See* New Age
Stewart, Charles 4, 6, 10, 70–1, 74, 80–1, 111
Stoller, Paul 60

supernatural 49, 76–81, 171
Sutcliffe, Steven 7, 48
syncretism 81, 172, 159, 174

tourism 14–15, 116, 127, 136–7
tradition 13, 40–1
Turner, Edith 77
Turner, Victor 87

Veikou, Hristina 11–12, 62
Virgin Mary. *See Panagia*

Weber, Max 8, 161
witchcraft 21, 23
Wood, Matthew 7

yoga 47, 147–9

www.ingramcontent.com/pod-product-compliance
Lightning Source LLC
Chambersburg PA
CBHW070636300426
44111CB00013B/2132